OUTER SPACE AND INNER SANCTUMS

OUTER SPACE AND INNER SANCTUMS:

Government, Business, and Satellite Communication

MICHAEL E. KINSLEY

Foreword by Ralph Nader
Introduction by Nicholas Johnson

A Wiley-Interscience Publication

JOHN WILEY & SONS, New York • London • Sydney • Toronto

Published by John Wiley & Sons, Inc.
Copyright © 1976 by Center for Study of Responsive Law.

Library of Congress Cataloging in Publication Data

Kinsley, Michael E
  Outer space and inner sanctums.

  "A Wiley-Interscience publication."
  Includes bibliographical references and index.
  1. Artificial satellites in telecommunication.
2. Industry and state—United States. 3. Communication
Satellite Corporation. 4. United States. Federal
Communication Commission. I. Title

HE9721.U5K54   384.54'56'0973   75-26717
ISBN 0-471-48060-6

Printed in the United States of America

10 9 8 7 6 5 4 3 2 1

Foreword

Our cumulative ability to communicate is the factor which most dramatically distinguishes the evolution of homo sapiens. Communication is power not only as conveyance but also as substance, because inequalities beween people in access to conveyances become inequalities in ability to convey information to the public. As information is the currency of democracy, so communication systems become the filaments of a just society.

The First Amendment guarantees the right of free speech but it does not guarantee the right to "megaphones"—even those built with the taxpayers' revenues and operating through publicly owned resources like communication satellites. There is a "decibel dimension" to free speech provided by a monopolized modern technology that has made most persons second class citizens under the First Amendment. These are the people who can speak to their neighbors but cannot speak to millions of their fellow Americans through the electronic media without paying a giant toll and obtaining the permission of giant corporations. On the other hand, the powerful few can use their constitutional rights to command national audiences and decide the price, frequency and use of communications systems having such global reaches.

Ever growing differences in audience access between the many and the few can continue to be a subvisible subject, whose ominous consequences are not publicly related and debated, as long as the communications monopolies wish it so. It is a chicken *and* egg problem wrapped into one. Yet never has there been a greater urgency for the expeditious flow of substantial information and judgments. A complex society radiating events beyond people's awareness or control sows the seeds of early injustice and later deterioration unless it also radiates easier and cheaper access to communications facilities.

For years, technological abundance has been challenging the natural preference of corporations for controlled scarcity. The advantages of scarcity for corporate pricing policy are as obvious as the advantage to consumers of abundance. Cable TV, with its relative abundance, has long been stifled by network and local broadcasting companies who were busy marketing their scarcer and consequently more remunerative channels. It was likewise predictable that AT&T would react in similar fashion when communications satellites confronted the telephone company's rate based regulated capital investment. The company pursued a prolonged strategy of sequentially opposing, then delaying and now controlling, with a few other telecommunications corporations as junior partners, this wonderfully expansive and inherently cheaper human communication system.

AT&T, the world's largest corporation in assets, is not interested in a technology that can reduce the level of assets (such as underseas cables) on which its rates are calculated. Satellites can do this on their way to transmitting educational, cultural and civic programs to millions of people. So satellite potential has been held up unfulfilled while AT&T processes outer space through the wasteful interstices of its corporate maw.

While AT&T's struggle against prompt development of international and domestic satellite communications was going on in the sixties and early seventies, the public was scarcely informed. Corporate interests which could reach the public were just those interests that did not want to. An overweening technical and regulatory jargon did not help open any doors to the citizenry, either. Even progressive politicians were daunted by the contrived complexity of the jargon and interminable administrative procedures.

Out of the welter of delay and defeat for the public interest there persist some clear verities. First, as Michael Kinsley describes in this volume, the U.S. taxpayers paid and still pay for most of the development of outer space and the return on their investment is coming instead to AT&T and all other communication carriers such as ITT and RCA Global Communications. Have there been, for example, major reductions in long distance telephone rates which satellites could make very possible? The appropriation and manipulation of government authority and revenues by the companies that control the Communications Satellite Corporation (Comsat) is a chronicle of the modern corporate state in microcosm.

Far from pursuing its youthful and pioneering mission, Comsat wallows in mediocrity and subservience to the communications industry, led by AT&T. Comsat employees, interviewed by the author, described a company full of retired soldiers and former bureaucrats looking for a soft life, wracked by petty infighting, wasteful and unambitious. What such symptoms mean for the public's right to a broad range of inexpensive communications facilities is the question this book addresses.

Mr. Kinsley's analysis of the Comsat activity is a finely honed, timely and citizen-pertinent treatment of a subject that touches all Americans. This study was not easy; it faced the obstacles confronting any inquiry into corporate greed, monopoly, intransigence, and secrecy. Comsat itself, located in Washington, should have been the most open of companies, but it was not. An oft-described, semi-public corporation representing the U.S. government as manager of the international communications satellite consortium, Comsat behaved vis-à-vis Kinsley as if it were a cloistered combination of Citibank and General Motors. It has been an institution unaccustomed and untreated to Congressional or media scrutiny, much less the attention of an inquiring citizen. But through three "careers," as Harvard undergraduate, Rhodes Scholar and Harvard law student, Kinsley persisted to complete the first study of Comsat and AT&T for citizens and consumers.

RALPH NADER

Washington, D.C.
June 1975

Introduction

A thoroughly documented Nader Report on the history of communications satellites in this country is especially timely today. The decade of communications satellites—roughly 1963–1973—spans a time of dramatic change in the United States, and this change is evident from Mr. Kinsley's review of our communications satellite policy.

Consider the difference in certain of our attitudes today as compared with the halcyon days of early 1963. We are no longer so confident that every new technological marvel will be unambiguously beneficial to our well-being. Technological assessment now shows a concern for how technology will affect a whole range of social values. And we are only now beginning to ask how we can measure the quality of life within those social values.

Mr. Kinsley's description of the history of U.S. communications satellite policy—domestic and international—suggests that we have barely begun to evaluate the effects of technological change, nor have we established mechanisms for harnessing technological change to the public good. One measure of the tragedy of our times is that our vision now extends no further than the vision of those who can derive private profit from the exploitation of our natural resources, including the brilliance of trained and gifted people.

Exploitation for private profit is another theme of this study, and the result is an indictment of the regulatory process. If most governmental institutions have declined in public esteem over the past 10 years, few have suffered as much as regulatory agencies. This book is a case study of what is meant by the phrase "capture (of the regulatory agency) by the regulated interests." But Mr. Kinsley also shows how special interest "capture" extends far beyond the relatively unimportant Federal Communications Commission and reaches to the highest levels of government. The conclusion will surprise few readers, but rarely has the point been made more clearly or convincingly. The pattern that emerges illustrates a continuing, pervasive private control over public decision-making that transcends personalities and political administrations. We can hope that someday again men and women of vision and concern for the public good will direct regulatory policy. Until then all we can hope for are natural competitive limits to the exercise of private power.

Finally, Mr. Kinsley has a fascinating story to tell. If today's troubles ever end, we may remember that ours was the age of accelerating technological change. Communications satellites were and are a major contributor to that change, as the legend "via satellite" reminds us on every international report we see on television. We might also remember that the rest of the world sees us "via satellite" everyday as well. And that other countries—Canada and the Soviet Union—will have had domestic communications satellites in operation for years if and when a United States Domsat finally becomes operational.

I do not agree with all that is written here. Some events I know little about firsthand; others involved me intimately, and I thus have my own perspective. But Mr. Kinsley amply demonstrates the thoroughness with which he has pursued his endeavor, and my quibbles are relatively minor. I strongly recommend this study not only to readers who are interested in communications, but more generally to those who care about the interrelationships between government and private economic interests and what we should have learned about the events of the last 10 years.

NICHOLAS JOHNSON

Preface

Communication by satellite is one of the wonders of modern life. It is held to be, and is, a triumph of American technology. It is also held to be a triumph of American corporate capitalism, of American government, and of the working relationship between them. This book is a critical analysis of these latter propositions. Satellite communication is indeed a fine example of cooperation between business and all levels of government—the legislature, the regulatory agencies, the White House. My thesis, however, is that this cooperation has tended to thwart rather than to nurture technological advance, and to deny the benefits of satellite technology to the taxpayers whose investment in outer space made it possible.

The first commercial communications satellite, Early Bird, was launched in 1965. By 1973 satellites carried more than half of all communications between the United States and Europe, a volume which was itself many times greater than the total volume of trans-Atlantic communications just a few years before. In 1962 there were 99 trans-Atlantic voice communication circuits available on two undersea cables. In 1973 satellite capacity alone amounted to the equivalent of more than 10,000 voice circuits. A single satellite launched in 1975 was capable of carrying 7,500 voice circuits.

Yet the story of commercial satellite communication is not altogether one of a technological breakthrough successfully exploited. Even though satellites from the beginning have been far less expensive than the alternative—underwater cables—for international communication, the international communications companies, with government approval, continue to spend hundreds of millions of dollars on cables. These expenditures continue even while thousands of satellite circuits go empty. As a result, prices for international communication remain unnecessarily high and the volume of such communication is greatly reduced.

Even more important, the domestic communications interests —primarily the American Telephone and Telegraph Company —succeeded for almost a decade in preventing the use of satellites for communication within the continental United States. Once domestic satellite communication finally began (in July 1974), it should have had a dramatic impact on the communications services available and the prices we pay for them.

The capture of government regulatory agencies by the industries they are supposed to control is by now an old story. But I hope those interested in the subject will find this report on the performance of the Federal Communications Commission—along with the Senate of the United States, and Justice Department, the Defense Department, the State Department, and the White House Office of Telecommunications Policy—to be a recent, valuable and surprising example. Surprising because the subversion of technology has been accomplished amidst an atmosphere of celebration which began with passage of the Communications Satellite Act of 1962 and continues through the present day.

This book was begun in 1971 at the Center for Study of Responsive Law, under the direction of Ralph Nader. James M. Fogel conducted research during the summer of 1971. Joseph C. Goulden supplied a rare, almost complete edition of the Comsat filibuster and many of the congressional hearings that accompanied it. Many others in Washington and elsewhere—Comsat employees and former employees; competitors and customers in the communications industry; Washington lawyers; scientists and scholars at NASA and private institutions; policy-makers at the FCC, at the White House, and on Capitol Hill; members of the communications press; and representatives of foreign communications interests—were generous with their time and advice. Lou Early, the man Communications Satellite Corporation assigned to deal with me, was as helpful as he possibly could be within the constraints of his corporate obligation.

Any errors of judgment or fact, lapses of diction or taste, are my own.

MICHAEL E. KINSLEY

Cambridge, Massachusetts
July 1976

Contents

OUTER SPACE AND INNER SANCTUMS

1

A New Frontier

The legislative remains of the Communications Satellite Act of 1962 take up 4000 pages of committee hearings and reports, and 600 pages of the *Congressional Record*. Already yellowed, they comprise one of the richest documentary relics of the 1960s. A picture of Washington life in the early sixties emerges from these pages—colored by New Frontier optimism yet still darkened by the Cold War—as do insights into the Kennedy administration's attitudes toward Congress, toward business, and toward technology. The committee hearings leading up to the Comsat Act provide an example of the interplay between private and public officials in producing major legislation. The Comsat floor debate is more interesting for its portraits of colorful legislators now dead or defeated—Kefauver, Douglas, Gore, Morse, Dirksen, Celler, and others.

The Comsat debate is remembered in Washington primarily because of the unsuccessful filibuster of a small band of liberals who believed that the then-unique organization created by the act permitted private companies such as AT&T and ITT to benefit from "the biggest giveaway in the history of the United States."[1] Nevertheless, the Comsat Act passed both houses of Congress with overwhelming majorities. In fact, we can see in retrospect that it became a highly praised model for innovative legislation during the rest of the New Frontier and Great Society periods. Reincarnations of the Comsat model include such institutions as the Corporation for

Public Broadcasting,. Amtrak, the new Postal Service, and the National Corporation for Housing Partnerships.

"Space is our great New Frontier," President Kennedy said during the 1960 campaign, making the metaphor explicit.[2] The man-on-the-moon program was one of the New Frontier's answers to space. Comsat was another. Both partook of the New Frontier faith and imagery. "We are going into a new frontier, Senator," Attorney General Robert Kennedy soothed a Foreign Relations Committee member concerned about anti-trust oddities in the Comsat bill. "I suppose you always have qualms about it. But I think this is the best that we can do . . . after a good deal of study and a judgment by individuals who, it is my feeling, have the best interest of the United States at heart."[3] In an earlier hearing, NASA administrator James Webb angered a staff economist with a suggestion that the new space monopoly might require several years of government subsidy before the advantages of private enterprise became evident. He reassured the economist that the Federal Communications Commission would regulate international phone rates, only to be informed that they had never before seemed able to do so. Undaunted by his earlier declaration that he was "not the expert" on the FCC, Webb proclaimed,

> I believe they can do it. I think the New Frontier is not necessarily the years of the past. And I think the position of this Nation in the world requires us to do things we have not heretofore done.[4]

Part of the affirmative thrust generated from New Frontier imagery was to be directed toward beating the Russians. In a 1961 memo to President Kennedy about the moon program, written with Secretary of Defense McNamara, Webb said,

> Our attainments are a major element in the international competition between the Soviet system and our own. The non-military, non-commercial, non-scientific but "civilian" projects such as lunar and planetary exploration are, in this sense, part of the battle along the fluid front of the cold war.[5]

The British journalists who uncovered this quotation say it "articulated in finer detail exactly the philosophy underlying much of Kennedy's campaign against the Eisenhower record."[6] Kennedy himself wrote that "If the Soviets control space, they can control the earth. . . . We cannot afford to run second in this vital race."[7] A commercial project like satellite communication also was intended for duty along the "fluid front of the cold war." Both sides of the Comsat debate expressed concern that the Russians might be able to complete their system first and spread their propaganda uncorrected by our own. Wayne Morse warned Secretary of State Rusk during a hearing that "Russia in the not too distant future will be in competition with us in exporting her enslaver philosophy of communism through the development of the underdeveloped areas of the world through the satellite communications system."[8] Liberal dissidents even argued that the propaganda importance of communications satellites was a major reason for keeping them under government control. Late on the fourth day of the "extended debate," however, Senators Paul Douglas and Albert Gore engaged in a less than serious colloquy on the image of American culture we might gain from satellites controlled by private industry.

MR. DOUGLAS.   Does the Senator from Tennessee think it is quite dignified to appropriate the vast reaches of outer space for the advertisement of laxatives?

MR. GORE.   At least I think there is plenty of room, although I am not sure it is appropriate.

MR. DOUGLAS.   Does not the Senator from Tennessee know that the Senator from Illinois is not a squeamish person?

MR. GORE.   I never would have asserted that the Senator from Illinois was squeamish.

MR. DOUGLAS.   Is the Senator from Illinois correct in understanding that the Senator from Tennessee does not ascribe to the Senator from Illinois an attitude of being unduly prissy in his ideas about life?

MR. GORE.   That would be furthest from any attribute I ever heard ascribed to the Senator from Illinois.

MR. DOUGLAS.   But does the Senator from Tennessee think the Senator from Illinois is being unduly fastidious when he says he has doubt that outer space should be conquered by laxatives and deodorants?

MR. GORE.   I share the sentiment of the Senator from Illinois. I hope it is not prissy.[9]

Arthur C. Clarke, the popular science writer, usually gets credit for first expressing, in 1945, the idea that spaceships could be used to facilitate terrestrial communications.[10] Government experiments in the field began in 1958. But 1960 was the real beginning of the communications satellite era. That year saw the first flurry over Washington in the still-raging storm of legal documents on the subject. By then it was clear that satellite communication would be the first of the long-heralded practical benefits to result from the billions the U.S. government had invested in outer space research. It was clear that this breakthrough could deeply alter the communications industry and be a boon or a bane to its constituents, primarily the American Telephone and Telegraph Company. It was clear, too, that since taxpayer money had made this incipient miracle possible, the public interest was entitled to a strong voice in the matter.

But little of what was clear in 1960 stayed clear for very long. Did satellite communication really require a new monopoly? Should it be directed primarily toward communication over oceans, and its domestic possibilities ignored? These questions were barely considered. Nor was it obvious at this early stage that if satellite communication were to be turned over to a group of private business interests, they ought to be communications firms.

In 1961 the four major international communications common carriers (AT&T, Western Union International, ITT, and RCA) proposed that they be permitted to form an exclusive consortium to develop space satellite communication. The FCC endorsed this plan. AT&T was to own as much as 80 percent of the consortium. The aerospace manufacturing contractors (firms such as Lockheed, Boeing, Hughes Aircraft, and North American Aviation), which were already making a great deal of money from the space program, had similar aspirations. Their usual legislative sponsor was Senator Robert Kerr of Oklahoma, the richest man in the Senate, and one of the most powerful. Kerr had secured the directorship of NASA for his protégé James Webb, and together they had secured the Apollo development contract for North American Aviation in an arrangement that provoked controversy.[11]

That same autumn of 1961, Kerr performed similar services for AT&T during development of the Communications Satellite Act. ("I am sort of like Senator Robert Kerr on that," said Russell Long during one hearing. "He says he is against any combine he is not in on."[12]) After Kerr died, Webb remembered who his friend's friends were. In 1963, after bids had been submitted and opened for Apollo's communication system, Webb announced that AT&T—which had not bid at all—would get 20 percent off the top, with the competitors scrambling for the rest.[13] When Senator Long asked Senator John Pastore, the floor leader, who besides AT&T was "particularly interested" in the Comsat bill, Pastore snapped, "The President of the United States. Does the Senator from Louisiana want to go further than that?"[14] The dissidents, who did want to go further, did not have much further to go. Albert Gore said,

> There were two bills introduced in Congress, the Kennedy bill and the Kerr bill, both authored by distinguished friends of mine, and I must say, as I look at the progeny, it looks a little more like my friend Senator Kerr than it does like President Kennedy.[15]

At first the Kennedy administration resisted the communications carriers' pressure. President Kennedy released a statement in 1961 saying he favored private development of a satellite system, including "maximum possible competition" and "full compliance with antitrust legislation." What the Justice Department actually proposed, however, was that the federal government supervise the establishment of a single privately owned corporation to develop satellite communication. The company's stock would be available to anyone, but no one person or firm could own more than 15 or 20 percent of it.[16] This proposed corporation was labeled "publicly owned" (in the same limited sense that British private schools are called public schools), to contrast it to the communications carriers' consortium plan.

Kerr had the power to block all of Kennedy's legislative program, so the President was forced to compromise with him. The bill that eventually became the Communications Satellite Act passed the House of Representatives almost without opposition in April 1962. It provided for a private corporation to be set up in the District of Columbia. Half its stock would be reserved for *international* communications companies ("common carriers" in regulation parlance). The aerospace firms could buy into the other half of the company if they wished (they did not), along with the rest of the general public, but no one other than an international carrier could own more than 10 percent. No exclusively domestic carrier (that is, no domestic carrier besides AT&T, the only carrier with both domestic and international operations) could own stock in the company at all. This provision was based on AT&T's insistence that satellite communication was far too expensive for domestic use and that Comsat (as the Communications Satellite Corporation came to be known) would always be an international company. (This contention had no validity, and it did not make AT&T reluctant to claim later, when the television networks wanted to put up their own domestic satellite and take their transmission business away from AT&T, that Congress clearly had given Comsat a monopoly on *all* satellite communication, international and domestic.)

Finally, the board of directors of the company would include six representatives from the international carriers, six elected by the other stockholders, and three appointed by the President with the advice and consent of the Senate.[17]

Thus the Comsat solution, later praised and imitated as a creative and prototypical solution to modern American business problems, really was a simple 50-50 compromise between what the Kennedy administration wanted and what Ma Bell and Senator Kerr wanted, with three public directors included to disarm liberal critics.

The process of compromise is part of the public record.

When Kennedy forwarded his original bill to House Speaker John McCormack on January 7, 1962, it was already a serious compromise of the original Justice Department proposal because it reserved half the stock of the company for AT&T and the other carriers. At the time, Kennedy declared that the *only* reason the carriers had been allowed to invest in the corporation was to allow the high start-up costs to be dispersed through rate-base regulation, whereby a government-approved monopoly such as AT&T is permitted to charge whatever it needs to cover its legitimate costs plus a fair profit. This was another idea from AT&T, which had insisted that the company's enormous early losses might otherwise be burdensome. The idea had no validity—as AT&T should have known even if Kennedy did not—and was used only as the thin end of the wedge for the carriers. Three months later, when the carriers knew they were in, the rate-base provision was dropped in the final version of the bill. The carriers bought into Comsat anyway and never complained about the company's modest early losses.

Meanwhile, a more important change had taken place. In the original bill Kennedy had insisted that to prevent the carriers from having a harmful influence on the company their stock would have no voting rights. In the April "compromise" version, the carriers had been given the right to vote—which they used to great profit for a decade. Strangely, no one at the time seemed to think much had changed. *CQ Weekly* reported that the April bill differed from the January bill "in minor respects."[18]

Kennedy also announced in January, more or less as an article of faith echoing his policy statement the previous June, that the bill would have the effect of "strengthening competition in the communications industry." The act itself insists that its purpose is to "maintain and strengthen competition" and "be consistent with the Federal antitrust laws." In fact, as Washington lawyer Joseph Rauh pointed out to the Senate Foreign Relations Committee, the final Comsat Act "only does not violate the Clayton and Sherman Acts if you consider this an amendment of the Clayton and Sherman Acts," and it violated the President's earlier policy statement "in the most flagrant, obvious form."[19] Rauh was candid about his own opinion of the bill: "This bill is probably the biggest giveaway in the history of our Nation, for it gives away not only billions of taxpayers' money already spent to develop both space and space communications, but also the vast unknown discoveries of the future . . . the still undeveloped wonders of the space age."

Rauh was completely correct. The Comsat Act established a monopoly in international satellite communications; permitted competing communications entities to invest together and work closely on a single board of directors; and gave control of a new technology to owners of an old one with which it competed. Yet the long series of hearings reveals a slow capitulation by the Justice Department as to the malleability of antitrust laws. In August 1961, when the Justice Department still was hoping for a completely independent corporation, antitrust chief Lee Loevinger (later in the decade an FCC commissioner) told the Senate Monopoly Subcommittee that if the established carriers were allowed to influence use of this new technology,

> there would be a natural reluctance on the part of the companies with large investments in existing facilities to take speedy action which would make these facilities obsolete. A company controlled by AT&T could scarcely avoid considering the effect of satellite facilities on existing investments in cable facilities. . . . Suppose that in the early days in the development of motor transport service we had decreed that all motor transportation should be owned by railroads. I think it is self-evident that we would not have quite the same system of motor transportation that we do have today.[20]

Even without carrier control, Loevinger said, consortium arrangements were dangerous.

Personally, I have a suspicion that at least part of the tardiness of this country in developing the control systems and the techniques for space technology in relation to Russia is due to the fact that such agreements have hobbled American industry and that we have not gotten the best benefits out of our competitive system by permitting free competition between our best scientists and our best laboratories.[21]

In wanting to exclude equipment manufacturers, the FCC was committing

a violation of their own logic. This arises out of the fact that the largest equipment manufacturer in terms of assets in this field is Western Electric, which is a wholly owned subsidiary of AT&T.[22]

In March 1962, when the administration was still hoping to avoid giving AT&T voting power in the company, Attorney General Robert Kennedy warned the House Commerce Committee:

Unavoidably, the satellite system will compete with, as well as supplement, existing facilities. This creates a possible conflict of interest . . . for it would be only natural for AT&T to consider in its policies the extent to which speedy expansion of satellite facilities would make obsolete facilities in which it now has huge investments.

A corporation which was truly independent would have no such conflict of interest.[23]

By August the Attorney General's conversion had become complete. Kennedy told the Foreign Relations Committee he had been convinced by arguments

that the carriers, AT&T, RCA, and seven or eight others, had had tremendous experience in this field, had had tremendous expertise, that if you turned this corporation over and just permitted the public to buy generally that frequently you would miss all of this experience, all of this background, all of this expertise, all of this knowledge which might be necessary in order to make this corporation a success.[24]

The antitrust safeguards in the bill were sufficient, Kennedy had decided.

We received 90 percent of what we struggled for. . . . I do not think
that this company or corporation is being turned over to AT&T. I
think anybody who makes an objective study of this bill, this legislation, could not possibly reach that conclusion.[25]

Deputy Attorney General Nicholas Katzenbach, who is reported to have
negotiated the Comsat compromise with Kerr, suggested at this point that
giving AT&T and its friends half the pie was the only way to save even a
few crumbs for the public. If the compromise should fail, Katzenbach
wrote Senator Mansfield,

> Ironically, in view of the arguments made by those in opposition, the
> possibility of a system owned and operated exclusively by the exist-
> ing carriers would be greatly enhanced. . . . Either they will domi-
> nate the system through ownership, as the communications indus-
> tries initially proposed to the FCC, or under a government-owned
> system they will dominate it through contract.[26]

This was an unusual admission from Katzenbach—that contractors inevitably dominate the government agencies they deal with. No one asked
the Deputy Attorney General what the Justice Department was doing
about this deplorable situation. It was also at this point, after the compromise had been threatened with a filibuster, that much-admired FCC
Chairman Newton Minow testified that, as for the longstanding problem
of controlling AT&T, "this bill . . . is exactly what we need."[27]

AT&T Vice-President James E. Dingman, later to become a Comsat
director, testified several times to argue the carrier position. His story,
unlike that of the Justice Department, was always the same. Communications satellites, he revealed, were really no big breakthrough. They would
not make undersea cables obsolete, and they certainly had no potential for
domestic use. They "will merely provide the means by which broadband
microwave techniques employed for continental communications can be
extended across the oceans to supplement existing common carrier
facilities."[28] Asked point-blank about domestic use, Dingman remarked
that "the international carriers, by and large, are the ones that have been
in the overseas business."[29] Nevertheless, he argued, only the established
international communications carriers had the necessary expertise,
financial resources, and raw guts to develop this relatively insignificant
system, and therefore they should be given exclusive control.

The magnitude of this task is very great. It will require an organization having technical competence of the highest order. . . . Expertness in the communications art must be accompanied by a thorough understanding of the communications business and an ability to deal with our foreign counterparts. . . . Above all, the organization must be service-minded, must sincerely believe in the objectives of the whole program, and must be willing to take the very real risks inherent in the speedy establishment of this new and untried communications facility. There can be no conflicts in objectives within this organization, no overabundance of caution, no pennypinching spirit.[30]

The carriers, Dingman testified, were sincere and enthusiastic in their desire to help advance satellite communication.

This position may be construed by some as stemming from the selfish interests of my company which is the largest of the carriers involved. Let me assure you that it is not.

Let one thing be crystal clear: AT&T has no desire or intention of seeking to control the communications satellite system to its competitive advantage. . . . Hard as it may be for some to understand, our sole interest is in the earliest practicable establishment of a worldwide commercial satellite system useful to all international communications carriers and agencies both here and abroad.[31]

Nonetheless there were limits to the carriers' enthusiasm. Dingman's company and the other carriers "would have considerable difficulty in recommending any substantial investment" as long as Congress insisted on limiting them to merely half the stock. They were ready "to put up real money to back a satellite corporation," but not for an arrangement they regarded as "impractical and liable to be unworkable."[32] Even 60 percent "would be an improvement," but "I would not prefer it."[33] Furthermore, the carriers worried about all the government supervision; it "could result in conflict and confusion which might smother the initiative and leadership which are essential to the accomplishment of the national purpose involved."[34] Dingman left it to his colleague from ITT, Vice-President Henri Busignies, to argue that the only solution to potential conflicts between international carriers and other participants in the satellite system was to prevent anyone else from participating.[35]

Senator Long summarized the carrier arguments during liberals' filibuster against the bill. Their position, Long said, was "that the proposed satellite would not be very good; that it would be a long time before they could be expected to make money from it; nevertheless, they would like to have it, even though it may not be valuable."[36] Long did not mention the carriers' alleged fear that stifling regulation and less-than-total ownership might discourage them from investing at all. This had already proved groundless.

The Comsat bill faced virtually no opposition in the House, where, less than a month after leaving the Commerce Committee, it passed easily, despite Emanuel Celler's metaphor-packed warning that "We arm ourselves with a sea of troubles if we embrace any legislation in this field which does not tether AT&T and thereby safeguard the public interest. You know, there is an old saying, Mr. Chairman, the horse neighs according to its rider."[37]

Mike Mansfield introduced the House bill in the Senate on June 14, 1962. With Pastore referring constantly to "the man at 1600 Pennsylvania Avenue," few Democrats were interested in opposing the bill, and the Republicans liked it regardless. (Former President Truman blamed it all on the Republicans. "The Republicans will give everything away if you don't watch them, he commented from Independence.[38])

The hard core of dissidents included Senators Wayne Morse, Ralph Yarborough, Russell Long, Estes Kefauver, Maurine Neuberger, Ernest Gruening, and Albert Gore. Senator Paul Douglas also participated. It was an occasion for high rhetoric. Yarborough, for example, said at one point,

> It is rather depressing that on the threshold of the greatest scientific discoveries in the history of the human race we have a little greedy band that reaches out to the Congress and says, "Give it all to us. Let us have it. Let us take this boon given to humanity. Let us take this thing developed by the scientific brains of man, paid for by the taxpayers of America, too big and vast to be developed by any one private individual or company. Now that the American people have taxed themselves to the limit, and have bled themselves white to develop this instrument, give us all the vast increment of it, give us the prospects for the future. Give us the profits for the future in outer space." . . . Mr. President, is this the council hall of the States, or has the Senate become the council hall of the corporations?[39]

Russell Long said:

> I see in this bill both the method by which the largest monopoly on
> earth could get control of a potentially competitive system, and the
> means whereby this monopoly could frustrate or prevent the rapid
> development of the system in the event it could not obtain adequate
> control to suit its purposes.
>
> In fact, it is clearly within the realm of possibility that the largest
> single stockholder in the system would see fit to retard the growth of
> the system, rather than speed it. It is crucial to the growth and
> development of this nation that this sort of thing not be permitted.[40]

Long wanted the carriers excluded from the corporation. Kefauver
and Yarborough wanted the corporation replaced by a government
agency. The common goal of the liberal group was to postpone action on
the bill until after the November congressional elections, by which time,
they hoped, public pressure and private reason would have time to
reassert themselves, while political interference from local telephone
companies would be less oppressive.

On June 21 the dissidents agreed to a postponement of debate on the
Comsat bill while some important New Frontier legislation passed. When
the bill came up again on July 26, the filibuster began in earnest. Compared to the anti-civil-rights filibusters the Senate was used to (whose only
object was to fill up the time), it was a serious affair. Speakers filled the
hours with detailed discussions of every sin their staffs could determine
was ever perpetrated by a communications carrier, especially AT&T.
There were, however, some of the usual high-jinks. On the first day,
Morse insisted that the clerk read the record of the previous day, and
Gruening ordered him to slow down because "I do not want to miss a
word." At the completion of this ritual, Douglas parodied Southern
filibusters by engaging in a long colloquy on the fact that the record
"failed to contain a reference to the Deity."[41]

By Senate rules a filibusterer could not stop talking for any reason
other than a question without losing the right to the floor. Another
speaker was almost certainly waiting to take the floor and move for a vote.
"I feel the hot breath of the distinguished Senator from Illinois," Morse
declared of Senator Everett Dirksen at one point. "And let me make
perfectly clear that it is fragrant." Dirksen made fun of the dissenters'
dilemma. "I wonder how the minority leader can adequately express his

appreciation to the distinguished Senator from Oregon for his highly complimentary references," he interrupted after one piece of fluff, "and do it in the form of a question." But the bill's supporters also had a problem. They had to keep people on the floor at all times to prevent the filibusterers from moving to adjourn for the day because of the absence of a quorum. On the first day, July 26, Dirksen asked, in the form of a question, whether he dared to go have some lunch. "Oh, Mr. President," Morse crooned. "I will protect the Senator from Illinois. I will see to it that his rights are not impaired." Dirksen snorted, "I now say, 'I thank you'—and that is not a question."[42]

Since there were so few of them, each dissident Senator had to hold the floor for long hours, relieved only by occasional long questions from the other filibusterers. Wayne Morse concluded one long, uninterrupted stretch by saying,

> The Senator from Oregon earlier announced that he was not going to yield for some time. It has been some time. It has not been very long, but it has been some time. I have kept that faith, anyway.... I will let the Chair in on the secret. I have received written instructions suggesting that I yield to the Senator from Alaska [Gruening] to ask me a question. I will listen to the question with one ear, and with the other ear I will listen to the Senator from Tennessee [Kefauver], standing beside me, who has some instructions to give me. I have been waiting for these instructions, because I am only a member of a team and I am only seeking to carry out my part of the work. However, I yield to my friend, the Senator from Alaska. I hope that he has pondered his question, and that it *is* a question, and that he will ask it rather slowly while I listen to my friend from Tennessee.[43]

Another device for taking a break without losing the floor is to demand a roll call. Maurine Neuberger led up to one such demand with grace.

> When I was a schoolteacher I used to teach English. I remember a quotation I used to give; an example of anticlimax in writing. That statement was:
> Oh, dear, what shall I do?
> I have lost my beau and lipstick, too.
> A man standing here in the Senate as I have stood here today, would begin to show a five o'clock shadow. I feel that I have lost my lipstick

too, and that is unforgivable for a female Member of this organization.

I suggest the absence of a quorum.[44]

The bill's supporters did not say much; they did not need to. Kerr and Symington agreed that this new monopoly would help cut short America's drift away from "competitive private enterprise" toward "any socialistic or communistic system." Barry Goldwater announced that the dissidents themselves were "a bunch of reactionaries" who "by dilatory tactics are helping the Russians." And Pastore arose from time to time to insist on behalf of the President that AT&T would not dominate the company and that the regulatory controls were sufficient.[45] But mostly the supporters just waited for the opponents to talk themselves out. When that did not happen, they began to get impatient.

At the end of July the Comsat bill was referred off the floor and back to the Foreign Relations Committee. This was the result of an agreement between Wayne Morse and Mike Mansfield that the bill would get one more committee hearing, as the dissidents wanted, but that when it returned to the floor it would become officially the pending order of business—and thus eligible for cloture. When the bill did return from the committee to the floor on August 10, tempers were short. And the debate—in line with Senate tradition—achieved new excesses of politesse.

> MR. GORE.   I have enjoyed the colloquy between the distinguished Senator from Missouri (Symington) and the distinguished Senator from Oklahoma (Kerr).
>
> MR. KERR.   I am especially happy to have contributed to the enjoyment of the Senator from Tennessee.
>
> MR. GORE.   The enjoyment of the colloquy was slightly diminished by the fact that I have previously read such catechisms published by the U.S. Chamber of Commerce and the Republican National Committee.
>
> MR. KERR.   The Senator has a broader range of reading information than I had been aware of. He does not often give evidence of it.[46]

Mansfield extended the hours of the Senate to make the filibuster more difficult; then, on Saturday, August 11, he filed to limit debate. The Senate had imposed cloture only four times before in its history, most recently in 1927. Two cloture attempts during civil rights filibusters that very session had failed to get the support of a simple majority, let alone the necessary two-thirds. Morse was miffed.

> We are told that we must proceed with great haste in this effort to give away to a Government-created private monopoly the exclusive right to the use of space for commercial exploitation in the field of communications. We must move with consummate dispatch to create an exemption to the antitrust laws which would allow the communications carriers to join together in their efforts to extend the reaches of private monopoly power throughout our economy. We must hasten to insure complete dominance of our communications system by the American Telephone and Telegraph Company, which is already the world's largest private monopoly.[47]

Comments from outside Congress were almost totally against the dissenters. *Washington Star* columnist William S. White described their activities as "an increasingly savage filibuster," "a threat to the whole cooperative arrangement between government and business," and an "almost hysterical thrust at the heart of capitalist democracy." Marquis Childs accused them of being populists. (This is a fashionable term in the 1970s, but it was not in 1962.) "They are a bunch of soreheads," he explained, "braying before the images of a past that is gone forever." The *Washington Post* declared that the issue was not satellites and monopoly at all.

> The question is whether, in a time of continued world tensions and on the eve of a congressional election, the Senate will conduct itself as a responsible legislative body. . . . This is no time . . . to be squandering party unity and good will for a Pyrrhic victory.[48]

The response from the *New York Times* and elsewhere in the liberal press was similarly negative.

On Tuesday, August 14, the day of the cloture vote, five Southern senators, including J. William Fulbright, found it convenient to be absent from the floor so they would not be recorded as favoring the stifling of Senate debate. (Dirksen said dryly of their absence, "A lot of things can happen to a Senator on the way to the Senate. . . . Someone might stop a Senator and try to sell him a horse. You can lose a lot of time in a horse trade."[49]) Vice-President Johnson was in the chair so that every proadministration senator could cast a vote. AT&T had bought the back page of the *New York Times* to remind everyone that it was "by far the world's biggest business. Without it, we could not call home, or fight a nuclear war."[50] (Senator Neuberger said of the advertisement's claims that she did "not want a private corporation to have this hold upon me."[51]) Mansfield declared that debate had gone on as long as many Southern filibusters. He neglected to mention that these others had been successful. Long of Louisiana told his cloture-minded colleagues, "Senators would not do that for the NAACP. Why do they wish to do it for AT&T?"[52] Douglas said that while he opposed filibusters on principle, he would vote to sustain this one.

> I am tired of the one-sided application of the rules of the Senate . . .
> by the opponents of civil rights legislation. . . . While such tactics are
> conducted and legitimized, I do not wish to disarm those who favor
> progressive legislation. I believe in mutual disarmament.[53]

A two-thirds majority is required to invoke cloture. Shortly after one o'clock the cloture motion passed, 63 to 27, with the missing Southerners making the crucial difference.*

The opponents proposed amendments—to increase supervision, to assure reasonable rates to the government, to generate a subsidy for educational television. All were tabled without discussion. Morse kept on plugging.

> I say most good-naturedly and respectfully that if any senator really
> thinks that AT&T will not dominate the proposed corporation to be
> created by the Government under the bill, he is naive. And I know of
> no Member of the Senate who is naive.[54]

A few odds and ends were tidied up. Hubert Humphrey defended President Kennedy's "fine mind" against charges that he did not understand the bill, as the opponents (and Harry Truman) had chivalrously concluded.[55] On August 17, Pastore ended the debate.

---

*Ironically, this vote may have made possible the passage of the Civil Rights Act of 1964 by dampening the Senate's historic reluctance to "gag" its members, as the anticloture position used to be put. After using cloture against men like Estes Kefauver and Paul Douglas, some senators felt they could no longer refuse on grounds of historic principle to let a civil rights bill come to a vote. And so they did not.

This bill is what the administration has suggested. It is what President Kennedy has said time and again that he wants. Let him who wishes to do so give it a vicious name, or label it as he will. However, let me say this. All of us in a sense are sinners. None of us is perfect. But as my God looks at me tonight, with all that I have done in this bill and all that I have fought to do with this bill, and all that I know that is in this bill, I can look Him straight in the face.[56]

Pastore's climactic variation on the theme of invoking the chief executive brought his colleagues to the peak of enthusiasm. "Vote! Vote!" they shouted, and shortly afterward they did. The act passed, 66 to 11. James A. Weschler wrote that autumn of the senators who had tried to defeat it:

Their lost cause is probably already largely forgotten by most Americans, if, indeed, it was ever seriously noticed by many. Yet one ventures the prediction that we have not heard the last of this affair. It might be described as one of the greatest untold stories of the early space age—and, conceivably, the first momentous scandal of this new era. In a free society such episodes have a way of haunting the participants long after the deals have ostensibly been completed.[57]

Business Week predicted in October 1962, barely a month after the Comsat Act was signed, that members of Congress who opposed the bill "will be alert for evidence that they were right and that the program needs changing." This turned out not to be the case. (Many of them soon lost their offices. Kefauver died.) Except for an insignificant technical alteration in 1969, Congress never has amended the Comsat Act, despite the fact that subsequent events proved the opponents to be correct in almost all their contentions. Viewed from the perspective of more than a decade, some of their concerns seem a bit skewed. They had worried about the delegation of foreign-policy-making power, as well as the use of government patents and equal opportunity for procurement contracts. None of these has emerged as a major problem in the way the filibusterers had in mind. But they were right in their central complaint.

In retrospect, the provisions of the Communications Satellite Act seem to have been based on two myths: that the traditional communications carriers had to be in on satellite development because of the capital and technical expertise only they could provide; and that the government regulatory structure created by the act was sufficient to overcome any pernicious carrier influence.

The capital crisis was a fantasy engineered by and for the carriers, to justify their position. In 1961 the FCC appointed a committee of carriers to study commercial satellite communication, then endorsed the committee's inevitable conclusion that the carriers should control it. Commissioners praised the companies because they "express a willingness and indicate a capability to marshal their respective resources" to finance a system. In November 1962, after the act had become law, AT&T general counsel Horace Moulton (later a Comsat board member for many years) worried in print that noncarrier investors might be afraid of the risk and that the company might therefore go hungry for cash.[58] Meanwhile, it was suggested during Comsat's formative months, by the carriers among others, that the company would require a medium- or low-altitude satellite system costing up to $500 million.

Comsat settled on a stock offering of $200 million—10 million shares at $20 each—which it made in May 1964. Because it chose a cheaper high-altitude system (over AT&T's objections), and because other countries were allowed to share system ownership, even this seemingly conservative figure turned out to be far more than the company needed. Half of this money remained for a decade in "temporary" cash investments, not in satellites or related equipment.

Half of Comsat's stock was by law reserved for the carriers. (Though they billed themselves as the investors of last resort, they really were the investors of first opportunity.) AT&T offered to buy $85 million worth but was restrained and told that $58 million was its fair share of the industry's investment. This gave AT&T 29 percent. ITT went in for $21 million, or 11 percent. RCA, Western Union International, and 159 other small carriers picked up the crumbs.

The supposedly timid general public behaved exactly as everyone but the carriers, Congress, and the FCC had expected, making Comsat the most heavily oversubscribed stock offering in history (surpassing the occasion when Ford went public in 1956). "There isn't enough of this stock in the world to take care of our customers' demand," the *Wall Street Journal* quoted one broker. Demand was so heavy that the offering had to be postponed a month. The official limit was 50 shares per person, but many brokers reduced the quota even further and refused to sell to anyone but regular customers. The average holding turned out to be just 27 shares. (The average holding of AT&T—the most widely held company in the world—is around 200 shares.[59]) Possibly inspired by AT&T's example, one woman said she was buying in because it was "the patriotic duty of every American."[60] A more common refrain was that the stock was "futuristic" and therefore "for my kids." Even in 1971, more than one-fourth of Comsat noncarrier stockholders—30,136 out of 119,533—were holding shares as custodians for children under Uniform Gifts to Minors acts.[61] The prophets of terrible doom and gloom who had played such an important part in the discussions leading up to the Comsat Act were drowned out by a chorus of optimists. Comsat chairman Leo Welch said in a *Newsweek* cover story that the Comsat enterprise was "as novel as the concept of increasing the stars in the firmament, which is what we shall do."[62] All the publicity surrounding the stock offering created the image of a company owned by thousands of taxpayers; the role of the carriers themselves was deemphasized.

Demand for Comsat's stock remained so strong that by 1967, before a dividend had been declared, the carriers' $20 shares were selling for $78 on the New York Stock Exchange. ITT, which in 1961 had told the Senate that part ownership in the satellite system was essential to its operation under the Communications Act of 1934, and that the company was not attempting "any get-rich-quick scheme,"[63] decided in 1968 that it was not so essential after all. The company sold its Comsat stock at about 60, for a 200 percent return in four years. Western Union International sold its Comsat shares about the same time. The remaining large-carrier stock-holder, AT&T, agreed in 1973 to sell its shares as part of a domestic satellite compromise with the FCC. AT&T cleared a $67 million return on its original $58 million investment. (During the 1974 slump, Comsat's share price dipped back into the 20's.)

The carriers had argued in 1962 that the impossibility of raising money from private citizens meant only one thing—if carriers were not allowed to invest, the government would end up footing the bill. By agreeing to own the system, they argued, they were saving taxpayers millions of dollars. In fact, government investment in other space communications programs and the cost of regulation make any saving seem insignificant, if it exists at all. In the two years following passage of the Communications Satellite Act, the Defense Department spent $170 million on communications satellite technology, more than the entire cost of the U.S. share of the private system. In the same two years NASA spent another $110 million on satellite communication research.[64] High levels of government spending have continued. NASA's Applications Technology Satellite (ATS) program received $60 million (out of a total NASA budget of $3.3 billion) in fiscal year 1972 alone.

The late Senator Kefauver expressed concern during the Comsat debate that the government would have to pay a premium to a private company just to use satellite technology the government had paid to develop.[65] As it turns out, the FCC's Authorized Users decision means that the government pays *two* premiums—one to Comsat, which was partially owned by the carriers for most of its life, and one to the carriers directly. Political considerations aside, the argument that a government-owned system would cost the taxpayers a great deal of money is without foundation.

Other arguments against government ownership were self-contradictory. It was argued, for example, that a government-owned system would both deplete the Treasury for years before showing a profit, and deprive the Treasury of income taxes on the private system's enormous profits. Of course, a government-owned system might have returned to taxpayers *all* the profits of the system's operation, not just the taxes on them. Government ownership, too, would have eliminated regulatory logjams like the 10-year delay in launching a domestic satellite system, the costs of which are hard to measure.

Another advantage the carriers were expected to bring to the satellite communication system, besides great quantities of otherwise unavailable cash, was their experience in communications. Once again, the carriers themselves advanced the notion that technological progress was impossible without them. AT&T's Dingman told senators a satellite system would need

> technical competence of the highest order, and this competence must be recognized both here and by the communications agencies abroad. . . . I think it is obvious . . . that satellites will be evolutionary, not revolutionary in character. They will not constitute a communications system in themselves but will merely serve as an intermediate link in a system that provides complete communications service. The degree of their usefulness . . . will depend upon their proper integration, on an economically sound and operationally efficient basis, in the vast complex of domestic and international common carrier facilities.[66]

Their investment in the satellite company, the carriers continued, would give them a vested interest in applying their great technical expertise to satellite development.

The record of carrier impact on satellite technology however, bears out the more reasonable contrary assumption. AT&T's $58 million investment in Comsat was an insignificant fraction of its investment in older, cable technology. The latest trans-Atlantic cable alone cost $145 million, of which AT&T has invested $70 million. In 1966, when the Ford Foundation first suggested that the television networks could distribute their shows by satellite instead of using AT&T's facilities, this service alone was bringing AT&T $65 million a year which they were not inclined to give up.[67] Compared to these figures, AT&T's $58 million total investment in Comsat meant little, except the influence it gave AT&T in communications satellite policy. Nevertheless, Comsat itself advanced the argument as late as 1972.

> We believe that an equity holding in Comsat by major customers, and a concomitant representation on the Board of Directors, tends to motivate those customers to interest themselves in the use of the satellite system and its development to a greater extent than would be the case if they were not shareholders.[68]

By this reasoning, the scheduled airlines should be given control over the cheap charters, which would make them more sympathetic to these competitors and lead them to send business their way. The traditional carriers' "technical competence of the highest order" led them to advocate the more expensive low-altitude satellite system, and their experience in the field led them to claim that the time-delay factor made satellites unusable for phone conversations—a point on which AT&T was especially insistent.[69] Both positions turned out to be erroneous.

Even taken at face value, the carriers' "experience" arguments tend to collapse as a justification for their privileged role, because the real breakthrough that made communications satellites possible was not in communications but in aerospace; that is where the Comsat effort has been moving along the cutting edge of technology.[70] AT&T more or less admitted this with Dingman's insistence during the hearings that satellites were really just like long telephone poles in the sky.[71] This was part of AT&T's "nothing new" argument for control of satellites. But if this was the case, should not the aerospace firms, not the communications carriers, have been given control of the company? AT&T argued the reverse—that the aerospace firms should be *excluded*—and they argued it successfully.

In fact, Comsat insisted ten years after its birth that there had been virtually no technical collaboration with AT&T. "With respect to technical expertise, there have been several instances of limited contacts between the AT&T and Comsat staffs," Comsat told us. "There is no significant relationship between the technical staffs of AT&T and Comsat today."[72]

The additional carrier argument, that any satellite would need to operate closely with the terrestrial communications system, is of course beyond question. But here, too, the past ten years have found the older communications companies using this fact to encumber, rather than to encourage, satellite communication. As one example, AT&T argued strenuously before the FCC in 1966 to prevent Comsat from building an earth station in West Virginia, saying that such a station would cause frequency interference problems for their terrestrial microwave system. This objection disappeared shortly after Comsat agreed to share ownership of all its earth stations with AT&T and the other carriers.

To give itself an extra bargaining chip in other negotiations, AT&T has worked consistently for satellite frequency allocations which maximize potential interference rather than minimize it. The argument is that frequency interference forces earth stations to be located at some distance from population centers. The farther away the stations, the longer the "local loops" that "interface" satellites with the terrestrial system. AT&T provides the local loops, and longer loops cost more. More expensive local loops, furthermore, raise the cost of satellite technology in cost comparisons with AT&T's own cables and microwave systems. A Ford Foundation study in 1966 concluded that it was possible to build earth stations with no interference problems on several sites "within only one microwave hop from the Empire State Building."[73]

Having determined that the communications giants' role in satellite development was inevitable and desirable, the creators of the Comsat Act believed they had taken extraordinary and effective steps to prevent carrier domination of satellite communication. The failure of the FCC, the presidential directors, Congress, and the White House to do so is a major theme of this book. But it is interesting to record here the way these regulators, along with AT&T and Comsat itself, have dismissed the very possibility of carrier domination. During the final hearing sandwiched between the two halves of the 1962 filibuster, the Kennedy administration dismissed the notion of carrier domination—some of its spokesmen contradicting their own earlier testimony. Besides Robert Kennedy, quoted above, his deputy Nicholas Katzenbach wrote: "The bill contains effective safeguards against AT&T domination. AT&T is prohibited from electing more than 3 out of 15 directors." FCC Chairman Newton Minow wrote to Senator Mansfield that AT&T could be prevented from retarding satellite development and would not even want to. He thought that "development of the satellite system will not be retarded or dominated by a single carrier or group of carriers."[74]

After the act was passed, AT&T became more strident in responding to those who questioned its lack of authority. *Newsweek* reported in 1964 that AT&T's Dingman "fairly explodes at such talk: 'How in the world three directors, which is the most we can have, can dominate a board of fifteen seems kind of ridiculous [*sic*]' "[75] Today Comsat feels that its historical immunity to domination has vindicated its earliest defenders.

> Congress, after thorough consideration of all aspects of the problem, determined that it was in the public interest to let AT&T and other existing carriers share in the ownership of Comsat; and Congress also provided numerous and substantial safeguards with respect to such ownership. To date, the operations of Comsat have fully vindicated congressional judgment that such ownership would not impair either the independence of Comsat or its dedication to promoting satellite technology and satellite service.[76]

Comsat still refuses to see itself as in any way competitive with its large associate. "AT&T is not strictly a competitor of Comsat in the market for international services," Comsat has written. And, "with respect to the market for domestic communications services, it is impossible to say whether Comsat or AT&T may or may not become competitors."[77] These two Comsat quotes show the benefits of the Comsat Act's creative ambiguity. When the company wants the right to cooperate with AT&T in the domestic satellite business, it says it is proud of its record of competition with AT&T. When it wants to convince an interested outsider that there is nothing wrong with carrier ownership, it argues that there is really no competition involved

History aside, the notion that 3 out of 15 board members and 29 percent of the stock does not mean domination defies traditional business assumptions. By coincidence it came out during the 1962 filibuster that AT&T owned exactly 29 percent of the Cincinnati and Suburban Bell Telephone Company, which it considered to be a subsidiary. Of another subsidiary, Southern New England Telephone, it owned only 19 percent.[78] In the section of the U.S. Code pertaining to investment companies,

> "Control" means the power to exercise a controlling influence over the management of policies of a company, unless such power is solely the result of an official position with such company.
>
> Any person who owns beneficially, either directly or through one or more controlled companies, more than 25 per centum of the voting securities of a company shall be presumed to control such company.[79]

In its famous 1957 decision forcing du Pont to sell its interest in General Motors, the Supreme Court ruled that the chemical firm's 23 percent ownership gave it an unfair advantage in doing business with GM. Interestingly, the Court said that du Pont's influence was increased by the wide dispersion of the remaining shares.

> The potency of the influence of du Pont's 23 percent stock is greater today [than when first purchased] because of the diffusion of the remaining shares, which in 1947 were held by 436,510 stockholders; 92 percent owned no more than 100 shares each and 60 percent owned no more than 25 shares each.[80]

In 1971 *98 percent* of Comsat's stockholders—116,809 out of 119,553 noncarriers—held 100 shares or fewer, and *63 percent*—75,357—owned fewer than 25 shares. Even after all the carriers except AT&T had sold their huge blocks, the average holding was only 58 shares per person. And this was double the initial average holding of 27 shares.[81] Here, then, is the ultimate irony of the Comsat stock situation. The low selling price and wide distribution of Series I "public" stock, which was intended to give as many citizens as possible a piece of this "semipublic" corporation, along with the enormous demand that the carriers insisted would not materialize, *actually solidified private carrier control of the company* during its formative decade.

In December 1972 the FCC suggested that AT&T sell its shares of Comsat in exchange for the right to share a domestic satellite system with Comsat. This was a cosmetic reform. Ma Bell had gotten about as much as it could out of the arrangement in both the domestic and international arenas, and since all the other major carriers had sold their shares the anomaly was becoming unsupportable. Two months later, in February 1973, the White House Office of Telecommunications Policy asked Congress to let President Nixon abandon his right to appoint three representatives to Comsat's board. Both bodies argued that the time had passed when Comsat, an ordinary private company like any other, required the benevolent guidance of AT&T and the President of the United States. Neither suggested that there had been anything wrong with the arrangement up to that time.[82] (In 1971 Justice Department antitrust chief Richard McLaren wrote to Senator Mike Gravel that the carrier involvement in Comsat was "contrary to the normal antitrust prohibitions" of the Clayton Act, but when Gravel released the letter the White House announced immediately that this perception was not the official policy of the Nixon administration.[83]) AT&T used its eleven-year control of Comsat and its continuing influence at the FCC in such a way that its effect on satellite communications will continue to be felt for a long time.

2
International Communications: Earth Stations

E arly Bird, the first communications satellite in the international system, was launched in April 1965. Commercial communication by satellite began on a regular basis two months later. The development of international satellite communication has been remarkable in many ways ever since. When the Comsat Act became law in 1962 there were only 99 two-way voice circuits across the Atlantic. These circuits were on two submarine cables owned by AT&T. In 1973 *each* of three Intelsat IV satellites over the Atlantic had a capacity of more than 4000 circuits, and the next generation of satellites was being designed for capacities of up to 40,000 each. Many underdeveloped countries, which had almost no communication with the outside world or could communicate with near neighbors only by sending messages via their former colonizers in Europe now have earth stations and full-fledged worldwide communications channels. In the United States, fewer than 8 million overseas telephone calls were placed in 1963. The total jumped to 39 million by 1972, and AT&T expects it to reach 200 million calls annually by 1980.[1] Meanwhile, we have witnessed great moments of global theater provided on television by athletes, beauty queens, and politicians. Many of the events might never have taken place at all had they not been broadcast around the world via satellite.

The mechanics of satellite communication are fairly straightforward. To transmit a message from, say, a sender in New York to a receiver in London, the message first must be sent through the terrestrial communications system to one of the satellite "earth stations" along the east coast of the United States. The connection between the user and the earth station is known as the "local loop." The earth station is a large, dish-shaped broadcasting and receiving antenna aimed at a satellite circling 22,300 miles above the earth. The message is sent via the earth station to the satellite. The satellite contains relay equipment to receive the signal, amplify it, and rebroadcast it back down to the British earth station in Goonhilly, Scotland. From there it is carried via another local loop to the user in London.

One factor that keeps satellite communication simple is that the satellites are in "synchronous" orbit. The frequency with which a satellite circles the earth depends on the altitude of its orbit. Thus the moon, a quarter of a million miles away, completes an orbit every month, while a manned space capsule several hundred miles up completes one in a little more than an hour. At 22,300 miles it takes a satellite exactly as long to circle the earth as it takes the earth to rotate on its axis—24 hours. A satellite placed at this altitude in an orbit around the equator appears to be standing still when viewed from the earth. A communications system involving nonsynchronous satellites would require many more satellites as well as complicated movable antennas. AT&T's insistence during the early 1960s on the necessity of using a nonsynchronous system was a major reason for the delay in using satellites for domestic communication, as we see in Chapter 6.

A satellite system, besides being much cheaper to use (a hotly contested issue we shall examine in detail), has three important mechanical advantages over equivalent terrestrial methods. The technical terms for these advantages are "distance insensitivity," "broadcasting ability," and "flexible routing."

"Distance insensitivity" means that it costs exactly the same to communicate via satellite between two locations, no matter how far apart these locations are. The cost of building and laying a cable rises almost directly with the length of the cable. But the cost of building two earth stations and launching a satellite remains pretty much the same no matter where the earth stations are located. Also unlike a cable, which can carry communications only between two specific locations, a satellite can receive a message and relay it simultaneously—"broadcast" it—to all other locations within its radius of "sight."

Third, a satellite poised to service a wide area can be used for communication between any of the earth stations in that area until its capacity is filled. Thus its circuits can be allocated, in whole or in part, to any communications routes that need it at any given time. Cables, once installed, are permanently allocated to a specific route. Since satellite circuits can be switched to different routes as traffic patterns change, they are said to have "flexible routing." Terrestrial circuits must be plentiful enough on every route to meet peak demand on that particular route, and as a result may go empty much of the time.

The commercial process of international satellite communication is as intricate and confusing as the mechanical process is straightforward.

The satellites themselves are owned by the International Telecommunications Satellite Consortium (Intelsat), an international organization founded in 1964 under the auspices of the State Department, with representatives from practically every country in the world outside the Communist bloc. Intelsat members own shares in the system proportional to their use of it. The United States owns about 40 percent. National representatives of the other members of Intelsat are government agencies, which also own the earth stations in their own countries. The U.S. representative is Comsat, which shares ownership of the earth stations in the United States with the terrestrial communications carriers—primarily AT&T—that long shared ownership of Comsat itself.

Comsat buys the services of the earth stations from the Earth Station Ownership Consortium (ESOC), of which it is half-owner, and buys satellite channels from Intelset, of which it is almost half-owner. It sells these combined services back to the very same international carriers that own the other half of the earth stations (and at one time owned up to half of Comsat itself), which then sell them to the general public. A contractual arrangement with a government telecommunications agency in a foreign country completes the financial circuit.

This chapter and the two that follow consider how this complex arrangement evolved, and why it may serve the interests of AT&T and the other carriers more than those of the general public. It might be said that international satellite communication has been the victim of the willingness of its regulatory agency, the Federal Communications Commission, to ignore facts that do not fit the policy it wishes to follow.

For example, Comsat made 15 percent of its operating income in 1971 by supplying emergency service during underwater cable breakdowns—including four failures by the newest TAT-5 cable—while maintaining 99.8 percent continuity of service in its own system.[2] Yet the FCC decided that the $70 million TAT-5 cable was required to protect against satellite failures and insure the "reliability of international communications."[3] Demand for a service such as international communications clearly depends on its price. In fact, how much something costs usually is considered to be one of the most interesting and useful things one can know about it. Yet the FCC has used demand as an unrelated and somewhat vague consideration that can be invoked or ignored, and FCC commissioners have said in choosing between cables and satellites that they "do not believe that any useful purpose would be served by going over relative costs."[4]

The facts the FCC chooses to ignore may even include the very meanings of words. For example, a phrase in the 1962 Comsat Act authorizing the company "to contract with authorized users, including the United States Government, for the services of the communications satellite system"[5] would seem to imply that the federal government is an authorized user. Yet the FCC interpreted the act in 1966 to mean that the government is *not* an authorized user.

On occasion the meanings of words are set loose from their moorings and allowed to float free on the turbulent seas of the adversary system. In a Report and Order of July 1972, the FCC mediated between the views of various parties about what had been meant by "reasonable parity," a term it had used just twelve months before.

> AT&T notes that the U.S. carriers do not accept the 1:1:1 approach; that it is in violation of the "reasonable parity" language adopted by the Commission in its Statement of Policy and Guidelines; . . . ITT further asserts that "parity" means "almost or approximately equal." . . . Comsat reaffirms its belief. . . .[6]

By relying on debate between the interested parties to determine what its policy *should be before* it has been set, and then renewing the debate in the form of a discussion of what the words *mean after* the policy has been made, the FCC erodes its ability to make policy at all.

These violations of fact, logic, and language form a pattern. They have served consistently either to solidify the control of the established international carriers over satellite technology, or to discourage satellite communication in favor of antiquated and expensive methods more profitable to the carriers. In the years since Early Bird was launched, the Comsat arrangement has failed the requirements of the act that it "reflect . . . the benefit of this new technology in both quality of services and charges for such services" and "strengthen competition in the provision of communications services to the public."[7] It has failed even in the field of international transoceanic communication, where satellite progress has been greatest.

The FCC's decisions, examined in the next three chapters, occasionally have their own internal logic (often they do not), but this logic usually conflicts with real-world facts, with the logic of other FCC decisions, or with both. For example, commissioners have allowed the carriers to argue both that it is unfair to let Comsat sell directly to users while they are left paying off debts on an older, more expensive technology; and that the older technology is really less expensive and they should therefore be allowed to incur further debts to build more of it.

In 1971 Comsat included as part of one of its massive briefs in the domestic satellite controversy a nine-page discussion, the purpose of which was to show how often it had opposed AT&T on various topics in front of the FCC. Of all the controversies Comsat mentioned, it had lost every decision but one, which was still pending. Within a year after the brief, it lost that one, too.

Comsat called its summary "a record of vigorous assertion of its corporate position by Comsat, win or lose."[8] But in fact Comsat's failure to act competitively was a recurring theme throughout the first decade of satellite communication. A critic of the several Earth Station decisions has complained that "it is hard to fault a compromise apparently accepted by the party most adversely affected." Comsat's objections to TAT-5, the carriers' most extravagant cable application, was so timid that the FCC was able to conclude that "Comsat does not request denial of the instant applications," and "the difference between the two (Comsat and AT&T) is more apparent than real."[9] Comsat's failure, despite the best legal counsel in Washington, to take strong positions and offer its own best arguments in opposition to the carriers, along with its consistent reluctance to seek judicial relief from unfavorable FCC decisions (Comsat never has appealed a decision to court), create a suspicion that the Comsat Act's opponents were correct in feeling that to allow the carriers a major influence in the company would have anticompetitive effects. On some issues there is direct evidence to support this suspicion.

The FCC was established by Congress in the Communications Act of 1934. Its seven commissioners serve staggered seven-year terms. They are appointed by the President with the "advice and consent" of the Senate. No more than four may be from one political party. The immediate impetus for creating the FCC was the need for orderly distribution of frequencies for commercial radio. But the FCC also was entrusted with the equally important function of regulating interstate and international telecommunications traffic. It has the power to determine the services communications carriers may offer, as well as the rates they charge. The Communications Satellite Act of 1962 extended this power to include regulation of satellite communication.

What exactly is the job FCC commissioners are supposed to perform? The purpose of regulation in a free-market economy is to prevent monopoly profits and to encourage efficiency in industries where unregulated competition is considered unsuitable. This situation can arise because of "natural monopoly" conditions or because of the need to distribute scarce public resources by government franchise. The FCC regulates the telephone network for the first reason, and television and radio licensees (users of the public airwaves) for the second.

The FCC's modus operandi, and that of many federal regulatory agencies, is known as "rate-base" regulation. Under this system, a firm's profit is supposed to be a function of its "rate base"—the total value of its investment in equipment that services customers. The commission determines a fair "rate of return" on this investment, one that reflects the cost of using money plus a factor for risk. The firm's profit is its total revenues for the year minus the cost of noninvestment expenses such as salaries and payments to other firms. The firm is allowed to set its prices so that its profit amounts to not more than the official "rate of return" on its "rate base."

Rate-base regulation causes serious administrative difficulties. The regulator not only must determine what is a "fair" rate of return in a world of multiple and constantly changing interest rates, but must in theory pass judgment on every single investment and expense incurred by a regulated firm, to determine whether it is necessary and contributes to maximum efficiency. It is clear that in a monopoly situation, locked into a predetermined maximum rate of profit, a firm will have little incentive to eliminate unnecessary expenses. In fact, it will usually have a *positive* incentive to try to get away with unnecessary investments, because these will add to its rate base. (More on this later.) Finally, the FCC must approve prices for the firm's various services which, given demand (which it must also try to predict), will produce the appropriate return on investment.

The task is difficult. The FCC began a study in 1965 to determine how rate-base regulation should be applied to the novel problems posed by Comsat. A decade later it was still studying.[10] In 1965 the FCC also began to investigate a subject it should have been more familiar with: AT&T's long-distance rates. The Common Carrier Bureau produced a 202-page report on this subject in July 1971, but the following December the Commission tried to drop the whole subject. After a good deal of negative reaction from AT&T critics, the investigation was reinstated, but it remained unclear what would come of it.[11]

If the FCC decides not to allow a certain investment or expense, which rarely happens, a firm may decide to spend the money anyway. This may, in fact, be a rational decision, even though such expenditure will not be included in the firm's rate base or allowable expenses for regulation purposes. Money spent on advertising, for example, may generate demand for services that will in turn create an opportunity for investments that *may* be included in the firm's rate base. (Whether advertising is an allowable expense is unclear. In its study of the rate-base rules for Comsat, the FCC staff proposed to forbid the deduction of such expenses for rate-base purposes. But AT&T, which lacks competition for most of its services, is permitted to deduct advertising in computing its rate of return, thus shifting the cost to telephone users.)

The rate of return a regulatory agency allows is almost always higher than the prevailing cost of money, because of the risk factor, but lower than what an unregulated monopoly could achieve. This leaves the regulated firm with (or rather, without) what economists call "unexploited monopoly profits." To get at these, the regulated firm has an artificial incentive to inflate its rate base. Specifically, the firm finds it profitable to make expensive, inefficient investments that a competitive firm would not make, because it will be entitled to a return on this investment higher than the cost of financing it. It will make this higher return by exploiting its monopoly position a bit more. Since the FCC is concerned only with the firm's *overall* rate of return on investment, the firm will find it profitable to provide services which, taken alone, would be unprofitable, as long as this expands its rate base. The firm can more than balance its loss in one area by extracting higher-than-allowed profits in others, and still come out ahead. This is called "cross-subsidization." Economists consider cross-subsidization inefficient, but the FCC encourages it in some areas—for example, by allowing profits on heavily used long-distance lines to cross-subsidize telephone service to sparsely populated rural areas.

The tendency of regulated companies to invest inefficiently and excessively, and to pass the cost on to customers, is known as the Averch-Johnson effect, after the economists who first defined it rigorously in 1962.[12] Few people have good things to say about it. Some point out the benefits of cross-subsidization noted above. Others say that the Averch-Johnson effect counterbalances a tendency of monopolies to invest *less* than is socially optimal. (As a monopoly keeps raising its rates to exploit monopoly profits, demand for its services—and thus the investment needed to satisfy that demand—shrinks. When monopoly profits are fully exploited, the price is higher and the volume lower than if the industry were competitive.) But most economists and regulators find the Averch-Johnson effect a nuisance.

Among other things, the Averch-Johnson effect creates a strong preference among regulated firms for ownership of equipment, rather than leasing or similar arrangements. The cost of buying equipment can be included in the rate base and thus generates a profit; rental costs can only be deducted as expenses. The impact of this preference on the attitude of the traditional common carriers toward communications satellites is obvious. Since they are prevented by law from owning satellite circuits (or from including Comsat stock in their rate bases), they naturally will prefer to build more undersea cable circuits rather than lease more satellite circuits from Comsat. It might seem, then, that in this respect at least the sensible thing would have been to let them own the satellites, too, as they originally wanted. But even if the carriers owned both, they would still prefer cables *precisely because they are more expensive.*

The only solution is to take decision-making power concerning alternative technologies away from the established carriers, as the FCC is supposed to do (or to dissolve such power into the market system, which may be impossible). Yet the effect of FCC decisions since 1965 has been just the opposite—to consolidate such power among the carriers. The Averch-Johnson effect explains many of the puzzles surrounding Comsat. It partially explains, for example, why AT&T was so reluctant to permit satellites to be used domestically, and why the other domestic phone companies offered so little resistance. In fact, it offers a general explanation of why established companies in regulated industries oppose technological change.[13] Specifically, it may explain why the carriers fought so desperately for control of U.S. earth stations in the international satellite system.

The earth station controversy apparently took Comsat completely by surprise. The company's first chairman, Leo D. Welch (formerly chairman of Standard Oil of New Jersey), told *Newsweek* before the stock issue in 1964, "We don't expect any trouble over who owns them." There was little reason for such optimism, as there had been trouble about the earth stations even before Comsat was founded. The act itself is vague on the matter, instructing the FCC to authorize ownership by the company, the carriers, or both "without preference to either." The Kerr bill would have given both satellites and earth stations to the carriers, while the original Kennedy bill explicitly reserved the stations for the new company. AT&T's Dingman had made clear, during hearings on the various bills, that even if the carriers got full ownership of the company (and especially if they did not), "We believe that the ground stations . . . should be owned and operated by the carriers and other authorized users and not by the Corporation." Furthermore, Dingman argued, any compromise involving shared ownership would be technically disastrous.

> Based on my personal experience of many years with our long lines department coordinating the operations of our domestic and oversea long-distance networks, I strongly believe that any other arrangements providing for divided responsibility for operation of these facilities will prove impractical and will degrade service to the public.[14]

The trouble that Leo Welch said he did not expect materialized immediately after Comsat requested ownership and control of the U.S. ground stations in September 1964. Of the six carriers that filed comments on the Comsat FCC application—including AT&T and ITT—all except Western Union International opposed it. Comsat, too, originally insisted it was essential to have undivided ownership and control, without which "it cannot manage the quality and quantity of the service provided by satellites, and will be unable to improve the design and operation of the terminal stations."[15] Comsat's firm position on its right to complete ownership of the satellite system lasted exactly one month. In reply comments of October 27, the company assured the FCC and the carriers that it had no wish to foreclose its competitors and part-owners from controlling earth stations of their own once the initial system was in operation.[16] This early concession was the essential renunciation, making possible the final "compromise" solution two years later, which removed any danger to the carriers of having to compete with an independent, integrated satellite system.

ITT saw a special danger in Comsat ownership. Its lawyers told the FCC in November 1964:

> It is foreseeable, should Comsat achieve the monopoly it presently seeks, the end result may well be that the international record carriers will be forced from the field and that two entities, AT&T and Comsat, will completely control international communications traffic (to and from the United States).[17]

Early in 1965 AT&T suddenly dropped its objection to Comsat control of the initial earth stations. Even "divided responsibility" did not seem as "impractical" and "degrading" as it had in 1962. In fact, AT&T proposed that Comsat manage the stations at the outset, so long as the carriers could share ownership immediately, up to 50 percent, and participate in control after three or four years.[18] It took the FCC until December 1966 to reach almost exactly the same conclusion.

A lot was at stake for both Comsat and the carriers in the earth station controversy, though the real issues were seldom discussed in their respective arguments. For both, there was the question of rate base. For the international carriers, a piece of the earth-station action offered the only chance to make a profit in satellite communication during the near future as the law stood, while satellites might be cutting deeply into their business and reducing the chance for new cable investments. The rate base, however, was not greatly affected by their investment in earth stations: the half-ownership in six earth stations they eventually got increased the carriers' rate bases an average of less than 4 percent each, far less than the incremental benefit to them of even a single new cable.

For Comsat, however, the rate base was crucial. Not only did the estimated $39 million cost of the six proposed earth stations represent a sizable chunk of its estimated final rate base of under $100 million (and three times its 1966 rate base of $13 million), but the company still had intact practically all of that $200 million it had raised. (Half of it remained intact for nine more years.) Using these figures, the final disposition of the earth stations reduced Comsat's rate base "by at least 25 percent, while adding relatively little to most of the carriers."[19] The carriers' rate-base plea has even less validity than this would indicate. According to the act, if Comsat could expand its rate base enough to issue more stock or bonds, the carriers would be entitled to invest in these securities. And—unlike their accounting of the original issue—they could include the investment in their own rate bases.

A great deal of misunderstanding about rate bases is evident in these controversies and in the commentaries on them. At least in theory, the public interest concerning which company is entitled to include an item in its rate base should be limited to determining which one will accept the lowest return on its investment, or which one can be expected to generate the lowest operating expenses. Neither of these considerations ever arose in FCC rulings on the earth stations. Rate-base regulation involves an implicit policy that the profit a regulated company deserves to make should depend on how much money it has invested (not how large its management task is, nor how many customers it has), and that its investment should be the minimum necessary to satisfy the demand for its services. There can be, then, no valid "need" to increase one's rate base, unconnected to provision of services, except to justify inflated overhead or to satisfy a desire for expansion. The claims that a company needs internal incentives to behave properly, or has a lot of money lying around, are not valid public-interest considerations in determining who is entitled to make an investment. That necessary capital investment in a satellite system is small compared to the volume of business it can handle does not serve as an argument against rate-base regulation for Comsat, as its president said it did in 1965.[20] It simply means that satellite communication is very cheap.

The rate-base issue was a diversion from the more important one. The real stake in the earth station controversy—for Comsat, for the carriers, and for the public—was the existence of an independent, fully integrated satellite system that could truly "strengthen competition in the provision of communications services." One former Comsat executive put it this way in an interview:

> What is Comsat selling? The law says it's selling "channels of communications." Without the earth station, there is no channel. If another guy has the earth station, you're selling him only the opportunity to look at a satellite, not a channel.

More important, do you see yourself as expanding into new areas, acting competitively? If you don't have control of distribution on the ground, how can you possibly sell your services?[21]

With full ownership and control of the earth stations and the "local loops" connecting them to the large customers and telephone switching centers they were meant to serve, Comsat could offer service fully equivalent to that of the international carriers, including Ma Bell. It could, therefore, reintroduce competition in this area, or at least allow for vigorous and independent assertion of satellite economies before the FCC. The benefits would be obvious, both to the company and to the public, and would fulfill the provisions of the Comsat Act.

Without the local loops, and sharing control of the earth stations, the satellite company—unless there was very close government regulation—would be at the mercy of its competitors. Comsat has day-to-day management responsibility for the earth stations but shares long-range planning and oversight with other members of the ownership consortium (ESOC). The carriers can use their influence in the consortium to discourage construction of earth stations in different parts of the country and close to centers of use. In this manner they increase the satellite system's dependence on terrestrial systems, thus increasing their own profit from it. More important, they thereby increase the cost of satellite communication as a whole relative to terrestrial and submarine methods completely under their control. All these methods for keeping satellites under control depended, however, on keeping Comsat from controlling the earth stations and terrestrial connections.

When the rumor spread in April 1965 that the FCC was planning to give Comsat full ownership of earth stations, the carriers were reported to be "hopping mad over the matter and likely will challenge it in court."[22] (Comsat tried neither hopping nor litigation when the tables were turned.) The first earth station decision came on May 12. It gave Comsat "sole responsibility for the design, construction, and operation of the three stations to be located in the Northeastern and Northwestern parts of the coterminous United States and in Hawaii."[23] Read literally, the decision does not explicitly award Comsat ownership. But the press at the time universally interpreted it that way, as did the FCC itself later.[24] Furthermore, despite a provision for review after two years, the decision was widely regarded to be "interim" only in that the Commission reserved the right to approve different ownership of future stations, "including one in the southeastern part of the United States which may be required during the period the interim policy is in effect." It seemed as if the first three stations were Comsat's for keeps. What's more, Comsat also was authorized to supply the local loops. Commissioners Hyde and Lee dissented and took what seemed to be an extreme procarrier position: that Comsat ownership should be limited to 51 percent.

The carriers were upset partially because the FCC appeared to have accepted and held against them some of their own dubious arguments from the 1962 debate. For example, the carriers suggested in 1965 that their own participation in the earth stations was required so that the satellite system could benefit from their communications expertise, and to insure their willingness to give business to the satellite system. The FCC replied that their expertise would surely express itself through their representatives on Comsat's board, and that their investment in Comsat itself would give them adequate incentive to use the satellite system, as the carriers themselves had claimed in 1962. The Commission also repeated AT&T's own warning about the dangers of divided responsibility.

> As a practical matter, we believe that any arrangement calling for a substantial ownership interest on the part of the carriers, however effectively it may function, involves the risk of diluting responsibility, with the resultant risk of possible delays and undesirable compromises in the decisions affecting the stations and the system during the interim period. We think this will be particularly true if, as has been suggested, the carriers were to have 50 percent ownership of the earth stations.[25]

The Commission showed that, at the time, it thought of Comsat ownership as a permanent solution for at least the first three stations, and shared ownership as a temporary measure in any event.

> Joint station ownership would require some type of temporary or ad hoc arrangement, the formulation and functioning of which could involve unnecessary delays, uncertainties, and possible conflicts among the parties greatly out of proportion to the temporary conditions it is designed to meet.[26]

After 19 months the permanent solution turned out to be temporary, and the temporary one permanent. AT&T immediately petitioned the

FCC to reconsider its decision to let Comsat own the local loops. The carriers also proceeded to arrange for construction of the local loops they had been denied permission to have, while ITT applied to own the earth station on the ship meeting the Gemini V spacecraft splashdown. Comsat protested in both cases that the carriers were doing things *it* was supposed to do, but its argument was weakened somewhat by the fact that it had failed to indicate any interest in the Gemini earth station until ITT applied. ITT also beat Comsat in applying for an earth station in Puerto Rico.[27]

Faced with the carriers' local loop arrangements, the FCC reversed itself in February 1966 and declared that the "interface" between the satellite system and the common carrier facilities would be considered to be the earth station site, rather than the "gateway" city. This meant that the carriers would own and manage the connections between city and station. Commissioners Hyde and Lee concurred in this, though they continued to insist that the carriers were entitled to up to 49 percent ownership of the stations themselves. The majority, however, confirmed their earlier preference for full Comsat ownership and the reasoning behind it. Praising their own foresight in classic regulatory prose, they said,

> The rapid technological and accelerated requirements for the availability of facilities, particularly in connection with the Apollo program, indicate to us that the advantages we envisage would result from a centralization of responsibility and control in Comsat are even greater than appeared when we first considered the matter.[28]

The loss of the local loops has haunted Comsat ever since. Not only did it reduce the company's rate base and prevent it from offering service competitive and fully equivalent to that of the carriers, but it has given the carriers a perfect opportunity to cause problems for the satellite system. Whenever the carriers and the FCC want to ignore cost considerations and approve construction of a new cable while satellite circuits go empty, they bring up the factor of satellite "reliability." Though it has never been proved that cables are more reliable than satellites (if anything, the opposite seems to be true), it is a fact that most satellite "outages" or periods of poor transmission quality are caused not by satellite breakdowns but by breakdowns in the ground connection facilities owned by the carriers.[29]

Thus the telephone companies use their inability to meet their own standard of quality control on a small part of the international satellite system as a way of arguing for a larger part.

The issue over which the carriers arranged to complete their defeat of Comsat on the ground-connections issue was the site of a second East Coast earth station. Comsat applied for a station in Etam, West Virginia, in January 1966.[30] All the carriers objected, saying there was no need to perpetuate a Comsat monopoly beyond its extensive trial period of nine months. But AT&T said its objection went beyond the mere question of ownership.

> Regardless of ownership and control, if the application (for the West Virginia station) is granted on the basis of the technical characteristics herein, there exists a serious hazard that the proposed facilities will interfere with existing domestic terrestrial communications facilities and that existing domestic terrestrial facilities will interfere with such a ground station. Petitioner owns and operates facilities which may be involved with harmful interference.[31]

At the same time, the carriers applied for their own earth station near Woodland, Georgia, or Moorefield, West Virginia.

In June Comsat was still calling "ridiculous" the carrier reasoning that it did not deserve complete control, but by August it was arranging with the carriers to make the ridiculous come true. Under the FCC's auspices, Comsat and the carriers formed two committees to solve the West Virginia problem. One was to consider technical issues and site selection; the other, policy questions of "interim organization and *joint financing*" (emphasis added). The wording of this mandate saved Comsat the trouble of having to negotiate away sole ownership, and made the result a foregone conclusion. The FCC offered the ambiguous (and ultimately worthless) reassurance that negotiated settlement "would not prejudice the interest of any entity in the final decision as to ownership and operation."[32]

Now events moved swiftly. By the beginning of September, *Broadcasting* magazine was reporting that the "carriers and Comsat seem to have agreed on joint ownership of stations," the only question being "how much each will contribute." Note the use of the plural noun "stations." Originally only the West Virginia station was under contention; now all were under contention. A "compromise" shared-ownership solution actually was proposed by Comsat at a meeting toward the end of September between Comsat President Charyk and the president of Western Union International.[33] Comsat more or less withdrew its West Virginia application on October 6, applying instead for a second antenna at its station (bought from AT&T) in Andover, Maine, on the ground that this would avoid delay resulting from conflicting applications.[34] Both RCA and WUI opposed this application, though RCA said in a separate filing that if the application were approved, it wanted to participate in ownership and operation.[35]

The FCC's second earth station decision on December 8, 1966, put an official imprimatur on the negotiated "compromise." In a total reversal of its earlier reasoning and conclusions, the FCC limited Comsat to 50 percent ownership of the earth stations, distributing the rest among the international carriers proportional to anticipated use (the same formula used for distributing the carrier half of Comsat stock). This formula applied not just to West Virginia but to all U.S. stations in operation, under construction, or proposed. And it took effect immediately, without regard to the two-year life supposedly given to the first decision. Thus Comsat had managed to negotiate away more by December than its most extreme opponents on the Commission, Hyde and Lee, would have taken by edict just the previous January. While Comsat retained management of the earth stations, the FCC gave the Earth Station Ownership Consortium as a whole responsibility for "formulating overall policy and deciding on major investments, types of major equipment and *location of new stations,* and the establishment of day-to-day operations of the stations" (emphasis added).[36]

The second earth station decision repeated the same arguments the FCC had refuted earlier. A carrier share in the earth stations was needed, the Commission said, so they could "make meaningful contribution to the development of the art." If the carriers were unable to expand their rate bases in this area.

> their incentives to aid in the growth of satellite communications would be severely limited. They would be faced with the prospect of ever diminishing rate bases, both in the absolute and relative senses, and would be driven to seek alternative means not necessarily dictated by efficiency but by need for survival.[37]

The commissioners offered several other ironies here. They argued simultaneously that satellite success required carrier involvement, and that without carrier involvement satellite success would be so great as to threaten carrier survival. They accepted as a given the supremacy of satellite technology, which they would later reject, and perceived the carrier motives for preferring inefficient cables, which they would later ignore. They embraced the carriers' rate-base arguments, overlooking the relative contributions of earth stations and cables to carrier rate bases. "Ownership participation and investment would provide powerful incentives to maximum use," they argued. "Orderly planning of needed new cables, satellites, and other facilities would be facilitated so that the inherent advantages of each could be exploited to the maximum."

While facilitating the facilities, the consortium arrangement "would be in a position to deal on equal terms with its foreign correspondents which, for the most part, have unified cable and satellite interests"—a conclusion precisely opposite to that of the first decision, which used the same reasoning to conclude that undivided Comsat ownership would best serve American interests. Finally, the commissioners concluded, questionably, that a Comsat monopoly violated the "spirit and intent" of the 1962 Comsat Act. As Herman Schwartz pointed out in the *Yale Law Journal,* not only was there no basis for this conclusion—the law *explicitly permitted* a Comsat earth station monopoly as one of the FCC's alternatives—but the conclusion implied directly that the Commission violated the law with its first decision of May 1965.[38]

A Comsat internal memorandum distributed in 1968 said the earth station verdict "clearly restricted Comsat's ability to market its services and to initiate new types of satellite services. Its effect was to insulate the corporation from potential customers."[39] In answer to my questions, the company would only say that a decision "more completely favorable to Comsat might have resulted, according to our view . . . in more efficient administration of the U.S. earth station operations." Many Comsat employees saw the controversial legal reasoning of the second earth station decision as offering an opportunity for appeal in court—just as AT&T said it would appeal an unfavorable earth station ruling. Comsat's legal help apparently felt differently. The company explained:

> In every instance in which Comsat has not *fully* prevailed in an FCC proceeding, consideration has been given to an appeal to the courts and the decision whether or not to appeal has been based on advice of counsel as to whether there were adequate legal grounds for overturning the decision.[40]

Privately, Comsat supporters say that unless the company had agreed to make a settlement sharing ownership and control of the earth stations, the carriers could have used various legal techniques to delay indefinitely the development of the entire satellite system. A court case, they argue, would have had the same effect. Their acknowledgment of AT&T's habit of seeking full legal and regulatory redress on all occasions contrasts oddly with Comsat's own consistent failure to do so. One would suppose that this technique would be a valuable piece of "experience" Ma Bell could share with her young foster child.

But Comsat did not appeal, and it is easy to see why not. After the ownership question was settled, AT&T's concern over the "serious hazards" of technical interference at the West Virginia station was never heard again. Similarly forgotten was a brief Western Union International complaint that a proposed Comsat station in California suffered from "16 actual cases of harmful interference and one case of potential interference" that should prevent FCC approval "unless and until these problems are resolved."[41] FCC chairman Rosel Hyde said a year and a half later that the success of this type of blackmail proved the wisdom of the FCC's policy.

> It is interesting to note that a whole series of claims and contentions about interference which the proposed earth stations might cause to the terrestrial facilities of the other carriers were quickly resolved after the later (shared ownership) policy was adopted, and earth station construction is now proceeding on schedule.
>
> It is also worthy of note that the other carriers, who as customers of Comsat heretofore expressed doubt, if not serious objection, about the twelve and a half percent return sought by Comsat, are now not only silent on this, but have adopted it as a figure reasonably applicable to their investment in the earth stations.[42]

Even Comsat's limited concern for "efficient administration of the U.S. earth station operations" may be misplaced, for there have been complaints that its own administration has been inefficient. Again, inefficiency raises the cost of satellite operations, aiding the carriers in their struggle to justify more cables. So they have every incentive as members of the consortium to make the earth station operation as inefficient as possible (a point the FCC apparently ignored). In November 1964 Hughes offered to build Comsat ground stations for less than $2 million each. The same month Comsat said its stations would cost $4 to $5 million each. They ended up costing about $6.5 million each. [43] Hughes did not get the contracts. Western Electric, AT&T's fully owned manufacturing subsidiary, got a major share of them.[44]

Foreign representatives to the Intelsat consortium have had occasion to look into the efficiency of Comsat's earth-station management. One of them said of the company, "They run the most expensive earth stations in the world." During an FCC hearing on Comsat's rates in March 1972, company representatives were forced to defend themselves against Commission staff charges that their stations were "overdesigned," which Comsat's spokesman justified on the basis of "redundancy" and "reliability." *Telecommunications Reports* summarized his testimony.

He observed that "complexity and reliability go in opposite directions" because "increased complexity leads to less reliability," but "advanced technology improves reliability." He also added that "It doesn't always follow that increased redundancy enhances reliability."[45]

Comsat's high earth-station costs and weak regulatory gamesmanship combined to deprive it of even the management of an earth station in the U.S. territory of Guam, allowing the carriers—in this case RCA Globcom—to take another little chunk out of the satellite system. Comsat insisted at first, in May 1968, that a station was not needed merely to provide the 31 additional circuits RCA claimed the Defense Department would require before 1973, and that constructing a multimillion-dollar station would do nothing but increase satellite system costs. (Much of the traffic that was supposedly overloading cables touching Guam was really relay traffic between two other points, both of which had earth stations mutually aimed at a satellite with a great number of empty circuits that the carriers refused to use.)

When ITT came to RCA's defense, no reference was made to cost. Rather, it was argued that a station was needed "both to meet defense requirements and to provide diversity of communications facilities." RCA offered to share station ownership with ITT and WUI. (Another ITT division got the contract to build the station.) Bowing to the inevitable, Comsat said that if there was to be a station, it ought to be manager and part-owner under provisions consistent with the FCC's second earth station policy. The carriers naturally disagreed, suggesting that a different arrangement might provide an interesting cost comparison between Comsat's management and their own. Comsat quickly declared that it "does not consider this an appropriate time" for such experimentation; besides, costs had gone down since it built its first stations. Costs certainly did decrease over the next few months, as Comsat and RCA played leapfrog down the cost curve in successive submissions to the FCC. After 13 months of furious filing over who was to satisfy this "emergency" demand, RCA won "interim" approval in June 1969 to construct the Guam station, on the ground that it was most capable of building the station in the five months remaining before the Defense Department claimed it was needed. The Common Carrier Bureau ruling added, "We also believe a slight preference should be accorded to RCA with regard to the cost factors." This "interim" lasted exactly a month. At the beginning of July the parties were reported to have reached an agreement whereby Comsat would get half-ownership of the Guam station and the three carriers would split the rest. But RCA, not Comsat, would run the station, and assume responsibility for "all services directly related to the day-to-day construction and operation. . . ." Comsat was declared to be the station's "system manager," in charge of relations with other station owners and Intelsat members.[46]

The Guam arrangement thus entered the larger "interim" in which the FCC had placed all the earth stations following its second decision of December 1966. This interim was to last three years. But in December 1969 the Commission announced a review of its earth-station ownership policy and asked interested parties to submit their opinions.[47] Comsat suggested that it still wanted full earth-station ownership, and received a reprimand from the carrier. Said AT&T:

> As the whole tenor of its statement indicates, Comsat seems to lose sight of the public interest in the maintenance by the carriers of a balanced network of cable and satellite circuits. It unjustifiably considers the balanced network as a device for furthering the carriers' interest in submarine cables. . . . With this attitude, Comsat looks upon the carriers as "competitors" rather than "customers" and regards every disagreement between itself and the carriers as an effort by the carriers to obstruct the development of the satellite system.[48]

RCA Globcom called Comsat's views "oversimplified" and "rooted in its apparent desire to view the means of communication as in competition with each other," such competition being "artificial and pointless."[49] So much for the FCC's argument that share ownership would produce harmony. The review sputtered on for a while, but the policy today remains unchanged. The carriers had requested exclusive carrier ownership, while AT&T said it liked things as they were. As usual, AT&T and the *status quo interim* won.

The record carriers—ITT, RCA, and WUI—continued to show their concern as earth-station owners for developing the satellite system. In 1972, for example, they opposed Comsat's application to add antennas to the East Coast stations and to buy other equipment. Comsat president Charyk said of this:

> It is ironic that our application to the FCC for authority to construct the necessary facilities, although supported by AT&T, is being opposed by the record carriers who, at the same time, are advocating the construction of other communications facilities in the name of redundancy and flexibility. This is being done despite the fact the FCC has permitted the record carriers to have an ownership interest in the satellite earth station facilities under the premise that this would provide these carriers an incentive to work for the improvement of service through facilities in terms of quality, reliability and efficiency. We hope the FCC will re-examine, in light of this picture, the validity of the premise.[50]

There was little basis for this hope.

3
Authorized Users

To appreciate the illogic of the FCC's Authorized Users decision of June 1966, which prevented Comsat from selling its services to anyone but the international carriers, it is helpful to look ahead to 1968. At that time the FCC commissioners—echoing the carriers' arguments of 1961—were still talking about satellites in terms of "this high cost period [which] must be passed" and "hopes for economies [from satellites] in the more distant future."[1] In its Authorized Users decision two years before, the Commission had proclaimed that the day of cheap satellite communication had already arrived. Yet the *effect* of the Authorized Users decision was to keep satellite economies obscure, preventing satellites from competing with the carriers' cables. What little competition there has been has occurred indirectly.

On at least three occasions since 1966 the international carriers have reacted to the threat of losing exclusive retailing rights to satellite business by promising to lower their cable/satellite composite retail rates. Does this mean that satellite communication is cheaper than that by cable? Or does it mean that carriers' rates previously were too high? Or does it simply mean that the carriers are shifting revenue requirements to other services where they have no competition, and raising rates there? AT&T denies all these possibilities. And the FCC, instead of forcing its clients to explain such contradictions, creates its own contradictions. Thus the commission-

47

ers force Comsat to sell virtually all its services through carrier middlemen as the best way to "reflect the economies of satellite communication to all users." Then they insist that cables have a cost edge over satellites because "cable costs include but a single corporate overhead, whereas satellite facilities include two corporate overheads."[2]

The payment of even one corporate overhead by the government, which had spent billions developing the technology it was turning over to a private firm, was of great concern during the 1961–62 congressional debate. This is why the law creating Comsat refers to "authorized users, including the United States Government." Efforts by the dissenting senators to include a statutory discount for the government got nowhere. Both sides were somewhat misdirected on this point, as witnessed by the following exchange.

> MR. GORE. The U.S. Government will pay a few large American corporations for the privilege of utilizing the facility in international communications which may determine the outcome of the cold war; a facility the technology of which has been developed almost exclusively, to this day, by the taxpayers' money.
>
> MR. PASTORE. . . . When the Government uses the facilities of NBC, of CBS or of ABC, we do not mind. But when we propose to use the facilities of AT&T, everyone gets excited. What is wrong? Are we or are we not for free enterprise?[3]

The first firm to raise the important question of whom Comsat could sell its services to was not Comsat itself but one of the television networks. In February 1965, two months before the launching of Early Bird, Comsat's first satellite, CBS filed a petition in the docket concerning the earth station controversy. The network requested to be considered an "authorized user" with whom Comsat could do business. Reports surfaced that the networks, the wire services, and IBM all were "looking at this portion of the law" because the satellite firm "might be able to undersell AT&T." Comsat's response to these customers was laconic; the company's only public statement on the subject up to that point had been in a speech the previous October by Chairman Leo Welch, in which he had said that Comsat's "principal income" would come from "telephone and telegraph companies leasing satellite circuits."

Applications increased as inauguration of satellite service approached. The first official authorized user application came from the Associated

Press in April. UPI, the *Washington Post,* and even Eastern Airlines soon applied. (The *Post's* late publisher, Philip Graham, had been one of Comsat's presidentially appointed incorporators. His widow and successor as publisher, Katherine Graham, asked for an early ruling from the FCC.) Meanwhile, AT&T and RCA Globcom confirmed, when asked, that they planned to apply for authorized user status, though they had not done so yet. AT&T was confident there would be no trouble. Chairman Frederic Kappel told the corporation's annual meeting in April, two weeks after the Early Bird launch, that the company's "continuing efforts throughout the years to improve satellite communications by no means diminishes its deep interest in or need for other forms of communications." Asked if this did not suggest potential conflict of interest within Comsat, Kappel replied that it did not as long as Comsat "sticks to the business they're set up to do," which was to be a "carrier's carrier."[4]

AT&T's confidence in Comsat and the FCC was well placed. With the television networks, the newspapers and wire services, and the large business communications users on the opposing side, a lesser monopoly might have compromised. But it took Ma Bell only a year to achieve total victory. Comsat was in a strong position to request the right to rent Early Bird circuits directly to the networks, the largest potential customers, because the percentage of the satellite's capacity needed for a television signal was greater than that which any one carrier would control if it was allocated by the Commission's usual "predicted use" formula, and greater than any undersea cable could carry.

At first the FCC let Comsat sell directly. But in July, less than a month after Early Bird began service, it reversed itself and ordered the carriers to take turns as satellite middlemen, so that each could get practice at it, though none would be given an advantage in a final solution. Comsat, meanwhile, produced initial rates the networks labeled "ridiculous," "chaotic," and "completely uneconomic." The FCC agreed, saying that Comsat had overestimated the likelihood of launch failure, underestimated potential growth to fill up the channels, and allowed itself too large a profit. Nevertheless, it let the rates stand temporarily. As a result, the networks fulfilled their promise of "severely reduced" use. *Variety's* classic headline summed up the story:

COMSAT, COMME CI, COMME CA
Webs Give It The Bird, Early[5]

This infelicitous early rate policy was not designed to encourage maximum use of the satellite system, spread the benefits of satellite technology as widely as possible, or encourage alliances between Comsat and ultimate users against the carrier middlemen in the authorized users controversy.

Twenty-seven different interest groups filed comments in the Authorized Users docket by the FCC's November 1965 deadline. The international carriers insisted that the intent of the 1962 act had been to protect their investments in international communications by giving them exclusive rights to buy and resell Comsat circuits. They made much of the fact that Senator Pastore himself had used the phrase "carrier's carrier" back in 1962. This is an interesting argument. Although a majority of legislators had seen the carrier role as necessary, it is important to remember that not even the carriers themselves were offering the protectionist rationale before the act was safely passed. Even if this was their real motive, and that of some of their supporters in Congress, it was not a significant part of the original public debate. By 1966 the carriers were offering their $100 million investment and their seats on Comsat's board as "proof that it would have been inconceivable for them to create competition for themselves."[6] (Recall Dingman's 1962 complaint that their offer of millions was "construed by some as stemming from the selfish interest of my company." "Let me assure you that it is not," he had said.) The carriers warned of the serious consequences to them and their customers if they were denied any part of the satellite business. A number of large users, meanwhile, insisted that they would rather make a new arrangement with Comsat than enlarge their long-standing relationship with AT&T and the other carriers.

Caught between the users who supported it and the carriers who opposed it, Comsat took what is known in Washington as "a middle position": it capitulated to the carriers.[7] It said that "as a general rule," the carriers should be given "the first opportunity" to buy Comsat's services and resell them to all customers except the government. All Comsat asked was the chance to offer services directly if for some reason the carriers were not interested in doing so. This provision was necessary to insure that the carriers were not able to prevent satellite services from being offered at all by refusing to act as middlemen.

Meanwhile, Early Bird circuits were going unused. The FCC sent an unpublicized letter to AT&T in March 1966 asking it to lower international rates to increase business for the satellite. But a more pressing problem was that AT&T had just completed TAT-4, its first cable to continental Europe, and it was filling up the cable before directing business to the satellite.[8] The ability to do this was, of course, one of the main advantages of having exclusive retailing rights to satellite circuits. To avoid this problem, the FCC later instituted complicated and constantly redefined "fill" policies to determine—in the absence of competition——where international communications business should go.

The FCC's Authorized Users decision of June 1966 ruled that Comsat could furnish satellite services and channels only to the other international common carriers except in "unique or exceptional circumstances," or when a customer desired a service that no other carrier was willing to provide.[9] This limited Comsat to four customers: AT&T's Long Lines division, ITT World Communications, Inc., RCA Global Communications, Inc., and Western Union International. A subsidiary decision, seemingly reasonable, authorized the carriers to sell equivalent services at equivalent "composite" rates, whether they were provided by cable, satel-lite, or microwave relay.

(International communications carriers charge users on the basis of "half-circuits," a metaphorical rate for bringing communication from the middle of the ocean, or from the satellite, to the American user and back to the middle again. The foreign communications entity that completes the circuit may charge whatever it wishes for its half, and the total circuit rate is the sum of these two.)

The only business at issue was that of large users who wished to lease circuits for long periods of time. There was never any question that individual telephone callers and cablegram senders would have to deal through the established carriers. But large users constitute a much greater percentage of international than of domestic communication, and the FCC's decision to keep Comsat isolated from them was a serious blow to the company and to the opportunity for increased competition in international communication.

ITT had argued that the carriers provided the service of transforming a "raw" satellite channel into a "useable circuit."[10] But users such as IBM had replied that they would rather purchase raw channels from Comsat, even if they had to supply their own local loops. The FCC's own defense of its Authorized Users decision was based on the economic argument that direct Comsat service to large users would be "cream skimming." Their argument is worth quoting at length. Repeating the carriers' own position, the FCC said,

> Sound policy indicates that . . . they should not be required to depend solely on Comsat for satellite circuits while Comsat is simul-

taneously allowed to syphon the most profitable part of the business from them. . . .

We find that revenues from leased circuits provide an important, if not indispensable, part of the carriers' total receipts. . . . Reports to the Commission show that in 1965 these carriers, as a whole, had net operating revenues, before Federal income taxes, of about $20,300,000. Their revenues from leased circuit service for that same year were $20,200,000. . . . Because of the relatively low nonfixed or variable costs associated with this service, the loss of such business could come close to wiping out completely the record carriers' earnings. . . .

The danger of loss by the terrestrial carriers of existing or additional leased circuit business to satellite facilities is not merely theoretical. A recent complaint . . . and a press release by Comsat . . . indicate that Comsat would propose to charge both authorized users and carriers approximately the same amount for leased circuits and that the amount is substantially below current or recently proposed charges for leased cable circuits. Accordingly, the terrestrial carriers could reasonably be expected to lose a substantial share of their leased circuit revenues to Comsat. Under these conditions and in light of the data set forth above, it could very well be necessary to permit these carriers to increase rates charged other users in order to enable them to earn a fair return. Certainly, such a detriment to the vast majority of users for the apparent benefit of a few large users would be in derogation of the objectives of the Act.[11]

Asher Ende, former assistant chief of the FCC's Common Carrier Bureau, summarized this argument.

We told Comsat, "The law says you have a monopoly in space, Mr. Comsat. But you, Mr. Comsat, are not entitled to supply the whole service." The carriers provide the service for the same price Comsat would have. What is the effect on the general public? If the international carriers lose all their leased circuit service, they're still entitled to a fair rate of return. Therefore it will drive their price up and Mr. John Small Businessman will pay with higher rates. It's worse than cream skimming, because of the regulatory system and the way it works.[12]

In exchange for their victory in the Authorized Users case, the FCC instructed the carriers to cut their prices.

> We therefore expect the common carriers promptly to give further review to their current rate schedules and file revisions which fully reflect the economies made available through the leasing of satellite circuits. Failure of the carriers to do so promptly and effectively will require the Commission to take such actions as are appropriate. Even though satellite circuits are not now and will not for some time be available to all points to which users presently lease circuits, carriers should also reduce charges to many points to which satellite circuits are not now available.[13]

To understand the Authorized Users decisions we must try to understand something about regulatory economics. Take the last sentence quoted above. This would seem to indicate that reduced rates were not a result of cheap satellite communication but rather an exchange for a favorable decision. Otherwise, why should rates be reduced where satellites were not being used? Did this mean the FCC had been letting the carriers charge too much beforehand? Was their rate base or permitted return too high? Or had the Commission detected a previously unnoticed cross-subsidization of other customers? The Commission did not admit to any of these possibilities, or even mention them.

If it was the introduction of satellites that made the rate reduction possible, and if satellite competition would have the devastating effect on the carriers they suggested, the assumption seems to have been that satellites were cheaper than cables for international communication. And if so, why has the FCC approved carrier investment in $170 million worth of cables since 1966 ($90 million for TAT-5, $80 million for TAT-6 and CANTAT-2[14]), for which their users will be forced to pay them a profit during the next 20 years? It is precisely the purpose of regulation to prevent such uneconomic expenditures, which a monopoly will have every incentive to make. If Comsat had made this point when the new cables were up for approval, which it did not (and could not, given its position in 1966), the carriers might have argued that the new generation of cables was cheaper than the latest generation of satellites, whatever the cost comparison had been in 1966. But if at any moment in history a circuit in the latest and most efficient cable is cheaper than a circuit in the latest and most efficient satellite, why should it be necessary to protect the cable companies from satellite competition? How could this competition be unfair to the cable?

One might argue this way. Suppose that the average cost of a satellite circuit is less than the average circuit cost of *all* the cables still included in the carrier's rate base, including the older, more expensive models. In this case, if competition were allowed, the satellite firm could sell circuits at a price less than that of the cable firm, even if the *latest* cable were cheaper per circuit than the latest satellite. This would drive business to the satellite firm and mislead society as a whole into investing in more satellites when the marginal cost of adding more cable circuits would be cheaper. But the job of the FCC is to prevent such misallocation by refusing to approve investment in the more expensive technology. Some commissioners have implied that they thought this was indeed the situation but they were approving a few satellites to be built in the hope that the new technology *might some day* be cheaper than the latest cable. Even in this extreme and improbable case, a limitation of the satellite firm's right to do business as great as that in the Authorized Users decision would be unjustified. The FCC could easily limit Comsat to one satellite of any particular generation and instruct it not to undersell the composite cable rate, perhaps applying any abnormal profit to research and development. (If you are going to approve satellites even though they are more expensive, however, it still makes economic sense to let them be used fully before approving more cables, even if the cables are cheaper.) All these "if's" might be interesting to economists and lawyers, but they show how far we have come from the real situation, which is that satellites, when fully used, have almost since the beginning been demonstrably cheaper per circuit than a fully used cable.

The real reason for the Authorized Users ruling is said to have been the protection of the carriers—WUI, divisions of the ITT and RCA conglomerates—which would have gone under had Comsat taken away a large chunk of their leased circuit business.[15] The section of the decision quoted above supports this interpretation. The question of whether, economically, the non-voice carriers deserved such protection is discussed below. A more important point is that the Authorized Users decision—whatever its validity taken alone—contradicts the FCC's later cable decisions, and stands as an early admission by the Commission and its carrier clients that satellite technology is in fact cheaper.

Taken by itself, the validity of the decision is a more difficult question. In what sense would direct Comsat sales to ultimate users be "cream skimming"? And is it the job of the government regulator to prevent such competitive behavior? Once again, one must extrapolate from the FCC's own reasoning to give its decision the greatest benefit of the doubt. By any official ruling, the FCC has already lost the economic argument by default. It says little for the adversary system as a method of economic decision-making that a year of filings and counterfilings by the various interested parties should have produced a final decision that failed to deal with some of the most important issues involved.

Open competition between Comsat and the international carriers might have produced "cream skimming" in two ways. When technological breakthroughs reduce the cost of new equipment in a regulated industry, regulatory commissions traditionally have permitted firms to retain the undepreciated portion of the more costly older technology in their rate bases at the old high value, rather than reducing it to the "replacement cost" of newer and cheaper equipment capable of performing equivalent service. The rationale is that scientific innovation should not be punished. Otherwise the company that introduced the cost-saving equipment not only would diminish the potential for future increases in its rate base, but would risk actual overnight reductions in its rate base—and therefore in its profit. International cable circuit prices, therefore, were allowed to reflect not just the average cost of the newest and most efficient cable, but the average "historic" cost of all cables still in use. Rates were to decrease gradually as new cables were installed and older ones fully depreciated. (As the first cable was installed across the Atlantic in 1956, and they are presumed to last 20 to 24 years, all the cables are still included in AT&T's rate base.)

The FCC presumably saw the Authorized Users decision as a way of incorporating satellites into this scheme. If a competitor like Comsat could offer rates reflecting only the latest and most efficient technology—skimming the cream—the older carriers would be forced to reduce their rates to meet the competition. They could afford to do this because the cables had already been installed and, once there, cost practically nothing to operate. (In economists' language, the rate would still cover the carriers' short-run marginal cost, which is very small because the cable business is highly capital intensive.) But then, because the cables were still in the companies' rate bases, the regulatory agency would have to allow them to raise rates for other monopoly services in order to generate a fair return. This would be unfair to users of the other services. These other users might include the small businessman referred to above, who might find his own occasional-use rates going up in order to compensate AT&T for its losses on leased circuits that had suddenly become so competitive.

Alternatively, the FCC could reduce the carriers' rate bases to reflect the reduced value of their older equipment, then refuse to allow them price hikes elsewhere to compensate for their revenues lost in competition. But if this became a habit, it would discourage them from seeking new breakthroughs that might suddenly reduce the value of their rate bases. The Commission might also refuse the older carriers permission to reduce their rates to meet the new competition, but then the new firm would be flooded with business and would purchase more equipment while the older equipment sat unused, which would be a waste. And if the FCC refused the new firm permission to build equipment to meet demand, leaving some business to the older firms, it would be creating irrational price discrimination. Thus one argument against cream skimming.

This argument is nice in theory, but it fails as justification for the Authorized Users decision. It is difficult to see how open competition——with an appropriate reduction in carrier rate bases to prevent them from shifting the cost to other users—would be more stifling to progress than the effect of the Authorized Users decision. Unless very close supervision is exercised, that decision gives the owners of the cables complete control over how much business will go to each mode. Competition unquestionably would be damaging to the companies, perhaps fatal to the carriers. But competition, even fatal competition, from newer technologies is considered to be a necessary risk of doing business in unregulated industries. It cannot be considered predatory cream-skimming unless the regulatory restriction is what prevents the firm from competing successfully, or unless a third party or the general public also is harmed. Neither condition applies in this case. (The carriers' exclusion from satellites is not relevant here. Even if they could put up their own satellites, the carriers would still have the burden of their earlier, more expensive investments, which Comsat would not. While such circuits remain empty, in fact, there would be no reason for them to put up a satellite even if they were permitted to do so. And anyway, they claim satellites are not cheaper.)

The FCC defends its protection of carrier clients by saying that if any of them were to go out of business, competition would be reduced. This is a dubious proposition. As the earth-station discussion has shown, and later examples will show further, the international communications industry is far more often characterized by government-administered market sharing than by true competition.

The other type of cream skimming feared by defenders of the Authorized Users decision involves cross-subsidization of some communications users by others. Richard Posner, an economist and law professor, has explained:

> The record carriers have long provided telegram service at a loss which they recoup by charging supra-competitive prices for other services, principally leased lines, where their costs, as mentioned, are small. As a result, there is a class of customers who receive a service for which they would have to pay much higher prices were it provided in a free market; possibly the service would not be offered at all.[16]

"Cream skimming" in this sense means to offer the more profitable service at a more competitive price, without offering the service that the more profitable one is cross-subsidizing. Completely unshackled, Comsat would only be able—and only want—to service the large users of leased circuits. Is this fair to the small users? First, the Authorized Users rule is a remarkably inefficient method of subsidizing senders of international telegrams, since up to 85 percent of the benefit accrues to AT&T and only 15 percent to the other carriers. Second, it follows that if it is public policy that senders of international telegrams should be subsidized, the policy should be carried out openly and not secretly through regulation.

For a regulated company to offer two or more different services that share common costs makes perfect economic sense. When is one service cross-subsidizing another? This depends on how the common costs are apportioned between users of the different services. A minimum standard, however, is that cross-subsidization exists if one group of customers is paying more than it would cost to serve them alone, because then they are paying more for the sharing arrangement than they are benefiting from it. They would be better off without it. Either some other group of customers is being cross-subsidized, or the company is making abnormally high profits.

How can you tell if such unhealthy cross-subsidization exists? If a separate company is willing to offer equivalent service to one class of customers at a lower price, without benefit of any cost-sharing arrangement, these customers must have been cross-subsidizing the others. If Comsat were willing to lease circuits to large users at a lower price than the carriers were charging, this would be proof that the leased circuit users were cross-subsidizing the occasional users. Allowing Comsat to compete for the leased-circuit business would have driven down the price and eliminated this cross-subsidization.

Of course Comsat was not willing to offer such service. But a good many users seemed to think Comsat could have done so, and there is evidence of strong pressure on Comsat from its AT&T board members (not the carriers) not to request the chance to compete for leased-line business.[17] Furthermore, if Comsat did not wish to offer the service, there was no need to make a rule preventing it from doing so; and if the company ever changed its mind, that would be evidence that the ruling was incorrect. The incredible surge of international communications in recent years has shown that demand is very responsive to reductions in price. Through cross-subsidization and composite rates, the Authorized Users decision kept international leased-circuit rates abnormally high. This slowed the growth of Comsat and discouraged maximum benefit to world users of the communications satellite system. Both effects directly violated the intentions of the Communications Satellite Act. Economist Alfred Kahn said of the Authorized Users decision, "It also must uneconomically have retarded the application of that new technology, since its cost savings were not passed on fully in rates to those customers who alone were in a position to take advantage of it."[18]

There is a third type of cream skimming: the cream skimmer will enter a market served by regulated companies and—because it too is regulated—will be able to undersell the going rate by raising prices on noncompetitive services. Unless the regulatory agency prevents them, other firms will do the same. This would *create* artificial cross-subsidization (of the competitive service by noncompetitive ones) and is regarded by economists as the only kind of cream skimming that is truly damaging. It clearly does not apply to the Authorized Users situation.

The important thing to remember, in the end, is that the absence of competition is what creates the blurred distinctions of regulatory economics. It is difficult to know exactly when competition needs to be restricted, but it is clear that the Washington regulatory commissions are rarely averse to imposing restrictions. And, as Kahn points out, "The burden of any mistakes that are made under competition is borne, in large measure, by the businessmen themselves; the burden of the mistakes of monopoly or of its ineffective regulation is borne principally by the consumer."[19]

The FCC offered similar sentiments in its surprising 1969 Specialized Common Carriers decision, when it rejected AT&T's cream skimming arguments in approving an application by Microwave Communications, Inc. (MCI), to construct a microwave connection for large leased-line users between Chicago and St. Louis. In this very similar case, the Commission concluded,

> it would be inconsistent with the public interest to deny MCI's application and thus deprive the applicant of an opportunity to demonstrate that its proposed microwave facilities will bring to its subscribers the substantial benefits which it predicts and which we have found to be supported by the evidence in this proceeding.[20]

Finally, the Authorized Users decision forbade Comsat to sell its services directly to the U.S. government, despite explicit language in the act referring to "authorized users, including the United States Government." (A minor exception was made for NASA's Apollo program.) The FCC said that

> because the Government is a principal source of overseas traffic and revenues to the common carriers, substantial diversion of Government telecommunications business to Comsat could seriously jeopardize the viability of those carriers who are expected to maintain and operate an efficient network of both cables and satellite circuits serving the general public at reasonable rates.[21]

Comsat had asked for the right to serve the government directly, but later claimed not to regard the loss as very important—despite the fact that the importance of government business seems to have been the FCC's rationale for denying it to Comsat. "The FCC's final decision gave Comsat essentially what it had requested," the company wrote.[22] Comsat never appealed this obvious violation of the letter of the law to a higher forum, despite a virtual invitation from the White House to do so. Shortly after the decision, President Johnson's communications adviser, General J. D. O'Connell, wrote a letter urging the FCC to reconsider its ruling "so we can avoid the necessity of a lengthy review of this matter in the courts and in the Congress."[23] The Commission declined to reconsider, and the "lengthy review" never materialized.

Comsat, in fact, has never taken advantage of opportunities for legislative relief written into the 1962 act. The act instructs the corporation to file a report with the President and Congress annually "and at such other times as it deems desirable," while instructing the President to report to Congress annually with "any recommendations for additional legislative or other action which the President may consider necessary or desirable."[24] According to one former Comsat insider, this report arrangement is "the one power Comsat has that no other carrier has. They could open any can of worms they wanted looking like a good guy. But every year, they just say that everything is a big bed of roses."[25] This source maintains that at the end of 1966, following the decisions on earth stations and authorized users, Pastore and his staff director on the Senate Communications Subcommittee, Nicholas Zapple, actually put out feelers to the company urging it to ask for congressional action to reverse the FCC (though it is difficult to see how Congress could make its intentions about authorized users any clearer than they already were). "Pastore started getting disillusioned. He expected Comsat to get on its high horse and come to Congress for remedial legislation, but they never did."[26]

The Defense Department almost saved the day. Less than two weeks after the Authorized Users decision, in what the *Wall Street Journal* quoted "one observer" as calling "a refusal to even concede the existence of the FCC," the Defense Department announced it was renting directly from Comsat 30 circuits from Hawaii to the Far East for use in running the Vietnam War. The "30 circuits" episode, another regulatory filing marathon, is the only example we have of the effect competition can have on international communications rates. Ironically, it was pressure from Congress in support of the carriers, which had lobbied skillfully, that eventually caused the FCC to override the Pentagon's wishes.

The Defense Department's reason for preferring Comsat is clear. When it invited bids to provide the service, Comsat's price was $4200 a month per half-circuit. The lowest price offered by an established carrier (ITT) was $10,000. Hawaiian Telephone wanted $12,700. The average carrier price was almost three times that of Comsat. All the carriers planned to buy their circuits from Comsat and sell them immediately to Defense; it bothered them that Comsat wanted to charge them the exact same price it was planning to charge the Pentagon directly. RCA offered to beat Comsat's price if the FCC would let it build an earth station in Hawaii, but the Defense Communication Agency demurred, saying it had no power over the FCC.[27]

After the FCC's Authorized Users decision and its talk of "composite rates," ITT reduced its bid to $7100, conditioned upon its right to buy from Comsat and immediately resell to Defense all 30 circuits. WUI offered to meet ITT's bid for all 30, or handle just 10 for slightly more per half-circuit. But much more important, both carriers offered to apply this drastically lower rate to all government and private business over the contested routes, not just to Defense's 30 circuits.[28] It may seem odd that the carriers would be willing to lose 60 percent of all their revenues on this route just to get 30 extra circuits of business from the government, especially when they had not abandoned their claim that cables were cheaper than satellites. What they really wanted was to protect the ability to make this claim at all, which would disappear once cables and satellites were in true competition.

The new carrier offers gave the government an ingenious argument for backing out of its contract with Comsat. As Representative Chet Holifield's Military Operations Subcommittee of the House Government Operations Committee pointed out in a report of October 1966—after weeks of testimony and other advice from Comsat and the carriers—the government would save more on its entire Pacific communications bill by the carrier composite rates than it would on the lower Comsat rate applied only to the 30 circuits.[29] In September 1966 the government was using 118 cable circuits in the Pacific. The composite rate would save the government $4.9 million a year over the current bill, plus another $4.6 million if the foreign communications firms followed the U.S. carriers' lead in their charges for the other half-circuits. The Comsat tariff for the 30 circuits alone would save the government only $2 million over the best carrier offer. The rate reduction, of course, depended on giving the carriers the 30 circuits too. So the Holifield committee recommended that the 30 circuits be assigned to one or more of the international carriers in exchange for substantial reductions in Pacific rates for cables and satellites.

The FCC, in its decision of February 1967, did the Holifield committee one better. Instead of requiring the carriers to compete at least among themselves for the Defense Department business, it ordered a "composite" rate of $7100 per half-circuit and split the traffic evenly three ways—ten circuits each for ITT, RCA, and WUI. It required Comsat to sell these circuits to the carriers at $3800—$400 less than its original offer, which had started the whole rate war—and told Comsat it could supply the service directly while the carriers developed the arrangements with foreign communications entities that Comsat already had.[30]

The FCC's reasoning was entirely specious. Thirty times the difference between Comsat's wholesale rate and the old composite cable rate represents the maximum possible saving to the carriers or the government resulting from the introduction of 30 satellite circuits instead of cable circuits into Pacific service. (This is irrespective of the actual Comsat rate. If the FCC ultimately decided it should have been $3800 for the carriers, it should have decided the same thing for the government.) If Comsat and the government had dealt directly, the government would have received the entire benefit of this saving. For the carriers to offer the government a greater savings suggests that either they were charging too much for the service earlier, or they were planning to overcharge for some other service later to make up the difference. In the absence of competition and of detailed cable cost/rate studies by the FCC, there is every reason to assume that Pacific communication rates had been too high—way too high. The Commission might have demanded rate reductions and *still* give the 30 circuits to Comsat.

To make the composite rate structure work, the FCC could not allow the three carriers to compete among themselves for the Defense Department's satellite business. If it had, they eventually would have struggled their way back down to the rate Comsat was charging, since they incur no costs themselves except for a little bookkeeping. Yet despite the economic disadvantages of this cartellike structure, FCC Chairman Rosel Hyde announced in 1968—with consummate illogic—that because of pooling arrangements such as the 30-circuit case, the Authorized Users decision was saving communications users $20 million annually.[31] Meanwhile, in November 1968 Comsat asked for repeal of a similar pooling arrangement of carrier middlemen which excluded it from providing television service direct to the networks. Comsat pointed out, sensibly, that a "composite rate" for cables and satellites serving TV was nonsense because no cable had sufficient capacity to carry television broadcasts anyway. In January 1969 the carrier pool suddenly cut its television rates 30 to 60 percent.[32] The FCC did nothing.

4

Cables

The Earth Stations and Authorized Users decisions left the international communications carriers exactly where they wanted to be in relation to satellite technology. In 1967, they were buying trans-Atlantic half-circuits from Comsat for $2700 a month, then turning around and selling them to users for $8000.[1] In the years since, they have won approval of two expensive, low-capacity cables across the Atlantic and several others off other United States coastlines. Despite important developments in both satellite and cable technology, the actual costs of satellite circuits have remained, by any rational measure, consistently and dramatically lower than those of cables. The carriers have used a variety of arguments to show that it still makes sense to build these cables. When their cost arguments were not sufficient, they offered other and perhaps more questionable noneconomic reasoning. In most cases, the FCC has conceded, and on occasion even Comsat has conceded too.

In the early 1970s more international satellite circuits were empty than there were circuits in all the cables now built or under construction. The cost of using empty circuits already available is approximately zero, yet cables costing hundreds of millions have continued to be built. Per-circuit costs plummet, yet prices for customers remain high.

As recently as 1956, the only reliable method of communication between continents was underwater telegraph cables. In that year AT&T, a

Canadian company, and the British Post Office installed two one-way cables across the Atlantic. When fully developed, these cables supplied 51 telephone circuits in all. The cost per circuit per mile was $305.[2] By the time Early Bird was launched into orbit above the Atlantic in April 1965, AT&T had built, in cooperation with European telecommunications entities, three cables with a total capacity of 240 "voice-grade" circuits, at a total cost of $133 million. The fourth trans-Atlantic telecable, TAT-4, came into service at about the same time as Early Bird. It had 138 circuits and cost $46 million.[3] At the insistence of the FCC, AT&T shared ownership with Western Union International, ITT Wordcom, and RCA Globcom.

Comsat, because of the Authorized Users rule, was completely dependent on other carriers, primarily AT&T, to use the more than 100 circuits available in its new satellite. In December 1963, before the corporation had even issued its stock or decided whether to build a medium- or high-altitude system, AT&T declared that it would be willing, "in order to provide diversity of facilities," to use satellite circuits over the North Atlantic if they could be provided at a cost "reasonably related to the costs of providing communication circuits by alternative means." The company said its preference for satellites over cables would continue "until North Atlantic routes were served by approximately equal numbers of cable system voice circuits and satellite system voice circuits."[4] In other words, AT&T felt that half the business in the world's major international communications corridor should go to cables, and half to satellites.

This was to become the FCC's official policy, following years of legal maneuvering. In the mid-1960s AT&T's proposed policy was considered beneficial to Comsat. But in fact it was exactly the opposite. Because of the huge volume of later generations of satellites, the number of satellite circuits soon surpassed the number of cable circuits available, while the average cost of satellite circuits plunged far below that of circuits in cables. Within two years of Early Bird, AT&T was using its proposed 50-50 policy as an argument for constructing more cables and delaying satellite development, so that the number of cable circuits could catch up. Since 1970, the FCC's "reasonable parity" guideline, based on AT&T's 50-50 policy, has been the telephone company's only justification for new cables. The enormous proliferation of satellite circuits, rather than reducing the need for new cables, made it essential for new cables to be built, to maintain the proper ratio of cable to satellite circuits in use.

It is possible to distill, from the many filings and comments made by the international carriers since 1965, the basic outline of their case in favor of constructing more underwater cables—a case the FCC has time after time found convincing. This is not to suggest that the case ever has been presented in definitive fashion at any one time. Rather, the carriers have depended on a series of independent arguments that disappear and reemerge through the years, each time a little older and a little balder, like characters in a long-running soap opera. Some are false and some are circular, while others merely are inconsistent with one another.

The carriers still like to claim, on occasion, that cables are cheaper to use than satellites, for similar types of communication. (This, of course, directly contradicts the basis upon which they argued for the Authorized Users policy.) They usually base this contention on a fallacious comparison between the fee they pay Comsat per satellite circuit and what they say it would cost them to build and operate a circuit in a fully-used cable. But this is like comparing apples and oranges. Or rather, it is like comparing apples and applesauce.

Four different relevant figures must be compared. First is the so-called annual "revenue requirement" of any given cable circuit. This is the amount of money the cable must earn every year to pay off the construction and operating costs over its lifetime, plus a fair profit for the owners, all divided by the number of circuits in the cable. The annual revenue requirement of a satellite circuit is the cost of building, launching, and maintaining the satellite and affiliated earth stations, divided by the number of circuits it provides and amortized over its expected lifetime. If every circuit of a cable or satellite brings in its own revenue requirement every year, the owners will make back their investment plus a fair "rate of return." The other two relevant figures are the price Comsat charges the carriers for satellite circuits, and the price the carriers charge their customers for equivalent cable and satellite circuits.

In seeking FCC approval for a new cable, the carriers argue that the revenue requirement of a circuit in the proposed cable is less than Comsat's current price per circuit. This is fallacious because the proper comparison is between the revenue requirement of a satellite circuit and that of a circuit in the cable. This comparison would consistently show satellites to be cheaper. The prices charged both by Comsat and by the carriers diverge significantly from their revenue requirements. The reason in Comsat's case is clear; in that of the carriers, it is less so.

Comsat faces the problem that most of its available satellite circuits have been unused. In 1974 Comsat was leasing barely 3000 circuits, three-fifths the capacity of a single Intelsat IV satellite, even though the corporation had several satellites of all four generations in orbit.[5] Since it costs almost as much to operate an almost empty satellite as a full one, Comsat must charge the carriers many times its average fully-loaded revenue requirement to make any money. Under this system, the cables begin to justify one another. The more cables built, the more satellite circuits go empty. The more empty satellite circuits, the more Comsat must charge to make a profit. And the more Comsat charges, the more cables the FCC approves.

The only real incentive Comsat has to lower its rates toward a closer approximation of long-run marginal cost (or its full-capacity revenue requirement) is the hope that this will dissuade the FCC from approving new cables. Comsat may have failed to seize this opportunity to the extent that it should. But the disincentives to cutting prices also are great. In the short run, Comsat cannot undersell the carriers' marginal cost of using their own cables already installed, as this is practically zero. And even if Comsat could, the carriers would have no incentive to increase their use of satellite circuits, because of the Averch-Johnson effect discussed in Chapter 2. Occasionally, Comsat has made a timely rate reduction, or the offer of one, in an attempt to thwart a cable approval. But in general, realizing that the demand of the carriers—Comsat's only customers—will not be affected by price cuts, the company maintains rates high enough to cover its expenses and generate a profit with only a small fraction of its circuits in use.

The international carriers, which retail Comsat circuits to users in the United States, have been remarkably tolerant of Comsat's reluctance to reduce rates in pace with technological cost reduction. The reason for this tolerance is that the carriers use the high rates Comsat charges them as an argument in favor of permitting them to build more cables. Whatever the real cost of satellite circuits, they argue, the cost *to them* is greater than that of building their own cables. From time to time they offer Comsat's maintenance of high rates as evidence that there has been no progress in satellite technology. Western Union International told the FCC in 1971,

> Although Comsat has consistently heralded the economic advantages of satellites over cables, Comsat has yet to initiate any reductions in its rates to the carriers for full-time satellite voice-grade channels. . . . Comsat's continued failure to reduce its rates belies its statement that reduced rates flow faster from satellite than cable technology.[6]

While the FCC allows the carriers to make the fallacious comparison between Comsat's annual rates and their own cable revenue requirements, it regards without suspicion the huge disparity between the carriers' revenue requirements and the rates they charge to the using public. The carriers do not share Comsat's main problem; their cables operate at relatively full capacity. (Were it otherwise, they would be hard put to ask for the right to build more.) As discussed in Chapter 3, cable rates have been based on so-called "historical costs," which represent the average circuit cost of all cables still in use, rather than the cost, or revenue requirement, of the latest and most efficient cable alone. This is so as not to penalize innovation by reducing rate bases as a result. And the firms are entitled to something for overhead, promotion, and so forth. Nevertheless, in June 1965, when Comsat filed its initial Early Bird rate to the carriers of $4200 a month for a leased circuit between New York and Paris, the carriers were charging their customers $10,000 for an equivalent service by cable. The composite cable/satellite rate was set at $8000 and then—when Comsat lowered its price to $3800—lowered to $6000, for a 40 percent cut.[7] This pattern continued in episodes like the 30-circuits controversy. If the carriers' cable revenue requirements were consistently lower than Comsat's rates, the FCC should have asked, why were their own rates so much higher?

In several other ways, the cost comparisons with which the continuing cable-satellite stew has been peppered are designed to make cables look more economical than they really are in comparison to satellites. An underwater cable can only provide a communications circuit between a point near the coast of one continent and another point near the nearest coast of another. A satellite can be far more flexible. Comparing the cost of satellite and cable communication between, say, Paris and New York, ignores the fact that a satellite could communicate just as easily between Paris and Chicago (if AT&T had allowed Intelsat earth stations to be built in the American interior). A satellite, in fact, could establish direct communications circuits between every point in Europe and every point in the United States where there was an earth station. A cable, even if it had the same circuit capacity for the same cost, would have to be supplemented by expensive and complicated land interconnection and switching facilities from the cable head-end on the Atlantic coast. (These facilities, of course, are supplied by AT&T.)

Satellite flexibility has a time dimension as well. Cables are presumed to last much longer than satellites. In fact, both the first trans-Atlantic cable,

TAT-1, and the first commercial satellite, Early Bird, were still operable well into the 1970s, though Early Bird was not being used because of the great superfluity of satellite circuits available. In computing annual revenue requirements, the cost of building and laying the latest cable is spread across 24 years; that of building and launching the latest satellite is spread over 7 years. This reduces per-year cable costs. But assuming that cables really do last almost four times as long as satellites and assuming that this might make the annual circuit cost of the latest technology in each mode approximately equal, the short life span of satellites is a tremendous advantage. This is because technology is reducing circuit costs so fast in both new cables and new satellites. A satellite circuit can be fully written off and replaced by one in a cheaper model, while an equivalent cable circuit would have to generate the higher annual revenue for another 17 years. Already we can see the disadvantage of this in practice. Early Bird, built in 1965, has been written off, even though it still works. TAT-1, built in 1956, still is part of the carrier rate bases and composite rates must be set high enough to pay its annual revenue requirement, even though this is many times higher than that of the latest cables, let alone the latest satellites.

Operable satellites that have fully served their original purpose and been replaced can be moved to places where they are still needed. Thus, when the new Intelsat IVA satellites with about 8000 circuits go into operation over the North Atlantic, one of the 4000-circuit Intelsat IV's will be moved to a position over the Indian Ocean. Certainly this cannot be done with cables.

In part because of these considerations, the international carriers do not rely on cost estimates when applying for a new cable.

The carriers do present a series of noneconomic arguments to bolster the case for cables. In fact, the noneconomic issues have dominated the FCC's cable decisions, and the discussions leading up to them.

The carriers insist that additional cables are needed because satellite communication lacks the security necessary for U.S. military needs. The Defense Department has supported this contention, while simultaneously insisting on millions from Congress to build a completely independent international military communications system *by satellite.* Comsat has pointed out in vain that even if this contention were true, it would be possible to supply all the military's needs on existing cables, by transferring more commercial business to satellites.

Why the military should consider cable circuits more secure than satellite circuits is something of a mystery. In time of war, slicing a cable anywhere on the ocean floor would seem far easier than trying to destroy simultaneously a satellite 22,300 miles in the air and all the associated earth stations on at least one side of the ocean. Jamming or intercepting satellite signals would be almost as difficult, and so far there has been no public indication that it has been attempted. But Jack Anderson reported in 1973 that, "Russian trawlers have located our undersea cables by electronic devices and have cut them at least three times in the last 15 years." He quoted an "informant" as saying, "They were just practicing for the real thing."[8]

The carriers claim that in general underwater cables are more reliable, less likely to break down, than are satellites, and support this contention with various figures on satellite versus cable breakdowns. Comsat counters with other figures that indicate the reverse. The fact remains that the very same week in 1968 when the FCC approved the fifth Atlantic cable, TAT-5, two of the other four broke down when they were cut by trawlers. Service was quickly restored by vacant Comsat circuits.

Even today, a significant part of Comsat's revenues comes from emergency cable restoration. The satellite system has been planned so there is always an operational spare satellite of the latest generation over the Atlantic. Usually, another is in storage on the ground, along with satellites of earlier generations that have been written off but can be reactivated. All these precautions are included in satellite revenue requirements; no such similar precautions are taken for cables, nor could they be because cables are so expensive.

This brings us to "redundancy" and "diversity." Redundancy means that there should be more circuits available than you expect to need, in case of unexpected increases in demand or unexpected breakdowns of equipment. Diversity means that circuits should be supplied by various routes, so that if one facility breaks down, there will be alternatives. The carriers dealt with these two straightforward concepts in less than straightforward ways. They have suggested, for example, that an 825-circuit cable is a wiser social investment than a 4000-circuit satellite, even if it costs more, because a breakdown of the former knocks out fewer circuits than does a breakdown of the latter. More successfully, they have propagated the fundamental fallacy that diversity of facilities—the need for several indpendent communication "pathways" along major communication routes—implies diversity of modes—that is, having approximately equal numbers of cable and satellite circuits serving major routes.

They have not explained why the cause of diversity is not better served by, say, two 4000-circuit satellites than it is by a 4000-circuit satellite and an 825-circuit cable. Suppose that a Federal regulatory agency has refused a barge corporation permission to build a $50 million canal along a certain route, on the grounds that a $10 million railroad link could do the same job. The barge company replies that both a barge canal and a railroad are needed in case one breaks down. As the White House economist who proposed this example has written, this is hardly a convincing reason to build the canal. For two-fifths of the cost of one canal, on this route, the public can have two separate railroads; for the full cost of one canal, the public can buy five separate railroads. If separate railroads do not suffer from service interruptions simultaneously as the result of some phenomenon, then two railroads provide the same reliability as one railroad and one canal, at a lower cost.[9]

Note that this point follows a discussion of why the proposed rates charged by owners of the cheaper mode might be higher than those of the more expensive one. This discussion ignores the most immediately relevant reason: if, by government fiat, the canal was provided with a full complement of business, while the railroad went nine-tenths empty, the $50 million canal owner could break even by charging rates only half as high as those required by the $10 million railroad. Nevertheless the economist, Walter Hinchman, is correct in his more general point that, "The rates approved and required by regulatory authorities thus depart from the prices which would be set in a free competitive market. The latter prices are efficient signals [for investment decisions]; the former are not."[10] This, of course, is exactly why agencies given power over a company's rates must also have veto power over its investments.

Another carrier noneconomic argument, which cannot be dismissed so easily, is that the European countries with whom the United States does most of its international communicating strongly prefer cables to satellites. Their timely intervention has saved the carriers from some unfavorable FCC decisions. The U.S. government, naturally, does not want to appear to be dictating modes of communication to its European partners. The Europeans feel that they can proceed with cable development on an approximately equal basis with the United States (the British Post Office and AT&T are the two major developers of new cables), whereas increasing use of satellites leaves them totally under American domination. This is partly because, of the Western nations, only the United States can place a satellite in synchronous orbit, and U.S. companies are masters of satellite communication technology. But the European attitude is also partly due to Comsat's imperious behavior, as U.S. representative and system manager, in the Intelsat international satellite consortium (see Chapter 5).

By contrast, AT&T manages to maintain excellent relations with the Europeans. "They have an impeccable reputation," said Dr. Reinhold Steiner, former Intelsat representative from Switzerland. "They have been known to bend over backwards. The philosophy started with radio communications and continued with cables. Whenever I go back to Berne and discuss various Comsat misdeeds, the PTT boss always says, 'why can't they behave like AT&T, RCA and WUI'?" [11]

The European communications systems are run by government entities, which have a tendency to place nationalistic and foreign policy considerations ahead of economic ones. AT&T understands this. It argued for the TAT-5 cable between the United States and Spain on the ground that the southern Europeans felt hurt that all their cable communication with the United States had to be channeled through England and France. (There was also a timely reminder of all our defense installations that depended on the continuing good will of the Franco regime.) Before TAT-5 had even gone into operation, the carriers had applied for a similar 825-circuit cable to France, on the ground that the northern Europeans would be annoyed if they too did not have direct access to the latest model cable.

The foreign relations problem is purely an artificial one, a function of the way an international "half-circuit" is defined—from the middle of the ocean to a user on one side and back again. The communications entity in each country is responsible for half of a complete international circuit and may charge whatever it pleases for that half. (Already, the Europeans charge more for their half of a complete circuit than do the American carriers.) The total fee is the sum of the two half-circuit charges. But under this arrangement, both sides must agree on which facility should be used for any particular phone call, and therefore on the total division of traffic between cables and satellites. If the half-circuit were redefined to mean a one-way trip across the ocean, the Europeans could pursue any sort of uneconomic communications policy they wished, without interference from us. Not only could they use available circuits at whatever ratio they preferred, but they could build and own their own cables and use them exclusively to provide the Europe-to-America half of a two-way conversation. (Of course an American placing a call to Europe would still have to pay their higher rates for the return half of her call, but she must pay their higher rates under the present system as well.) The White House Office of Telecommunications Policy said in 1971 that it was going to call a conference on redefining the half-circuit, but like many of Clay Whitehead's plans, it did not pan out.

Even without redefining the half-circuit, the Europeans could be told that they are free to build and operate cables landing on our shores if they like, and that the American carriers would be permitted to lease half-circuits on them as long as the rate was less than what Comsat was charging for satellite half-circuits. Since this would be a losing proposition, the Europeans would be paying exactly the economic cost of their own alleged preference for cables. It would be interesting to see how strong this preference remained under those circumstances. As things stand now, most of the cost of these new cables is paid by the American carriers. In fact, the carriers even have obtained a substantial investment in the only recent trans-Atlantic cable *not* to touch the United States—a 1974 link between Canada and Great Britain.

The carriers and the FCC often tend to place overwhelming importance on European opinion, whether manufactured or real. There is no reason why our own economic considerations should not be as important to us as are the idiosynchrasies of our communicating partners.

The Telephone Company also argues that if the FCC does not keep approving new undersea cables, whatever the need for them or their cost relative to satellites, it will stop conducting research and development for newer cables, thus denying the American people some potential technological breakthroughs. This is not an ennobling argument. Why would AT&T halt research on new cables, if it really expected a major cost breakthrough, just because a less economical cable had been denied to it? A competitive firm would be inclined to redouble its efforts. The suggestion that AT&T would voluntarily abandon its interest in cables is ludicrous. AT&T said in 1971 that if its second 825-circuit cable to Europe was rejected, it would not pursue a 4000-circuit cable in which the FCC had expressed interest. When the smaller cable was denied, and when a petition for reconsideration was also denied, the company immediately applied for—and won approval of—the larger cable, arguing among other things that it was needed so as not to discourage further cable research.

Even accepting AT&T's insistence that it needs artificial stimulation to continue research in cables, letting the carriers install cables when it is not otherwise economic to do so is likely to have exactly the opposite effect. Safe in the knowledge that its cables will continue to be approved whatever their economic disadvantage, AT&T has little incentive to make them cheaper.[12]

The FCC's decisions allowing the international carriers to construct new transoceanic cables are even more extravagant than the relative costs of new cable and satellite circuits would indicate. This is because the cables are built while satellites already in orbit have more unused circuits than an entire new cable will be able to provide. Because both cables and satellites are almost completely capital-intensive, the cost of using circuits already in existence is practically nothing. Thus to regulate properly, the FCC must make two separate decisions: whether new facilities are needed; and, if so, which type they should be. Because of the Averch-Johnson effect discussed in Chapter 2, a regulatory agency must resist the efforts of its charges to overinvest in costly equipment. AT&T has not even attempted in most cases to argue that there is a positive *need* for its proposed cables, in the sense that without them someone's phone call could not go through. Certainly this would be a hard argument to make, considering AT&T's own demand estimates and that adding a new cable to the rate base, by keeping prices higher, would reduce demand rather than the reverse. Instead, AT&T argues that the lack of a new cable will create a "dangerous dependence" on satellites.

Why have so many satellite circuits been put into operation if they were not going to be used? Isn't this as wasteful as building unneeded cables? The fact is, the carriers have never opposed strenuously the development of new satellite generations, though they occasionally have challenged Comsat's right to launch satellites already designed or even built. For them to do so would defeat their claim that they are equally concerned with cable and satellite development, and would also encourage more comparisons of relative cable and satellite costs. Better to ignore costs and urge massive investment on all fronts. Besides, satellites serve many routes—primarily underdeveloped countries outside the North Atlantic or countries in the interior of continents—which even the cable companies admit would be uneconomical to serve by cable. Once in position, however, a satellite can serve any earth station in its region of the world. A satellite launched to communicate between South America and Africa can simultaneously communicate between the United States and Europe. In fact, building a cable instead of using empty satellite circuits raises the rate the underdeveloped countries in Africa and South America must pay to use the satellite. Intelsat has a policy of worldwide rate averaging. This is partly because satellite communication is distance insensitive, and partly a conscious attempt to fulfill the aims of the Comsat Act to foster communication in the underdeveloped parts of the world. It makes the rates on heavily used channels higher than they otherwise might be. But as the White House economist Hinchman pointed out, the FCC should be smart enough not to take these rates, compared to cable rates, as appropriate "signals" for investment decisions.

In February 1966, less than a year after Early Bird, AT&T applied to build a cable of about 800 circuits from Florida to Puerto Rico and the Virgin Islands. (ITT owns both these Caribbean phone systems.) This was the first major international cable to be proposed following the establishment of the international satellite system, and Comsat opposed it. The Caribbean controversy displayed in miniature many of the elements of later trans-Atlantic cable debates.

The controversy involved three applications. AT&T and ITT applied jointly for the cable, Comsat applied for a satellite earth station in the Virgin Islands, and ITT applied for an earth station in Puerto Rico. Each party filed a petition urging that all other parties' application be rejected. (AT&T later urged that ITT's earth station request be approved; apparently it did not oppose bringing the Caribbean into the satellite system, it just wanted its cable, too.) Comsat pointed out that its earth station would cost $6 million, while the cable would cost much more. For this money, the Caribbean could be connected not just with Florida, but with many earth stations all over the Western hemisphere. To deny the satellite system the Caribbean–United States traffic (which even AT&T pointed out constituted 98.5 percent of the communications traffic out of the area) would be to delay the day the satellite system would become profitable. Comsat said the Caribbean traffic (carried, of course, at virtually no marginal cost) might reduce rates in the entire satellite system by 25 percent. AT&T called this "an academic exercise in arithmetic." Comsat said that dramatic decreases in cost could be expected in the satellite system, whereas "because of the relatively fixed characteristics of the proposed cable, a comparable decrease in annual carrying charges cannot be expected" from the cable, whatever new cable developments took place.[13] What it all came down to was this. Everyone agreed there was going to be a substantial increase in Caribbean communications traffic. Everyone agreed that an earth station should be built. No one questioned that the satellite system was perfectly able to handle the increased traffic. Nevertheless, the carriers wanted the cable.

On December 7, 1966, after several rounds of filings, the FCC decided to approve both the cable and the satellite, saying that there was enough business for both,[14] although even AT&T had estimated the area would need only 588 new circuits by 1973. The commission justified the cable partly on the grounds that it was an experiment in new cable technology—the first 800-circuit model. In exchange, the carriers were to reduce their Caribbean rates by 25 percent, and split their business 50-50 between the cable and the satellite system. (This, despite the prediction that there would be enough business to justify both.) Ownership of the earth station was split, like that of the other U.S. earth stations, with Comsat getting half.

The result? An 825-circuit cable was built between Florida and St. Thomas, Virgin Islands. It cost $38.5 million. Phone users will be paying off the cost until 1992, plus a profit each year for its owners. An earth station was built in Cayey, Puerto Rico. It cost about $6 million and will be almost completely written off (even though still in operation) by 1980. In 1970, the cable and the earth station were carrying fewer than 200 circuits each—a small fraction of the cable's capacity, and an infinitesimal fraction of the satellite system's capacity. (In that year, 1740 satellite circuits went *unused* over the Atlantic alone.)[15] Clearly, the expense of the cable not only was enormous in comparison to that of the earth station, but was completely unjustified in terms of demand for communications circuits. In fact, this artificial means of keeping rates high greatly reduced potential demand.

In September 1967, the trade journals announced that the U.S. telecommunications firms and four European countries were on the verge of signing an agreement for construction of a $75 million, 720-circuit trans-Atlantic cable, to be known as TAT-5. *Telecommunications Reports,* in predicting that the announcement would spark a lengthy debate in front of the FCC, suggested that Comsat might be supported in its opposition to the cable by the State Department. State was expected to feel that cables, which drew business away from the satellite system, were annoying to the countries that did not benefit from them, and might damage the United States position in negotiations for a permanent Intelsat agreement.[16] (The FCC later used alleged foreign policy considerations impressed on them by the carriers as a reason for *approving* the cable.)

Apparently, Comsat first heard about the cable agreement the previous summer.[17] Unlike the head of AT&T Long Lines, Comsat's president could not sit in on all the competition's board meetings to keep himself informed of their plans. That the carriers knew exactly what Comsat was up to, while Comsat was completely in the dark about the carriers, may help to explain the exquisite timing of the TAT-5 proposal to take advantage of a weakness in the satellite system.

Another interested party, the FCC, also was caught somewhat by surprise. It told the carriers they would be well-advised not to make any formal arrangement with foreign governments before the Commission had approved their plans. In letters of October 4, 1967, to Comsat and AT&T, FCC Chairman Rosel Hyde asked both to state their plans for new trans-Atlantic equipment and to justify the plans in terms of cost and expected levels of demand.[18]

AT&T's defense of the TAT-5 cable came in its October 30 response to the chairman's letter. It is notable for two things: the lack of any cost comparison between cable and satellite technology, and the lack of any direct claim that the cable actually was needed to avoid a shortage of circuits. "There is no real issue of cable versus satellites confronting us," AT&T stated, "although unfortunately the situation seems to be developing along those lines. . . . The question is one of proper balance." This balance would provide "diversification of communications which is so important to service integrity." Unless the new cable was built, the letter warned, 75 percent of all trans-Atlantic phone calls would be going by satellite at the end of 1972. In other words, without the cable the satellite system would be perfectly capable of meeting all expected demand. AT&T justified its stance this way:

> It is our view that a proper overall balance for the transatlantic route is approximately half cable and half satellite circuits. With such a balance, in the event of a catastrophic failure of one type of facility not more than half the services would be lost.[19]

TAT-5 would make it possible to achieve this balance. The catastrophe that could simultaneously knock out all satellites or all cables (without knocking out all of both) was not specified.

Bell listed other points in favor of the cable. It would land in the Iberian peninsula, "where our defense agencies have substantial interests," and thus "would be of incalculable benefit to our government and our national security." AT&T had spoken with all the Defense Department communications heads and, "They have all encouraged us to proceed with this project."[20] This, of course, was an easy position for Defense to take, since it would not cost them a penny.

On another battle front, AT&T pointed out that TAT-5 "would give a substantial impetus to the development of our cable techniques and skills." While AT&T had patriotically maintained American leadership in cable research and manufacture, "We cannot overlook the fact . . . that the governments and communication interests in several foreign countries are diligently pursuing a vast program of cable development and construction throughout the world."[21] The FCC should not count on AT&T's continuing generosity in this regard.

> If the use of the work already done is denied or delayed further, there would be a serious question as to the justification of continuing to devote research effort to new submarine cable systems or retaining the special manufacturing facilities for submarine repeaters and cables. . . . skills once allowed to deteriorate for lack of use are soon lost.[22]

Having explained that we must prevent other countries from surpassing us in cable technology, AT&T then explained that we must respect and honor their preference for building cables because "the international communication business requires a high degree of mutual understanding and cooperation."[23] AT&T mentioned the "strong views" of the southern Europeans "with respect to the TAT-5 cable," but did not discuss the equally strong views in this respect of the South Americans who, according to *Congressional Quarterly*, "have vigorously opposed the cable on grounds it will be translatable into higher satellite costs."[24]

Almost in passing, the AT&T letter mentioned that TAT-5 would be cheaper than earlier cables.

> Because of its large capacity, the per circuit cost of this cable will be considerably less than that of the existing transatlantic cables. These lower costs could result in a substantial reduction in rates for transatlantic telephone service.[25]

AT&T applied its understanding that higher capacities can lead to lower prices to the 720 circuits in the TAT-5 cable, but not to the four or five thousand predicted in Comsat's planned Intelsat IV. AT&T concluded, as it had begun, by saying "it would be most unfortunate if the present situation were to be looked upon as a struggle between cables and satellites." Rather, "it should be viewed as an adjustment in the use of the two types of facilities to strike a more efficient balance from the viewpoints of service and cost"—even though the company had given no indication that "balance" would do anything but increase costs. To prove its commitment to balance, AT&T made a timely announcement on October 10, six days after the FCC's inquiry, that it was doubling the number of Atlantic satellite circuits it was leasing—to 170.[26]

Comsat responded to the cable plan by rushing an announcement of its Intelsat IV series of multipurpose satellites. Comsat said the program would cost $97.2 million. But this would be for several satellites around the world, each with a capacity of four to five thousand circuits, compared to $75 million for one 720-circuit cable. Katherine Johnsen of *Aviation Week* called Comsat's announcement "a tactical move in its eleventh-hour fight to block construction of TAT-5."[27]

Comsat also filed a 92-page response to the FCC's inquiry of October 4. The company began by echoing the carriers to the effect that "we have at no time regarded the question as one of cables versus satellites for all time—in the Atlantic or any other area." In particular, Comsat pointed out, it was certainly not a question of TAT-5 versus Intelsat IV, since even the carriers were conceding that TAT-5's 720 new circuits, taken alone, could not satisfy increases in demand for more than two years. Nor was anyone suggesting that Intelsat IV could not be built. Furthermore, Comsat said, it was not a question of whether a new cable and a new satellite could both be economically viable, because—and this was expressed somewhat more gently—rate-base regulation makes profitable almost any extravagant investment by allowing a monopoly to charge rates high enough to pay for it.

Rather, in our view, the central question is whether the satellite system of the late 1970s is to be allowed to realize its potential economy through optimum utilization, without being weighted down—at least in its early period of growth—by diversion of traffic to an unneeded cable.[28]

Unneeded, because even by carrier estimates, Intelsat IV and existing cables could satisfy all circuit requirements in the Atlantic through the mid-1970s. TAT-4, TAT-5 and the Caribbean cable, all proposed by the carriers for use after the satellite system began operation, would amount to $150 million in initial costs and more than a billion dollars (including profit) of payments by users to the carriers during the next 20 to 25 years. They would add only 1600 circuits, and satisfy the demand that could have been fully satisfied at little extra cost by the satellite system.

But while Comsat was objecting to the TAT-5 application in its filings with the FCC, it was arranging its own satellite plans so as to give the carriers an extra reason for demanding approval of Intelsat IV. This reason—not particularly convincing, but effective with the FCC—was that there might be a gap of a couple years in the early 1970s between the time current North Atlantic facilities were filled and the time Intelsat IV was ready for operation. Bell said that TAT-5 could be ready by 1970, but that Intelsat IV might not be ready until 1972. In further comments filed on December 26, 1967, AT&T said there was "serious question" whether the satellite system could meet its 1971 circuit demands.[29] On this basis and, increasingly as the legal briefs poured in, on this basis alone, the carriers were asking the FCC to approve a $75 million cable to be paid for by communications users over 24 years.

This "gap" emerged from a series of unfortunate planning decisions by Comsat. Comsat's announcement in October 1967 that its giant Intelsat IV series of satellites would be ready in 1970 was open to doubt. For the past year the company had been claiming that the series would not be ready until 1972 or 1973. Even before that, it had predicted a giant, multipurpose system for as early as 1969.[30] But in mid-1966, Comsat was trying to persuade the FCC of the necessity of another smaller-capacity generation of satellites, to be built by TRW Aerospace, before the larger Hughes system would be ready. The TRW system, Intelsat III, was to be launched in 1968 and depreciated over five years, so Comsat was anxious to insist that it would be needed for most of that time. To a Hughes charge that the TRW system was unnecessary, Comsat said that the higher capacity satellites had not yet been designed, that "performance and earliest production date are still uncertain," and that there was an "urgent necessity for proceeding at once."[31] When Intelsat III failed to meet expectations, the carriers were able to borrow these identical arguments; Comsat's claim that Intelsat IV could be ready by 1970 was open to doubt. (In the end, the satellite was launched in January 1971.)

The FCC approved Comsat's Intelsat III plans—under foreign relations pressure because Comsat already had got approval from the other Intelsat members—in June 1966. Only three of the eight Intelsat III satellites ever went into operation. As Asher Ende of the FCC said of this model, it "fell into the ocean fairly sickly . . . AT&T saw the gap of a year and jumped in."[32] In January 1968, when the TAT-5 issue was being debated, the Intelsat III program was beset by problems and delays, allowing the carriers to claim,

> It is difficult to share Comsat's "confident" view . . . that the Intelsat IV satellite can be launched by mid-1970, when Comsat's shorter-term prediction expressed at the same time, about a mid-1968 Intelsat III launch is now open to serious question.[33]

Comsat's decision to proceed with the Intelsat III, and the ensuing misfortunes of that satellite—the only Comsat generation not to be almost completely successful—could not have been more convenient for the carriers. "It just would not be prudent," said AT&T,

> to rely wholly upon such an uncertain program when an economic, reliable, fully developed facility—the submarine cable—is available to provide the additional circuits to the critical Mediterranean area when needed.[34]

Comsat pointed out the fallacy of this argument in its reply comments of January 4, 1968.

> AT&T's point is that insurance is required in the shape of TAT-5 to cover the risk of a slip in the INTELSAT IV program. But one must calculate the nature of the risk, and the coverage and the cost of the insurance. Does AT&T really mean that a burden of $260 million over a 20 to 25-year period should be imposed on users of communications to cover a chance of a few months' slippage in the satellite program? Viewed as insurance, it strikes us that TAT-5 is prohibitively expensive, directed at a risk that is not of major dimensions. Moreover, it is important to recall that, despite the obvious disadvantages of this alternative, an additional INTELSAT III satellite could handle at least half again as much traffic as TAT-5 at a fraction of the capital cost of TAT-5, and thus provide "insurance" at a far lower premium.[35]

In the December 1967 round of filings, the carriers did claim—
—incorrectly—that the circuit cost of the new cable would be less than that
of satellites. But since none of them contested the need for the new
satellites anyway, or questioned whether the new satellites with their
thousands of circuits would have sufficient capacity, it is difficult to see
how AT&T could claim that TAT-5 would enable it to lower trans-
Atlantic phone rates by 25 to 30 percent. As Comsat explained:

> When a new cable is laid to carry traffic that could otherwise be
> carried at no extra cost by satellite facilities which must be estab-
> lished in any case, the ultimate customer must bear the cable cost as
> an addition to the already committed costs of service.[36]

If AT&T was able to lower rates by 25 percent after building TAT-5, it
should be able to lower them even more if it did not build TAT-5. AT&T
charged that this argument was not directed merely against TAT-5, but
implied "for the foreseeable future a moratorium on all cables because
they would divert traffic from the satellite system. This would deprive
communications users of the manifold benefits we have outlined in previous filings and which would result from the healthy growth and development of both cables and satellites."[37] And if AT&T meant by this that its
various balance and diversity arguments were incompatible with those of
least cost to customers, it was completely correct. "We do not press any
rigid, formal division of satellites and cables," AT&T said, only to add
later that "under the present and foreseeable conditions there should be
about an equal division of cable and satellite circuits."

Comsat's January 4 filing was one of the better ones it has made.

In general, all of the data presented by Comsat, AT&T and the
record carriers to date can be associated with two economic questions:

(1) Can satellite technology provide communication services at a
lower cost than cable technology? AT&T and the record carriers are
planning a 720-circuit cable at an investment cost of some
$70,000,000 (not including interconnect facilities costing
$20,000,000). At the same time, Comsat is planning a 5000 to
6000-circuit satellite in the Atlantic for an additional investment of
approximately $29,000,000. Not only will the satellite involve lower
annual carrying costs than the cable, but the seven-fold higher
satellite capacity will result in substantially lower costs per circuit

than can be realized by the cable. Furthermore, the shorter satellite life allows satellites to take more frequent advantage of improving technology thus resulting in still further decreases in satellite costs. In short, there is no doubt that satellite technology can provide cheaper communications services than can cable technology.

(2) How much will TAT-5 add to the total communications bill paid by the public? The circuit requirements that would be met by TAT-5 will be well within the capacity of the INTELSAT IV. Thus, the revenue requirement of the TAT-5 cable will be an additional cost that will have to be borne by the public users of communications. The amount of this unnecessary burden is estimated to be some $260,000,000 over the lifetime of TAT-5, and none of the carriers has expressed disagreement with that figure.[38]

To no avail. On February 19, 1968, the FCC sent letters to all interested parties saying that the appropriate applications for a TAT-5 cable would be "entertained" by the Commission. Since this constituted informal approval, the carriers could confidently sign contracts with their European correspondents. The commission listed nine "factors" involved in its decision, involving such issues as the purported "gap," relative costs, diversity, and foreign policy. But it did not give any details of how it added these "factors" up, one way or another. Approval of the cable would be contingent on assurances from the carriers that it would be in operation by early 1970; that they would reduce rates to users by at least 25 percent as soon as it was installed; and that empty cable and satellite circuits would be filled at the same proportional rate until all facilities were filled.[39]

The proportional fill ruling later was skillfully confused by the carriers. Its purpose was to assure, in the absence of intermodal competition, that as long as some circuits were going empty, the business was being spread around. It had nothing to do, originally, with construction of new facilities—only with use of facilities already constructed. In fact, the Commission's letter to Comsat specifically said that its TAT-5 ruling should not be "construed as indicating that the Commission believes that any particular ratio of satellite to cable facilities is, or will in the future be, required in the Atlantic basin or elsewhere."[40] And since satellites already had far surpassed cables in terms of circuits available, the policy, if carried out, would have meant a preference of several to one for satellites over cables in allotting increases in traffic.

That the Commission should approve the cable on grounds of a shortage of circuits, then make its approval contingent on proportional fill agreements for sharing the burden of excess capacity, is just one of the anomalies of the TAT-5 approval.

The letters give no indication of the Commission's reasoning in approving construction of the cable. If the foreign relations element was downplayed (merely referred to as "the views of interested foreign entities *insofar as available*" [emphasis added]), it might be because the State Department actually had been pushing for the satellite, feeling that a new cable would compromise the U.S. position in Intelsat. A letter was sent to Under Secretary Eugene Rostow "to allay such fears and prevent possible misinterpretation" of the TAT-5 decision by reaffirming the FCC's commitment to the satellite system in general, and to Intelsat IV in particular.[41] There would be no such fears to allay if foreign policy interests truly weighed in on behalf of the cable. Likewise, no mention was made except in the most oblique manner ("potential benefits of the availability of different media") of the carrier claim that cables were more reliable. A week before the decision was released, both of the carriers' two latest jointly-owned cables, TAT-3 and TAT-4, were out of action after being cut by fishing trawlers. The Associated Press reported that communications between the United States and Europe "were plunged into chaos." The FCC gave AT&T emergency authorization to rent 130 extra satellite channels from Comsat; Early Bird, already fully depreciated and taken out of service, helped an Intelsat II satellite take up the extra load; and the satellite system, according to Comsat, "functioned precisely."[42]

The Commission decision, then, seems to have been based on two considerations: a possible lack of circuits during the early 1970s, and a carrier promise to reduce rates by 25 percent for both telephone calls and leased circuits. In a stinging dissent, Nicholas Johnson demolished both these reasons.[43] Assuming, Johnson said, the most extreme possibility: that a "shortage" of trans-Atlantic circuits could develop in 1969 and last as late as 1973—what was the best "insurance policy" against such a problem? The policy the Commission had bought, apparently, was a $70 million cable with 720 circuits. To be depreciated over 20 or 24 years, it entitles the carriers to a "return on investment" for that period. Before the cable is even built, Comsat will have two Intelsat III satellites operating over the Atlantic, each with more circuits than the cable. "The cost of adding an additional Intelsat III satellite and building two additional earth stations to handle all the traffic that would go on the point-to-point cable would be roughly $35 million." (And this would be using the satellite in the least efficient possible way.) Other satellite alternatives, such as expanding current earth stations or remodeling the second Intelsat III to double its capacity (an idea Comsat toyed with and dropped) might be even cheaper.

> Of course, by depreciating the cable over *twenty* years it appears that the per-year cost of the cable is lower than the per-year additional satellite cost over its projected *five* year life. The point is that—based on the record before us—neither will be needed as insurance for more than five years. It is acknowledged that Intelsat IV (now scheduled for late 1970) and successor satellites will be more than adequate to handle projected channel demand in the mid-1970's and early 1980's. If we compare the total cost of the cable to the total cost of the additional satellite the *extra* cost to consumers of using the cable circuit will be in the neighborhood of $85 million . . . . This cost will be paid by those who use international circuits, whether they use cables or satellites. There is simply no economic justification for meeting any possible channel shortage by laying a new trans-Atlantic cable.[44]

Furthermore, Johnson pointed out, there is no need to buy insurance until you are convinced you need it. "A cable" (as the carriers themselves pointed out in urging haste) "requires two years lead time. A satellite requires weeks or months." So the satellite costs could be avoided if the gap failed to appear (which it did); the cable costs could not.

As for the rate reduction, it came as a result not of the cable, but of the FCC's refusal to take a hard line on rates.

> The FCC would like to see those rates come down. We don't think that our regulatory capabilities are adequate to reduce them. Accordingly, we are "requiring" ATT to persuade its foreign partners to lower rates in return for our approval of TAT-5. (It should be noted that ATT *offered* to reduce the rates 25% without our intervention. The Commission now seeks no more in exchange for TAT-V than AT&T's first offer.) As a commentary on the regulatory capacity of the FCC, the point is obvious. We do not know what the rates *should* be. Perhaps they should be reduced 50% or 75%. In any event, even the 25% lowering of rates is a Pyrrhic victory, since in the end consumers will have to pay at least $80 million in unwarranted costs.[45]

Commissioner Kenneth Cox wrote a bitter reply to Johnson's dissent. This is the only peek we have at the thought process behind the majority decision. It dealt mainly with relative cable and satellite costs, though only three months later, in another reply to another Johnson dissent, Cox insisted that costs had nothing to do with the matter.

First off, Cox was hurt that Commissioner Johnson had dismissed all of the carriers' favorite noneconomic issues.

> I do not believe that requirements of national security, potential advantages of diversity, substantial rate reductions, the concerns of our major traffic partners, or the potential effect on future cable development deserve such cavalier treatment.[46]

Johnson had said of national security that if the Defense Department wanted to override strict economic considerations it should offer to pay the difference, which it had not done. The Commission itself had named none of the "potential" advantages of modal diversity, and neither did Commissioner Cox, because there are none. Johnson of course had discussed the rate reduction in detail; part of that discussion is quoted above. The foreign policy considerations had been evaluated by the State Department as being against the cable. Johnson specifically said that he did not dismiss the possibility that cables yet to be developed might be cheaper than satellites. "If ATT shares that belief," he wrote, "it is presumably developing such cables. Until that day . . . the American people are entitled to the most effective technology . . . available."[47]

As for costs, Cox wrote, "Satellites are not now, and will not for at least the next 5 to 7 years be, the most economic means of providing international communications service. . . . By the middle of the 1970's we hope and expect that satellites not yet authorized, much less built, will enable us to begin to realize some of the hoped for economies."[48] Cox's basis for arguing that cables were cheaper was that Comsat's annual charge to the carriers was $45,600 per half-circuit, while the carriers alleged that their revenue requirement per half-circuit on existing cables averaged about $28,000. This, of course, was the basic fallacy of equating the revenue requirement per satellite half-circuit with what Comsat was charging for half-circuits in use. But it was strange for another reason. AT&T's current annual charge to its leased-line customers for a voice-grade half-circuit was $78,000. It made the Commission appear complacent to be praising a 25 percent reduction in carrier rates, when by their own admission the carrier rates were nearly three times their annual revenue requirement—a figure that is supposed to include their profit. Comsat later contended that the carrier revenue requirement really was $61,100, to which Comsat's $45,600 must be compared,

> if a meaningful evaluation is to be made of the current cost to carriers of the respective facilities. Were this not the case, a serious question could be raised as to the justification in the public interest of permitting a tariff of $78,000 for a service costing only $28,000.[49]

Commissioner Cox completed his cost comparison with the meaningless (and possibly incorrect) claim that in 1973 the revenue requirement of the entire satellite system would be more than that of the latest cable taken alone. He said that the FCC had approved "such seemingly uneconomic ventures" as the satellite system only "in the hope of future benefits," but that meanwhile, there was no reason to "forego the savings available from the cable for the next decade because the satellite can handle the traffic, albeit at a higher cost."[50] He did not explain how the cost could possibly be higher if the satellite system was to be built in any event. Cox's own conclusion was that the TAT-5 cable actually would increase use of satellites, because the rate reduction following its introduction would increase demand for trans-Atlantic circuits more than the cable would increase supply.

The very idea that addition of the TAT-5 cable alone could justify a 25 percent rate reduction was fantasy. If pre-TAT-5 rates were a realistic reflection of pre-TAT-5 circuit costs, simple mathematics shows that it would take a 33 percent increase in capacity achieved at *no* additional cost to support a 25 percent cut across the board. TAT-5's 720 circuits represent a much smaller fraction of total trans-Atlantic capacity, and obviously these added circuits were not obtained free of charge. The trade-off of the rate reduction for the cable was purely political, not economic.

The carriers formally applied for permission to construct TAT-5 on April 8, 1968; the FCC approved the application at the end of May. (In the interim, at the end of April, TAT-1 was cut by a trawler and put out of operation for a day and a half.[51]) The total cost of the cable and related facilities would be $90 million and the cable could be finished by early 1970 if Commission approval came "in the next few weeks." The carriers agreed to reduce their rates by 25 to 30 percent, and to fill the new cable and any new satellites proportionally, so that all would fill up at the same time.[52]

The FCC's formal TAT-5 decision of May 31, 1968 is interesting for several reasons. It demonstrates how Comsat once again had more or less cooperated in producing a decision contrary to its own interest. Commissioners were able to write that "no objections to the Commission's letters of February 16, 1968, were filed by the applicants or by Comsat." Also, "Comsat does not request denial of the instant applications" for TAT-5, provided that the proportional fill requirements of the February letter were carried out. The FCC concluded that the differences of opinion between Comsat and the carriers were "more apparent than real."[53] As the Commission was giving the carriers exactly what they wanted, it is clear how the commissioners perceived Comsat's position.

Having demanded detailed cable and satellite cost estimates, the Commissioners wrote in their decision that, "we do not believe that any useful purpose would be served by going over relative costs or the revenue requirement data filed by the interested parties." Likewise, the Commission did not intend to waste its time "to make definitive findings on the relative economic merits of TAT-5 and present satellites [Intelsat II], those now being constructed [Intelsat III], and those proposed for the early 1970's [Intelsat IV]." Another series of issues "which," the decision said, "need no discussion here," were all the supposed noneconomic advantages of cables. These, however, unlike the economic advantages of satellites, were accepted without question and simply listed parenthetically:

> (e.g., added diversity of facilities, the desirability for additional non-satellite facilities for combination with satellite facilities to serve distant areas which cannot be reached via a single satellite in synchronous orbit, foreign policy consideration, enhanced ability to meet national defense and security requirements, and the opportunity for prompt and substantial rate reductions by both the United States carriers and the foreign counterparts).

The only nonparenthetical defense of the cable was the supposed likelihood of "a shortage of several hundred circuits in 1970"—a shortage which, like a fine wine, "will become greater as time goes on." Here, too, Comsat cooperated. The Commission pointed out that plans for Intelsat IV "are not presently definite and require agreement of the Intelsat partners before work can go forward," which might delay their operation "until well beyond the time frames . . . when additional capacity will be urgently required." Yet Comsat's formal application for Intelsat IV came in July 1968, less than two months later, and the Intelsat executive signed a construction contract with Hughes the following October.[55]

The Commission repeated Commissioner Cox's contention that the cable actually would increase satellite use because lower rates would stimulate demand for communications circuits. At the same time, it endorsed Comsat's contention that since the proportional fill requirement would force the carriers to use satellites for most of their future business, "the cost of satellite circuits rather than that of cable circuits is the controlling factor in the carriers' revenue requirements." Then it immediately turned around and said that "the estimated cable costs themselves fully justify the proposed rate reduction," and that, "there is no element of subsidy from the satellite circuits involved in these reductions."[56] To repeat: it is clearly impossible that the addition of merely 720 circuits at a cost of $90 million could possibly in itself justify a rate reduction of 25 percent across the board. The only justification (and certainly the only necessary one) was that carrier rates were much too high. As for subsidy of cable rates by the addition of satellite circuits, it is odd for the Commission to insist that this was not taking place, as it was precisely their justification for the Authorized Users ruling.

But in pursuing this particular line of argument, the FCC has acknowledged, however briefly, its recognition of a fairly major principle of economics: that demand for a product or service is likely to increase if the price goes down. In the case of communication, as the growth of U.S. long-distance calling in recent years has shown, demand is very sensitive to price reductions (high downward price-elasticity of demand, the economists say). Yet the Commission has based all its important international facility decisions, including TAT-5, on volume predictions supplied by the carriers, which do not even mention price as a variable factor. Commissioners have argued simultaneously that skyrocketing demand will create a "shortage" of circuits if a cable is not built, and that if it *is* built, a price reduction will create a demand for the remaining circuits that is even greater than it was before. In the real world, a "shortage" means that the price is too low, and unused capacity means the price is too high. Thus construction of expensive cables is doubly damaging to the satellite system: not only does it siphon off business that the satellite system might otherwise be carrying, but by adding unnecessarily to carrier rate bases and keeping prices unnecessarily high, it reduces the total demand for communication by cable *and* satellite.

As in February, Commissioner Johnson wrote a dissenting opinion to accompany the May decision and Commissioner Cox wrote a concurring opinion attacking Commissioner Johnson. Johnson's statement was a repeat of his earlier objections. He mentioned that "as an added bonus, AT&T is to provide most of the equipment (for TAT-5) from its manufacturing subsidiary." He also commended the majority for having "simply abandoned its earlier effort to provide economic justification for its action."[57]

This latter comment annoyed Kenneth Cox. He said he was "somewhat at a loss to understand the thrust" of it, "as even a cursory reading of the Commission's earlier letter . . . will indicate there was never any statement, or even intimation, that its position was based primarily upon the economic advantages of the proposed TAT-5 cable."[58] There was, indeed, no statement, or even intimation *of any sort* in the Commission's letter of why it was approving the cable. There was, however, Commissioner Cox's own insistence, in his earlier comments, that TAT-5 was more than just an insurance policy against a delay in Intelsat IV, because "satellites are not now, and will not for at least the next 5 to 7 years be, the most economic means of providing international communications service."[59] Apparently, the Commissioner had changed his mind. Or had he? As we have seen, the Commission had written that "we do not believe that any useful purpose would be served by going over relative costs or the revenue requirement data filed by the interested parties."[60] But Commissioner Cox cautioned that this should not "be taken to mean, as Commissioner Johnson intimates, that we ignored the economic and cost data submitted to us" in reaching the decision. In the ensuing discussion, he made several valuable points, including the one—in an attempt to justify comparing AT&T's cable revenue requirements with Comsat's satellite charges—that "cable costs include but a single corporate overhead, whereas satellite facilities include two corporate overheads." This, too, was a direct result of the Commission's own staunchly defended Authorized Users ruling, the purported intention of which was to guarantee lower costs to all communications users. Cox concluded:

> Finally, because of the need to serve many points, and the manner in which units of utilization must be assigned under present operating modes, the satellite may not be expected to achieve a fill of more than about 80% of design capacity, whereas the cable can and does achieve 100%.[61]

"Units of utilization . . . under the present operating modes" means that the carriers prefer to fill up their cables before using any satellite circuits, and are able to do so because cable capacities are relatively small. Comsat could defeat this argument by designing a satellite with half the capacity of Intelsat IV, at twice the price.

About this circuit "gap." In response to an FCC inquiry in 1970, Comsat and AT&T filed detailed information about the use of their facilities on May 30 of that year, a month after the opening of TAT-5. AT&T was using 245 circuits on the new cable and had idle 243 circuits of the portion of the cable it controlled. Comsat had 2129 circuits leased in two Intelsat III satellites, and 1740 going empty. So if TAT-5 had not been built, and the circuits it was supplying as of May 30 were supplied by satellite instead, there still would have been perhaps 1400 empty circuits still available on the satellites (accounting for TAT-5 volume of the record carriers). This is the capacity of *two* TAT-5 cables, or about $180 million of cable equipment.[62] It does not include the available but unused capacity of earlier satellite generations, and exists despite the significant failure of the Intelsat III system, in which most of the satellites either never functioned, or functioned at less than full capacity. Barely half a year later, in January 1970, Comsat was ready to launch its first Intelsat IV, with 5000 circuits. (The carriers petitioned the FCC to have this launch delayed.) There was, therefore, no "gap."

In fact, so many extra circuits were available after TAT-5 was installed that the record carriers tried to renege on their proportional fill agreements with Comsat and the Commission, and to prevent Comsat from launching one of its Intelsat III's. The record carriers argued that the proportional fill formula was supposed to apply only to the proposed Intelsat III½ and Intelsat IV, and that until they were launched the carriers should be free to fill up their cables without any further use of satellite circuits.[63] This was false. The FCC's decision said it applied between the cable and "any commercial satellite facilities." The Commission's February letter said its approval would be conditioned upon the carriers' promise—a promise they promptly made—to rent new satellite circuits "in numbers sufficient to assure that this cable and the satellite facilities provided to handle traffic between the United States and their respective countries shall each be filled at the same proportionate rate."[64]

The May decision had made clear that this meant more new satellite circuits put in use than cable circuits, since there were more satellite circuits than cable circuits going empty. If it was ambiguous about whether this rule applied to the Intelsat III's, this is because the carriers had convinced the Commission that the Intelsat III's would be fully used by the time TAT-5 opened. This was why they said the cable was needed. Comsat, attempting a compromise, said it was willing to accept a 50-50 division of new traffic between the opening of TAT-5 and the launching of a new satellite generation, so as not to "adversely affect this nation's foreign relations." The carriers, true to form, had signed cable contracts with the Europeans, then argued that it would be bad international politics to make them change the contracts. ITT and Western Union International solicited objections from 20 countries and submitted them to the Commission.[65]

When TAT-5 opened, the record carriers refused to use it, pending solution of the controversy. They also refused to initiate the rate cuts that the FCC had required as a condition of the cable's approval. ITT also asked the Commission to prevent launching of Comsat's second Atlantic Intelsat III, on grounds that, "there is no urgent requirement for additional capacity in that region."[66] Since the Intelsat III can handle 1500 circuits, about twice those in TAT-5, this would seem to mean that the need for TAT-5 had not been so urgent either. But no one pointed this out at the time.

The FCC agreed to let the record carriers postpone their rate reductions. In May 1970, the record carriers reported to the Commission that, without prejudice to their position on principle, they had reluctantly agreed to "undertake to acquire" *one* additional satellite circuit for every *two* circuits they activated in TAT-5. In return, the FCC assured ITT that any future proportional fill requirements would ignore the entire capacity of the second Intelsat III satellite—on which grounds it then authorized Comsat to launch the satellite.[67]

ITT has continued to lead the carriers' opposition to new satellites. ITT also led the way in getting the FCC to renege on the proportional fill promise it had made to Comsat when it approved the TAT-5 cable. In December 1970, ITT asked the Commission to delay launching of the first Intelsat IV until a permanent policy for new overseas facilities had been set. At the end of the year of the crucial and increasing "gap," ITT said there were 1500 unused circuits available for immediate use over the Atlantic. In a complete reversal of roles, ITT argued that delaying the new satellite would not damage the public interest: "it is likely that the burden on the users of satellite services, to reimburse Comsat for unnecessary expenses, would be lightened."[68] And Comsat invoked foreign policy, responding that a delay "could only embarrass the United States in its relations with its international partners in Intelsat."[69] Comsat also pointed out that the ITT effort was a clear attempt to overturn the FCC's explicit commitment to an early Intelsat IV, which was a quid pro quo included in the TAT-5 ruling. And while ITT complained of excess capacity, AT&T argued for a circuit-sharing technique to increase the capacity of TAT-5, saying that there was a "pressing need" for additional trans-Atlantic circuits.[70]

In January 1971, a week before the first Intelsat IV was scheduled to take off, ITT went directly to the White House with a request that it intercede with the FCC to make it delay the launch. This was about the time when ITT's influence at the White House was reaching its zenith, due to certain "noble commitments" (as Dita Beard described them in her famous memo) that later became part of the Watergate affair.[71] However, OTP director Clay Whitehead deflected the company's request, saying that "economic wastefulness" and "international complications" made it too late to do anything. But he added that his office was studying the "long-term issues" involved, that the White House had taken no position on principle, and that it "would welcome and, indeed, actively solicit whatever assistance you feel you can provide." So the first Intelsat IV was launched successfully on January 25, 1971, and went into perfect synchronous orbit shortly thereafter.[72]

Undaunted, ITT asked the Commission to delay giving Comsat permission for "acquiring units of utilization" in the satellite (that is, for using it). It also asked the FCC to suspend the proportional fill formula to which the carriers had agreed in exchange for TAT-5. (This is the formula the carriers had argued should apply only to Intelsat IV, and not to the earlier satellites.) The Commission agreed with the carriers once again, saying that Comsat could activate the Intelsat IV if it wished, but that the carriers were under no obligation to give it any business until the 1500 circuits already available in older satellites were used up at the old two-to-one cable-to-satellite rate that was supposed to last only until Intelsat IV was launched. The Commission was endorsing a clear effort by the carriers to break their promise to Comsat, and Comsat said so.[73]

For a brief period, AT&T appeared to be the compromiser in the controversy. The company offered to take five additional satellite circuits for each additional cable circuit it placed in operation. Comsat said the true ratio of unused satellite and cable circuits—the basis upon which the proportional fill formula was supposed to be computed—was more like 5.8 to one. But the satellite corporation agreed to the compromise, and the FCC made it official in May 1971.[74]

But this compromise lasted less than six months. The record carriers immediately went to work on their European counterparts, who informed the Commission—in a statement relayed by Western Union International—that they had not been consulted about the compromise and were not happy with it. After a meeting with these Europeans and with Comsat and the carriers in September, the commissioners said they had gained a "new appreciation" of the foreigners' views. This new appreciation manifested itself in an October 19 decision revoking the previous five-to-one policy and dictating that unused cable and satellite circuits should be filled on "an equitable basis"—that is, one-to-one.[75] This was for AT&T. The record carriers were relieved of any need to fill satellite circuits before using their quota of circuits on TAT-5. The ruling was based only in passing on what the Commission called "considerations of comity and foreign policy." Much greater emphasis was placed on two contradictory contentions: that it was unfair to burden the carriers with filling Intelsat IV when it had been launched before it was needed (itself an admission of failure in allowing construction of TAT-5); and that communications business was booming to such an extent that the Intelsat system would soon be filled anyway. The Commission also reported that since it had first committed itself to "proportional fill" in 1968,

New views have evolved with respect to the manner in which facilities should be used over the heavily trafficked trans-Atlantic route, particularly a view which postulates that to meet growing needs and assure continuity of service there should not be excessive reliance on any single facility.[76]

Had the decision not been so favorable to them, the carriers might have been disheartened that the Commission should just have stumbled across and labeled "new" a proposition they had been endorsing at great intensity, length, and expense for years. But they undoubtedly were relieved that the commissioners had failed to notice that even their most emphatic arguments in favor of diversity in constructing new facilities had no bearing on relative use of facilities already available.

In November 1972, ITT World Communication announced its opposition to Comsat's plans for an Intelsat IVA generation of satellites with up to 13,000 circuits. ITT said that the $100 million revenue requirement this satellite series would have to generate over its lifetime (as opposed to something like $250 million for the 800-circuit TAT-5) "would be wasteful and contrary to the public interest." Instead, ITT suggested that a substantial number of circuits be rented in a cable running from Canada to Great Britain. This is the cable the carriers said TAT-5 was supposed to prevent them from having to use for U.S. traffic. Under pressure from all the carriers, the FCC ordered Comsat not to ask for approval from the Intelsat board at its December quarterly meeting.[77] ITT later demanded the minutes of that meeting, and suggested that Comsat had no right at all to propose new satellites without prior consent from the carriers.

> This proposal was set forth unilaterally by Comsat, a carrier's carrier which does not serve the public itself, without the consent or agreement of the international record and voice carriers which do serve the public and which would thus be in a position to know whether or not additional satellite facilities are required and, if so, in what time frame.[78]

Convinced by Comsat arguments that more satellites were needed, that the additional cost of remodeling the Intelsat IV to more than double its capacity was only $12 million, and that the new satellite could be sent over to the Pacific if it was no longer needed over the Atlantic, the FCC overruled the carriers and gave Comsat permission to build the Intelsat IVA. The first one was launched in 1975.

Even before TAT-5 was open for business, the carriers revealed their intention to build several more trans-Atlantic cables. In September 1969, AT&T revealed that it was preparing to file for a second trans-Atlantic 720-circuit cable, this one to France.[80] AT&T said the Northern Europeans wanted a new cable because TAT-5 had gone to southern Europe. (TAT-5, of course, had been needed because the previous cables had gone north.) The need for this cable was so urgent that "it becomes impractical to wait until all the details are concluded before the necessary Commission approvals are obtained." This urgency, however, did not emerge from an actual shortage of circuits. Although AT&T said its trans-Atlantic circuit requirements would increase from 2100 to 15,000 by 1980, it could only warn of "a serious imbalance . . . between cable and satellite circuits" by that year. If no new cables were built, satellites would be carrying 84 percent of all trans-Atlantic traffic, and cables only 14 percent. And "we and our correspondents in these European countries are concerned about the hazardous situation which will develop."[81]

AT&T also threatened that it was going to shut down its cable factory if more approvals were not immediately forthcoming, and that foreign firms were ready to step into the breach. Western Electric, its manufacturing subsidiary, "is considering selling the cable production machinery and converting the Baltimore factory to other use when TAT-5 is completed," AT&T said, while "existing foreign cable factories have capacity for additional SF and SG (800- and 3500-circuit) cables." Yet at the very time Bell was telling the FCC it was thinking of closing down its Baltimore cable factory, it was privately telling the Japanese (who were interested in a new Pacific cable) of its plans to put a cable repeater factory on 24-hour operation to satisfy the demand it expected to create for new cables.[82]

In a reply to this announcement, Comsat pointed out that all of AT&T's talk about "reasonable balance . . . does not deal with the economic considerations." Comsat asked how much it was worth paying for diversity of cable and satellite facilities "when the satellite system will have its own redundancy and diversity on a global basis." Comsat also pointed out that to get TAT-5 approved, AT&T had argued that negotiations with foreigners had proceeded to the point where refusing it would embarrass the United States internationally. The satellite corporation asked the FCC not to allow this tactic again, and was successful.[83] The FCC told AT&T to stop negotiating for another cable[84] and, in June 1970, initiated a new docket dedicated to an investigation of "policy to be followed in future licensing of facilities for overseas communication."[85]

So again, Comsat and AT&T filed comments—this time a pair of two-inch-thick volumes. The record carriers filed at length, as did other interested parties. And everybody filed reply comments on everybody else's comments.

AT&T's comments of August 21, 1970 revealed that the company planned to lay ten more transoceanic cables before the end of 1979—three in the Atlantic, three in the Pacific, and four in the Caribbean. These new cables were needed, AT&T said, to maintain a policy—which the company strongly recommended—of adding new satellites and cables "so that circuit use will be approximately equal." AT&T's several suggestions in defense of this proposed policy were similar to those it had offered before. Without attempting to claim that satellite revenue requirements were higher than those of cables, or to explain why its own rates were so much higher than its alleged costs, AT&T repeated that "per circuit charges to the carriers for satellite circuits are substantially higher than the per circuit costs of modern cables." ("However," the company added, "it is hoped that the upcoming Intelsat IV programs will introduce new economies." And later, "there is every reason for optimism that planned satellite projects . . . will aid modern cables in dramatically reducing overseas circuit costs and providing diversity." [86])

There was the usual talk about diversity which, as usual, failed to explain why extra satellites, with more circuits at less cost, provide less diversity than extra cables. This time it was supplemented by a lengthy discourse on "a remarkable new device called TASI-B." A "compression" invention for squeezing extra conversations into the breathing space between others, TASI is what allowed Bell to increase the capacity of TAT-5 from 720 circuits to 825. Reference to it here is a good example of AT&T's technique of obfuscation. "Thus," Bell explained,

> 120 simultaneous conversations may be fed into a TASI-B system to be carried on 48 cable circuits and 48 satellite circuits. If either the cable or the satellite circuits fail, the TASI-B system will automatically switch all conversations without interruptions to the working circuits on the other facility, which will be able to carry all the calls through the TASI technique.[87]

This has nothing whatever to do with any need to maintain balance between cable and satellite circuits, as AT&T tried to imply in its brief. This passage tells us simply that TASI-B is a technique that turns 48 circuits into 120 circuits. It works on satellites and on cables. If a piece of equipment breaks down, this technique can be used to expand the capacity of other equipment and switch the disrupted traffic without delay. It does not say that 48 circuits each on two satellites (or, for that matter, on two cables) would not be just as good as 48 circuits each on one satellite and one cable.

AT&T argued that "cables have traditionally been vulnerable to the risk of damage by fishing trawlers," but "satellites are subject to different" but unspecified "kinds of troubles." That word "traditionally" led to an announcement that AT&T had developed a cable burial technique that would eliminate the trawler problem. But the announcement was premature. TAT-5 was cut in March 1971; in February 1972 both TAT-5 and TAT-2 were out, the newer cable for two weeks. In both cases, the satellite system took over the business with no problems.[88] AT&T and Comsat threw statistics at each other in this round of filings, each one contending that its system suffered fewer "outages" than the other. But what the AT&T could not deny was that when a satellite or earth station broke down, the satellite system always had been able to cover for it; but when a cable broke down, it required the satellites to come to the rescue.

AT&T had decided that it would need 20,000 circuits by 1980—up from 15,000 the previous fall. Since these demand estimates were made without reference to the price that might be set for such services, they were of little value. The company said this meant that satellites would be carrying 88 percent of the trans-Atlantic traffic if new cables were not built. This, of course, constitutes an admission that expansion of the satellite system which AT&T specifically endorsed could handle AT&T's own estimates of the increase in traffic, without the help of any new cables. But this would cause a "serious imbalance."

As in earlier filings, AT&T threatened to abandon cable research if its application was refused.

> If cable technology is to go forward and United States leadership in that technology is to be maintained, AT&T must continue to devote its talent and money to the cable program, and to justify such expenditures it must be clear that submarine cables are to continue as one of the primary means of overseas communications.

And it repeated its concern for appeasing the Europeans.

> Finally, a factor not to be overlooked is the fact that the availability of both cables and satellites facilitates accommodation of the views of foreign correspondents who for one reason or another may need to use a particular type of facility.[89]

The Commission had asked all those submitting comments to discuss whether the Authorized Users rule should be modified. So AT&T ended its lengthy treatise on the many advantages of cables over satellites for transoceanic communication by begging the FCC to protect it from satellite competition.

> Here there is an artificial restraint on the carriers who cannot be licensed to provide the space segment and therefore cannot compete with Comsat in providing satellite service on equal terms.[90]

Comsat, of course, cannot be licensed to lay cables, so the disadvantage of competition would be totally Comsat's if, as AT&T had claimed throughout its brief, cables held all the advantages.

Three weeks after filing its comments in Docket 18875, AT&T made a formal application for permission to build an 825-circuit TAT-6 between France and Rhode Island. Unlike the earlier cables, the company was not planning to share this one with the record carriers, who apparently had no need for it. Of its total cost of $86 million, more than $70 million was to become part of AT&T's rate base. The remaining fraction was to be shared by the French and the German telephone systems. AT&T did not explain why, if these foreign governments were so anxious for yet another cable, they were not anxious to pay for more of it. There was a "pressing need" for this new cable, which could not wait until the end of the FCC's inquiry (though AT&T assured the commissioners that their study would "prove highly beneficial to the carriers in planning future facility programs").[91]

In a 235-page filing the next month, Comsat said it "fully supports the development of the technology of all modes of communication," but "not by promises based on arbitrary formulas."

> By the time additional cables could become available according to AT&T's plans, i.e. late 1972-73, there will exist in the satellite system over all high density routes the capacity not only to meet all traffic requirements, but the capability to do so with sufficient diversity of routing through different satellites and earth stations and with sufficient redundancy to provide a degree of reliability heretofore unknown in overseas communications.[92]

Comsat said the annual circuit cost of an Intelsat IV satellite used point-to-point with two earth stations was $1450, compared to $21,696 for an 845-circuit cable and $5571 for the 3500-circuit cable AT&T claimed it would have perfected by 1976. (And by 1976, Comsat would have a satellite with double the Intelsat IV capacity and even lower circuit cost.) Comsat explained to the Commission that an arbitrary division of future circuits would make it impossible for these economies to be reflected in rates to consumers.

> To date, the public has not received the full benefits of the satellite system. . . . AT&T compares its own calculations of projected re-

venue requirements per half-circuit with Comsat's present tariff rate per half-circuit and concludes that cables are cheaper. While this may be a useful comparison for AT&T, it is of no value to the Commission in its efforts to determine public interest considerations. The most significant determinant of satellite service rates is the volume of use. . . . To the extent that a portion of the traffic on (major) routes is allocated to modes of communication other than satellites during these early years of the satellites during these early years of the satellite system, the regenerating cycle of "more demand—more service—lower rates—more demand" will not reach its full potential.[93]

In its reply comments of the next month (October 1970), AT&T did not contest Comsat's relative cost figures, or offer any of its own. Nor did it challenge Comsat's contention that the satellite system would be able to handle all the expected increase in demand for circuits. AT&T merely repeated that if a 50-50 mix were maintained, no catastrophe to all cables or all satellites simultaneously could knock out more than half the total circuits available. The catastrophe AT&T had in mind was not specified.

Ma Bell did not rely on reasoned argument alone. She also enlisted the pressure groups that had been cooperative in the past. Letters began arriving at the FCC from the European telephone systems, all endorsing 50-50 and TAT-6. Then there was the Defense Department. On December 18, 1970, Secretary of Defense Melvin Laird wrote to FCC Chairman Burch to supplement an earlier letter from an assistant expressing Defense's views concerning future cable and satellite licensing policy. According to Laird's letter, the earlier views were not terribly controversial: "Our views were that as a matter of policy we supported actions on the part of the FCC which stimulate and encourage the growth and expansion of telecommunications throughout the world." On this basis and on this basis alone—the more circuits, at any cost, the better—Laird said he "strongly" supported AT&T's application for TAT-6. He was careful to add for the record, however, that the endorsement was made "since the AT&T Company and other participating carriers wish to construct another high quality communications path across the Atlantic *without obligating the Department of Defense*" (emphasis added) which, Laird said, could continue to "selectively fulfill its needs."[94] Like that of the Europeans, Laird's enthusiasm for cables was not strong enough to make him willing to help pay for them. Only the carriers, with their rate bases to think about, were that enthusiastic. (Of course, the Defense Department will end up paying for the cable anyway, in higher rates.)

Laird's assistant, Louis A. deRosa, wrote again in May, after the Common Carrier Bureau had recommended (though not publicly) that the TAT-6 application be rejected. The two-paragraph letter was intended "to ensure that no misunderstanding exists regarding our continuing strong support of the TAT-6 applications." Mr. deRosa concluded, "Favorable action thereon by the Commission would lead to an early service availability using SF cable technology."[95] In other words: if the Commission approves the cable, the cable will be built. Defense offered this observation as an argument in favor of approving the cable. A promise that it *would not* be built might have been a stronger one.

Unfortunately for the telephone company, its arrangement with the Defense Department was overruled by the Office of Telecommunications Policy, which announced at the end of May that it was opposed to TAT-6, and made clear that it was speaking on behalf of the White House and for the entire executive branch. The OTP guidelines said pointedly, "The executive branch will inform the FCC of significant national security and foreign policy needs." Furthermore, "specialized government circuit requirements do not provide a basis for approval of inefficient facilities." If the government needed more of a certain kind of circuit than was available, it would build or lease them specially, "rather than burden the using public by adding commercially inefficient facilities to the carriers' rate base." As for foreign policy considerations, the OTP said it would arrange a conference to redefine the half-circuit so as to "alleviate much of the concern of our European communications partners"[95] at having to accept FCC policy.

Whitehead's office told the FCC bluntly that "tariff rates cannot be used as a valid public-interest criterion for approval of investments in new facilities," since they had no effect on the relative cost of new facilities. As economist Walter Hinchman put it in an accompanying study, "Rates are in fact dependent on costs, rather than the converse." The OTP said that while there was a limited need for excess capacity in case of breakdowns, "this does not necessarily require duplication of circuits on different types of facilities, and such a fixed policy would be unnecessarily costly to the public." Specifically, "public policy does not require a particular ratio between satellite and undersea cable circuit capacity."[96]

Turning to the specific policy implications of its proposals, the OTP said that there was no need for any new facilities to satisfy demand at least through 1977; that there were sufficient cable circuits already available for any national-security and commercial communications that had to go by cable; that the best way to restore disrupted satellite circuits was on other satellite circuits; and that if no new cables were built to draw away business, satellite rates could be "reduced substantially." Declaring that the SF (845-circuit) cable was "several times more expensive per circuit" than the Intelsat IV for use across the Atlantic, the report pointed out that "construction of additional cable capacity at the present time will be doubly costly to the public because of the higher costs of SF cable and the creation of excess capacity that will prevent early satellite rate reduction."[97]

The Hinchman study was responsible for the definitive statement about relative costs.[98] It also compared Intelsat IV to AT&T's proposed 3500-circuit (SG) cable for 1976. Hinchman's conclusion, as described in the OTP guidelines, was that the 1976 cable "appears comparable to Intelsat IV satellites in terms of cost and capability *at relevant demand levels*" (emphasis added). But a closer look at the study reveals a greater contrast. As Hinchman's study is the only attempt ever made by any government agency to compare relative cable and satellite costs, the closer look is worthwhile.

Hinchman constructed a hypothetical model in which he went out of his way to give the benefit of the doubt to cables, thus making the prosatellite results less open to dispute. He compared Intelsat IV with the two generations of cables for point-to-point communication over the Atlantic—clearly what cables do best—and ignored the multipoint capability of satellites. He assumed 100 percent satellite and earth station antenna redundancy, and none at all for cables. (That is, he counted two satellite circuits for every one cable circuit, to neutralize the carrier contention that satellites are less reliable.) He based his comparison on the 24-year lifetime of a cable, and assumed that an identical new satellite system would be launched every 7 years without any possibility for improvement in satellite technology over that quarter of a century. He added a 24 percent profit to the satellite investment and only 14 percent to the cable, based on Comsat's contention that it deserved a higher profit because of its larger risk.

Hinchman concluded that despite all these artificial handicaps he had placed on them, Comsat's current satellites would be about one-third as expensive as AT&T's current cables per used circuit "at 1976 traffic levels." They would cost about the same to use as the cables AT&T

proposed to have developed by 1976 (by which time Comsat proposed to have satellites with twice Intelsat IV capacity—satellites that did not enter into the Hinchman study). Note those words "at 1976 traffic levels." They mean that Hinchman was comparing the cost per used circuit of a substantially filled cable system with that of a half-empty satellite system. AT&T's 1976 traffic estimates were simple projections from past growth; they bore no connection to proposed rates. If rates were permitted to reflect the larger satellite capacity, demand clearly would increase until that capacity was filled. Comparing a *fully used* Intelsat IV system to an equivalent number of cable circuits, Hinchman determined that current satellite technology was almost *nine times* cheaper than current cable technology for the same trans-Atlantic service, and more than twice as cheap as the cable technology AT&T proposed to have ready five years later. (Since satellite costs are distance-insensitive, the Pacific comparison would be even more embarrassing to cables.)

In a second model, Hinchman relaxed some of his antisatellite assumptions. He figured on one spare for two satellites (50 percent redundancy), on the reasonable assumption that there was little chance both would go out at the same time. (There was still no cable redundancy at all.) He equalized the profit rates on cable and satellite investment. He limited his time frame to ten years, to allow for more technical progress. And he took partially into account the multipoint capability of a satellite (which reduces its total circuit capacity). Under these conditions, he determined that it would be cheaper to put up a 5000-circuit satellite (with the requisite earth stations) and use only 825 of its circuits than it would be to build a fully-used 825-circuit cable. To supply the circuits of which one multipoint satellite was capable would require *six* of these cables, costing more than six times as much. Once again, the Intelsat IV technology already available turned out to be less than half as expensive per circuit as the cable technology AT&T was planning to have available five years later.

ITT wrote to Chairman Burch in June, calling the OTP memo "an ill-concealed attempt to promote a monopoly of satellite communications facilities in international communications."[99] It said OTP's guidelines were "a virtual blueprint for disaster" and signaled acceptance of Comsat's "arrogant demand for the privileges of an unregulated monopoly." "As a responsible utility," ITT said, it begged to differ: "A balance between cable and satellite facilities is clearly required in the public interest." In defense of this familiar proposition, ITT offered a new series of arguments. Satellites could be jammed "by hostile powers or dissident domestic groups." "Subversives" might obtain the secret codes for controlling the satellites, set up their own antenna, and "disable all satellites in 'view'." Technical arguments involving such things as the shadow of the earth are harder to evaluate. However, if ITT really felt happy with these arguments, why had the company not used them in its voluminous previous filings? As for costs, ITT said simply "we do not propose to argue the point as to whether cables or satellites are more expensive," declaring conclusively that "any theory used to determine satellite costs cannot be verified"—a proposition which, if adopted by the FCC, would effectively prevent cost from entering its deliberations for all time.

The FCC was, in fact, on the verge of abandoning costs as a consideration. On June 17, 1971, Chairman Burch called an informal conference of commissioners and representatives of the carriers and Comsat to discuss the TAT-6. The transcript is part of the public record.[100] Comsat's representative was its president, Dr. Charyk. AT&T's was its vice-president, Richard Hough, a member of the Comsat board. The other vocal carrier representative was Ted B. Westfall of ITT, also a Comsat board member until ITT sold its shares. In the presence of these people, Charyk failed to assert the basic facts about satellites and cables that the neutral Hinchman study had made plain, while he allowed Hough, especially, to contradict them unchallenged. "Now, I would like to emphasize at this point," Hough began, "that when we recommend a fifty-fifty distribution between cables and satellites, we feel just as strongly that we must have fifty percent on satellites, as we do on cables."

After two hours of arguments, Chairman Burch commented that he had heard very little about relative costs. He asked the participants, somewhat confusingly, "Would it be fair to say, depending on how you want to figure it, would you say that cost is probably more or less a push at this stage?" Hough responded, "With us, the higher cost of satellites is not something we are jumping up and down about, because we think that is a part of the route you have to go to get them in, so I agree with you." Was this supposed to mean that the telephone company felt satellites cost more, but was willing to pay more just for the privilege of using them? If so, it was a precise distortion of every aspect of the true situation. Burch tried again.

> THE CHAIRMAN. Cost is probably not the decisive factor between satellites and cables at this stage?

MR. HOUGH.   Along the cost line, as we are looking at the future, the message telephone service will be the largest user and, of course, the line haul is only one part of the total cost of providing message telephone service. The overseas line, you have the domestic line haul, the directory assistance, operators, and all of these other things, so we are only talking about a fraction of the costs.

THE CHAIRMAN.   Would anybody object if I knocked cost off of my list?

Comsat's representative did not object.

DOCTOR CHARYK.   Our exhibits indicate, in the time frame, they are basically in the same ballpark.

It was left to Asher Ende of the Common Carrier Bureau to reassert the advantages of satellites. Dr. Charyk did not.

Mr. Hough raised once again the danger of AT&T's abandoning research for better cables if the current application was not approved. (In this he was aided by Westfall of ITT, who told the commissioners about cable work being done in Japan and South America and warned that if the commission did not hurry, "there are going to be cables all over the world that may not touch on the United States.") Commissioner Houser was alarmed. He told Hough:

I certainly agree with you on the desirability of maintaining United States leadership. Perhaps I misunderstood you, or did I get the wrong impression, you were about ready to throw in the towel if you did not get this TAT-6?

Hough blathered on for another page of transcript. Nicholas Johnson was incredulous.

COMMISSIONER JOHNSON.   You are not really arguing that your expenditure of R&D on a cable is dependent on our decision?

MR. HOUGH.   Yes, sir, I am.

COMMISSIONER JOHNSON.   If we were to tell you to lay an SG

(3500-circuit) cable, you would not go on doing research on the SG
cable?

MR. HOUGH. I doubt we would.

When it appeared that his company's predictions for larger cables might
jeopardize its application for a second smaller one, Hough explained that
the SG cable could be ready early in 1976 (as AT&T had claimed in its
attempt to establish competitiveness with satellites) only under "undue"
pressure.

In any event, Hough's claim that AT&T intended to abandon any
effort to develop a 3500-circuit cable if its second 825-circuit cable was not
approved was soon shown to be ingenuous, because within a week the
Commission rejected the telephone company's TAT-6 application. The
commissioners said, however, that they would approve a 3500-circuit
trans-Atlantic cable as soon as AT&T had developed one.

These decisions came in a "Statement of Policy and Guidelines" that
was supposed to be the culmination of the FCC's general inquiry on
future licensing policy, begun the year before.[101] But in fact it was shorter
than the announcement that initiated the inquiry and offered no permanent policy for dealing with future applications. It did not even mention
the relative economics of cables and satellites. The commissioners said
that the $200 million lifetime revenue requirement of the proposed
825-circuit TAT-6 clearly was unnecessary as an extra Intelsat IV could
satisfy more demand for less money. But they refused to apply the same
logic—or the additional fact of a new satellite generation already
designed—to AT&T's proposed 3500-circuit cable, or even to wait until
the cable had been developed and applied for to approve it. Instead, they
argued that

> A high capacity SG type cable available for service by or before 1976
> would be needed so as to supplement then existing cable and satellite
> facilities to accommodate projected growth in circuit requirements,
> and to provide the diversity and redundancy needed to assure
> continuity of service.

Therefore, they invited the carriers "to file an application for such a cable
promptly."

Comsat had offered earlier to reduce its rates by 25 percent if TAT-6 was refused. So, as it did with the carriers, the Commission ordered Comsat to do what the company had already said it would do. In terms of general policy, the FCC came out in favor of "continued development of both cable and satellite technologies and their most effective and timely application"; "the most modern and effective facilities available . . . with due regard for efficiency, economy, diversity and redundancy"; "due regard for the concerns of Administrations which operate the foreign end of cables"; "economies available from each advance in technology . . . reflected in charges for service." Rather than apply a "fixed or rigid formula," the FCC said, it would be "looking toward maintenance of reasonable parity between cable and satellite circuits on transatlantic routes."

AT&T applied for partial reconsideration of the Commission's decision. So did the other carriers, even though they were not involved in the application, because they feared the precedent of a cable rejection. Despite the FCC's insistence that "reasonable parity" was not "a fixed or rigid formula," AT&T declared that it meant "approximately a 50-50 split between cable and satellite circuits." Comsat opposed the petitions, but objected only conditionally and in passing to the SG cable approval.[102]

In December 1971, the telephone company applied for permission to build the larger cable for 1976,[103] the cable Hough had said six months earlier would not be developed if the original TAT-6 application were rejected. The other carriers were to share in ownership of this cable, which was to cost $145 million and have up to 4000 circuits. AT&T once again emphasized how badly the Europeans—who were picking up less than 40 percent of the tab—wanted this cable. This time, AT&T said its 1980 needs would be "about 9499" circuits—down from earlier estimates on different occasions of 15,000 and 20,000.

Simultaneous with its new TAT-6 application, AT&T requested permission to buy 200 circuits in a new 1840-circuit cable running from Canada to England, planned for 1974. The phone company had said in 1968 that approval of TAT-5 would eliminate any need to use circuits in a new Canadian cable. This request also ignored the Commission's intention to prevent any investment in cables smaller than the 3500-circuit SG, which was implied in its approval in advance of the larger cable. AT&T had estimated earlier that use of CANTAT-2 for regular U.S. business would involve building $50 million of connecting land lines between Massachusetts and Nova Scotia.[104] Once again, there was no claim that the 200 extra circuits actually were needed, only that they would be "desirable from the point of view of service reliability."

ITT joined Bell in applying for the new TAT-6, and also applied for 62 circuits in the Canada-to-England cable. (All the carriers emphasized how anxious the British were to have U.S. firms help them pay for their new cable.) But ITT said it suffered "grave concern" about whether these two cables would satisfy its needs for the decade. The company wrote:

> Experience has shown that, absent restrictive regulation or artificial formula, submarine cable systems tend to fill rapidly in meeting the increasing demand for overseas communication requirement.[105]

In other words, unless they are prevented from doing so, the carriers will fill up their cables and build more cables rather than use empty satellite circuits. On this basis, ITT said it expected that another SG cable would be needed before the end of the decade.

The FCC approved carrier plans for the new TAT-6 in March 1972, and authorized construction in July.[106] It also authorized the carriers to invest in slightly fewer CANTAT-2 circuits than they had requested. In their July decision (Nicholas Johnson dissenting without comment), Commissioners pointed out that Comsat had opposed neither construction of TAT-6 nor use by U.S. carriers of CANTAT-2. There was the usual discussion of which circuits would be used. "We do not believe that it is necessary or even appropriate for us to prescribe specific formulas or rules concerning the manner in which available circuitry should be utilized," they said. Then they went on to say that in general, "all additional traffic should be divided three ways, with one-third on TAT-6 and one-third each" on the two Intelsat satellites.

Then, in attempting to justify the cable on the basis of need, the Commission based its computations on the 50-50 cable-satellite split that the carriers had wanted all along. For it was clear once again from their own statistics that whatever the relative economies of Intelsat IV and the SG cable (and Walter Hinchman had demonstrated fairly conclusively that the data favored the satellite), or the availability of even more economical satellites on the drawing board, there were sufficient satellite circuits already available to satisfy all the carrier needs through the late 1970s. By ignoring the empty capacity available on satellites and accepting *"arguendo"* the carriers' demand that half of all increased business should go by cable, the FCC computed that—based on the carriers' own estimates of demand for circuits—the record carriers would need "up to 400" new cable circuits, and AT&T would need "about 2698." Adding these, we get "up to about" 3098. So the TAT-6 cable could satisfy this demand with almost 1000 circuits to spare. (Even the Commission conceded that all foreseeable demand by 1980 could be met "without reliance on CANTAT-2," then approved use of it anyway.)

Another look at those numbers reveals how unnecessary the TAT-6 cable is. Elsewhere in its 1972 decision, the Commission said there were "over 8000 unused circuits" in the two Atlantic Intelsat IV satellites at that time. How many of these will be used by 1980 under the Commission's current plans? There will be 3098 of them, presumably, used to match, on a one-for-one basis, the TAT-6 cable circuits the carriers were said to require on the same basis. Add 303 circuits to match, on the same one-for-one basis, the unused circuits in older cables at the time of the decision. This makes 3502, or less than half the available Intelsat IV capacity. If the 3098 circuits intended for TAT-6 went by satellite instead, there still would be more than 1400 Intelsat IV circuits remaining unused or available for growth in non-U.S. communication. And this does not count circuits available in older satellite models, or the new satellites that the Commission has approved for the late 1970s. Based on the FCC's own numbers, the $140 million trans-Atlantic cable currently under construction clearly cannot be justified on the basis of need. Nevertheless, it will enter the carriers' rate bases in 1976, and communications users will be paying for it with higher rates until it is fully amortized in the year 2000.

The traditional international carriers were late in paying the same careful attention to trans-Pacific communication that they had devoted to communication over the North Atlantic. Cables make even less sense in the Pacific than they do in the Atlantic. The distance across that ocean is far greater, and the distance separating the major communications centers on the Asian side are far greater than in Europe. This adds nothing to the cost of using satellites, but adds greatly to the cost of laying a cable system. Also, the lower volume of traffic made it even harder to justify placing cables in service in addition to the satellite system. So for several years after Early Bird, AT&T and others proposed no new cables at all.

Why do foreign telecommunications executives tend to develop such preferences for new cables? A memo from the files of the FCC may be enlightening.[107] It concerns a visit in June 1971 to Asher Ende of the Common Carrier Bureau by two representatives of the Japanese international communication company, Kokusai Denshin Denwa. This was three months before AT&T applied for a new cable to Hawaii and almost a year and a half before the carriers applied to extend it across the Pacific. But the two Japanese reported that they had been holding "informal discussions and consultations" with AT&T since the fall of 1970, and that "in December a consensus had been reached . . . that in the interest of diversity and to prevent too large a percentage of traffic from being handled via satellite one or more additional cable facilities would be required in the next few years across the Pacific." (No attempt was ever made throughout to claim that cables actually were cheaper to use across the Pacific.) So AT&T was carefully lobbying its Asian counterparts long before it ever applied for a new cable.

In September 1971, AT&T and Hawaiian Telephone applied for the right to lay a new cable between California and Hawaii. This was an 845-circuit cable (including those added by compression techniques) of the type the FCC had just refused the carriers permission to build across the Atlantic, on the grounds that cable technology soon would make it obsolete. And indeed, as AT&T was applying for an 845-circuit Pacific cable to be in service by 1974, it was simultaneously preparing an application for a 3500-circuit cable across the Atlantic which it said could be in service by the beginning of 1976. But AT&T said the smaller cable was necessary "to effectuate the orderly establishment of parity between cable and satellite circuits" between the mainland and Hawaii. Unlike TAT-5, no attempt was made to suggest that more circuits were needed than the satellite system could provide, or that cable circuits could be provided for less money. The carriers declared this was the first step in a comprehensive new Pacific cable program, under which no new satellite circuits would be leased from Comsat until the cables caught up. This, of course, was exactly the opposite of what AT&T's "parity" doctrine had meant when the company had first proposed it in the midsixties. But the number of satellite circuits had all too quickly overwhelmed the cables, and especially so in the Pacific. This first new Hawaii link was to cost $59 million, and be completely owned by American domestic and international firms.

At first, Comsat did not even object to the new cable. While "construction of any additional facilities is not warranted on purely economic grounds," the company said, the cable "would provide both diversity and balance within the available facilities."[108]

However, the communications users who would be affected by the cost of the new cable were able to step in as a group to protect their own interests. The governor of Hawaii, John Burns, filed a strong objection to the proposed cable. To the carriers' contention that the new cable would not raise the price Hawaiians would have to pay for communication with the mainland, Burns said that rates already were high and that discriminatory rates "will be sustained subsilentio through approval" of the cable. He went on,

> To suggest, as the carriers appear to do, that the construction of such an expensive facility has no cognizable relationship to the rates which the public will pay strains credulity. Obviously, the expense of the cable will be recaptured from consumers over the life of the cable.[109]

Burns said the cable would be especially superfluous because it would coincide with the advent of domestic satellite communication. The FCC already had determined that any domestic satellite system would have to service Hawaii.

In October 1972, the carriers applied for the second part of the Pacific cable, between Hawaii and Okinawa.[110] This part, also the older, 845-circuit model, would cost $121 million, making a grand total of $180 million for the whole trans-Pacific cable. (This is only the addition to U.S. and foreign carrier rate bases. The total revenue requirement, including maintenance costs and profit to the carriers over its 24-year lifetime, will be several times higher.) AT&T said it "has no choice but to proceed expeditiously" with the cable, in light of the "strong views" expressed by its foreign counterparts—in this case a private Japanese firm, and the Australian Overseas Telephone Commission.[111] In light of Governor Burns's objections. AT&T said it would be willing to use the cable only for international traffic and not for mainland-to-Hawaii traffic. Once it was in the rate base, of course, it made no difference to the company's profits what the cable was used for, or whether it was used at all.

Comsat opposed the application early in 1973, saying that the "basic question" was whether parity "is of such overwhelming importance as to justify an enormous burden on the ratepayer of close to two-thirds of a billion dollars over an eight year period," especially "in view of the availability or expected availability of more advanced communications technology in both submarine cables and communications satellites." Comsat pointed out that only 1849 of the 4500 circuits in its Pacific Intelsat IV were being used at the time the carriers wanted another 845-circuit cable.[112]

The FCC's decision approving both parts of the Pacific cable came in June 1973, two years after it had rejected a similar low capacity cable for the Atlantic on ground that it was old-fashiioned even by cable standards.

The commissioners admitted that the 845-circuit, $180-million cable now completed could not be justified on the basis of any real shortage of circuits in the area, and instead offered the familiar potpourri of rationalizations.

> The economic, political, and national security considerations which require modern high capacity, efficient, and economic facilities; the concomitant importance of reliability and continuity of service which require both diversity and redundancy as well as adequate capacity; the relatively low capacity as well as the age of cable facilities [already] available in the Pacific Ocean; the fact [unexplained] that the costs related to the proposed cables are commensurate with the benefits to be derived therefrom; and the rate reductions which will be made available to the public upon authorization and installation of these facilities.[113]

As with TAT-5, the carriers had won approval of their cable in exchange for a 25 percent rate reduction. This led Governor Burns to withdraw his opposition, although he had seemed to understand previously that a rate reduction which accompanied huge inflation of carrier rate bases would be a Pyrrhic victory. The Commission emphasized that the joint cable/satellite rate proposals had the strong support of the state of Hawaii, the Defense Department, and foreign governments. This rate reduction was even more explicitly unrelated to the cable than the earlier Atlantic one, because it was set to take place not when the cable was open (when its alleged economies would begin to manifest themselves) but five days after it was authorized. As for the carriers' long-range Pacific cable plans, the commissioners said they "explicitly reject" a commitment to maintain a 50-50 cable circuit-to-satellite circuit ratio in the Pacific, like the one they had made for the Atlantic. "Our concern here is to assure adequate diversity, redundancy, and flexibility and the availability of sufficient capacity therefore," they wrote.[114]

5

World Peace and Understanding

The International Communications Satellite Consortium (Intelsat) was established at the instigation of the U.S. government in 1964, along the model of other post-World War II international organizations such as the United Nations. Intelsat's purpose, according to its charter (and identical words used in the Communications Satellite Act), is nothing less than to bring about "world peace and understanding" through the creation of an international communications satellite system.

But since its founding, Intelsat has been a source not of peace and understanding, but of contention and controversy among the nations of the world. Some of its member nations have complained that Intelsat's real intention and effect has been to promote American domination of international satellite communication. (Britain's *The Economist,* for example, has called Intelsat " a kind of hoax."[1]) And some feel that the Communications Satellite Corporation, as U.S. representative in and manager of the consortium, has failed both to administer the system properly and to generate international goodwill toward the United States.

From the beginning, the State Department made it impossible for the Soviet Union to join the new international organization. The Russians were never specifically excluded, but in the days of the space race they could hardly be expected to join an organization so clearly dominated by the United States. And, frequent reference to "a single global system" notwithstanding, nobody did expect it.

By the rules of the interim agreement signed August 20, 1964 by the United States, Canada, Australia, Japan, and the Western European nations, voting power and investment in the consortium were distributed on the basis of prospective volume of use of the system. This gave the U.S. 61 percent of the voting power among the original members. The provision for new members limited them to 17 percent of the original investment of $200 million, which guaranteed that the U.S. share would never fall below 50 percent. For certain important decisions, support was required from 12.5 percent of the membership beyond that of the United States (dropping to 8.5 percent after 60 days for certain other decisions), but in any event the United States retained veto power over all the consortium's activities.[2] Comsat was made the U.S. representative to the consortium—the first time such sovereign state power had been delegated to a private corporation (though at the time Comsat was not being presented to the public as a private corporation). Comsat also was named the "manager" of the satellite system, on behalf of all the international representatives.

Comsat has denied any difficulty in serving simultaneously the interests of the U.S. Government and those of a supposedly international organization.

> Thus, by agreement of the United States Government, Comsat in its role as manager serves the entire INTELSAT organization and membership without discrimination, acts solely in the interests of efficiency, economy and effective operation of the global satellite system, and does not serve any United States foreign policy interests which are not fully consistent with the interests of INTELSAT. On the other hand, with respect to Comsat's role as an *owner* of INTELSAT, Sections 201 (a) (4) and 402 of the Communications Satellite Act of 1962 assure Comsat's responsiveness to the foreign policy interests of the United States.[3]

In fact, there was little conflict between Intelsat's interests and those of U.S. foreign policy because considerations of U.S. foreign policy in the

Cold War, space race division, played an important part in the founding of Intelsat. Senator Pastore, commenting on Intelsat's first launching eight months after the agreement was signed, objected to a suggestion by Arthur C. Clarke that satellites might make Russian the universal language. "Dramatic as these observations appeared to be, the fact today is that Early Bird is orbiting and is controlled by the Communications Satellite Corporation and can become the show window through which America can and will be seen throughout the world. And indeed it will be the mirror of our image."[4] To show off Early Bird's potential impact on world affairs, a panel was arranged of top Intelsat country foreign ministers, including Dean Rusk, each broadcasting from his own capitol. The headline in the Toronto Globe: "Five Debate on TV/Agree Reds in Asia Should Be Stopped."[5]

Although it was important to retain American control of the consortium, it was equally important to sign up as many other countries as possible. There was some fear that the Western European nations would develop a space capacity of their own in a few years (the French, as might be expected, were especially adamant in this effort); Intelsat was meant to rechannel their aspirations and give them a vested interest in the American system. Toward this end, Comsat argued for several years that the treaty's reference to "a single global . . . system" meant that consortium members were committed to plan all their satellite communication through Intelsat. Comsat had another reason for this argument: it could be used to show that Comsat was entitled to a monopoly on any U.S. domestic satellite system. The FCC found this idea less and less appealing, however, and other nations increasingly rejected the notion of permanent and total reliance on the United States for their satellite needs. This is why "single" is now taken on all sides to modify "global" and not "system."

The dozens of small nations that signed up for Intelsat were courted more for prestige of numbers than for economic considerations. The United States-controlled Intelsat has run rings around Intersputnik, Russia's international consortium, which has nine member nations, all Communist. (However attractive its membership scheme, Intersputnik did not begin operation until 1974, nine years after Intelsat.) As of June 1975, Intelsat had 90 members. Many of these nations have no earth stations, and some are so small that they may never need one. José Alegrett, Intelsat representative from Venezuela, said in an interview with me that Comsat's International Development Division (IDD) and the State Department bring heavy pressure on small countries to join up.

Alegrett, one of two or three perennial troublemakers for the United States in Intelsat, said that any prospective members should be required to sit in on a few Intelsat governing board meetings before being allowed to join. "If they saw what goes on," Alegrett said, "there'd be 20 members instead of 80."[6] But according to a former employee of the IDD, while Comsat representatives were busy enrolling underdeveloped countries in Intelsat, the carrier members on their board of directors often refused Comsat permission to provide technical and financial assistance for the construction of earth stations in these countries, despite Comsat's experience as earth station manager in the United States and the $100 million it had sitting in the bank for most of this time.[7] The carriers saw no need for haste in making their cable operations obsolete.

Along with Alegrett, the main thorn in Comsat's side in Intelsat has been Dr. Reinhold Steiner. Until 1973, Dr. Steiner represented Switzerland, Austria, and Liechtenstein. (Countries frequently pool their voting power to achieve the 1.5 percent necessary for representation on the board.) Dr. Steiner was the only full-time permanent representative to Intelsat who was not from the United States. "It was a misunderstanding," he said in an interview with me while still on the job. "The Swiss thought this was truly an international arrangement. But just keeping track of what Comsat is doing is a full-time job." He said of Comsat, "If you consider the interest of the U.S. in improving relations with other countries, Comsat has failed. Of all the international carriers, Comsat has the worst reputation."[8] According to Steiner and Alegrett, both Comsat and the State Department tried to get them relieved by complaining to their governments and national communication agencies about the men's unsporting behavior. For many years they failed. When the Swiss government wanted to transfer Steiner back to Berne in 1973 after 20 years in the United States, he quit the diplomatic service and became a Washington-based communications consultant. Alegrett, however, was elected vice-president of the Intelsat Board of Governors.

As a private company, Comsat has been less successful than an experienced government agency might be in dealing with foreign representatives. John A. Johnson, a Comsat vice-president and former NASA official who was U.S. representative to the Interim Communications Satellite Committee (ICSC), Intelsat's governing board, and who therefore became its first chairman, found dealing with the other national representatives especially trying. Dr. Steiner said flatly, "Mr. Johnson is the most xenophobic fellow I've ever met. He's a talented lawyer, but why he'd be in international relations I don't know because he hates foreigners—it's that simple."[9] Another ICSC members' favorite has been Louis Meyer, Comsat's director of administration. One of Meyer's own former underlings says of him, "When Lou Meyer came in front of the committee, even when he was telling the truth it sounded like lying. You could tell immediately his disdain for the other members. He treated them like little boys whom Comsat had deigned to tell what was going on."[10] A demeanor so much in keeping with the facts of a relationship clearly is out of place in the world of diplomacy. Allegret complained that Meyer frequently refused to supply information the ICSC members requested, and that Johnson misused his chairmanship to protect Comsat's interests.[11]

At first, Comsat insisted on having permanent chairmanship of the ICSC, and of all three of its subcommittees as well. Only after foreign representatives complained to the State Department did Comsat agree to a more equitable sharing arrangement. In 1969, over Comsat's objections (but not its veto), the ICSC paid the management consulting firm of Booz, Allen & Hamilton $63,000 to study Comsat's management of Intelsat. Booz-Allen concluded: "There appears to be no doubt that a number of the problems experienced by the manager and the ICSC have been made more difficult because of certain of the personalities involved." For $63,000 these experts recommended that "matters should be freely discussed . . . and a mutual accommodation arrived at."[12] Mr. Johnson has since been promoted out of the international arena.

The Booz-Allen study is more enlightening concerning another frequent ICSC complaint—that Comsat as manager is profligate. According to Alegrett, a section in the first draft of the report comparing Comsat executives' salaries with those of other U.S. telecommunications companies—and concluding that Comsat's were significantly higher—was left out of the final report distributed to Intelsat members, on Johnson's insistence that such information was irrelevant.[13]

Several Intelsat representatives complain that Comsat's basic research program on behalf of Intelsat is extravagant and unnecessary, given the enormous amounts of space application research being conducted by NASA and the Defense Department. They suggest its purpose is to "make work" for the elaborate laboratories Comsat has constructed in the Maryland countryside, as well as to subsidize Comsat's domestic satellite (an issue examined below).[14]

When Comsat was asked its reaction to the concern "expressed by some members of Intelsat and others, that it doesn't avail itself as much as it might of the R&D conducted by NASA," the company replied: "We doubt the existence of this so-called 'charge' and would be interested in knowing of any specific instance of such a charge by specific 'members' of INTELSAT or 'others.' "

The Booz-Allen study was not available to the public. But is said in reference to its interviews with Intelsat representatives:

> The issue is raised that INTELSAT's R&D efforts may be largely redundant when related to U.S. Government space applications programs. . . . A review of the available budget information and discussions with U.S. manufacturers show, of course, that the majority of this NASA and DOD spending does not have direct, peaceful communications-related use. It also shows, however, that a very large amount, in absolute terms, does have such use.[15]

Comsat's attitude has antagonized foreign governments and has been accused of slowing development of the international satellite system. Harvard Law professor and former State Department official Abe Chayes complained in 1967 of "a kind of studied unreality" that caused him to discount Comsat's intentions "by at least a grain or two of salt. . . . I think it will be hard for the nations of the world to surrender permanently the managerial control of the prime long-range international communication network to a U.S. corporation staffed primarily by U.S. citizens," Chayes said.[16] This attitude is one reason why some countries would prefer to build more expensive cables, rather than become completely dependent on the United States-dominated satellite system. The American cable carriers—AT&T, ITT, RCA—often have excellent relationships with their foreign counterparts. The ability to achieve these good relationships is an example of the kind of experience and expertise the carriers failed to pass on to Comsat. Nevertheless, Comsat has known when to use the government's concern to minimize the impression of U.S. dominance. Asher Ende of the FCC has complained:

> Sometimes they [Comsat] show up with a 200-page contract and give us 45 minutes to consider it. They have come into this commission at 10 A.M. saying they need an authorization by 5 P.M. to spend something for Intelsat IV. They got it that day because 78 other countries had approved it and we would be accused of dictatorial delay. Then

they told the other countries that the FCC was forcing this thing on them. ... What happened to Intelsat is that you have very good engineers who know what they're doing and get very impatient with the peons they have to deal with.

Mr. Ende says of his foreign counterparts:

Very definitely the arrogance of Intelsat makes the other countries like cables. France wouldn't like anything. But the British, the Canadians, the Philippines are all unhappy. If Comsat acted like an angel, that would have ameliorated the preference for cables somewhat. But their treatment is salt in the wounds.[17]

The other developed countries in Intelsat have been bitter about Comsat's failure to give a larger share of the construction contracts to non-U.S. companies. France and England worried that by joining Intelsat—especially with its early emphasis on a *single* international satellite system—they would be allowing their own aerospace industries to wither, leaving themselves far from the frontiers of communications technology indefinitely. They were persuaded to join Intelsat with the promise that not only would they have a fair share of the procurement contracts but that they would get to share the United States' superior expertise in this field.[18] In the preamble of the first Intelsat agreement, shortly after the words "world peace and understanding," the belief is expressed that all states should be allowed to invest and participate in the system "including the provision of equipment." These political considerations apparently overrode a warning by the RAND Corporation in 1963 that

the value of foreign technical contributions . . . has to be considered in relation to the need for early establishment of a working system, a prime objective of both the United States and the Corporation. Foreign participation in the research and development phase could delay the effective initiation of the system long enough to permit the Soviet Union to gain another "first" in space. Moreover, the sharing of decisions about research and development with nations that are less advanced than the United States and have different research and development interests might prove exceedingly disadvantageous to the system at this time.[19]

For the first three generations of Intelsat satellites, the United States had it both ways. The other countries of the world—developed and undeveloped—were in effect subsidizing our own space effort (though of course the amounts were relatively trivial and this was not the purpose of encouraging their involvement). Intelsat I included no non-U.S. contracts. For Intelsat III, foreign contracts amounted to only 4.6 percent (and about half of that if you include bills paid to NASA for launch costs). For the first four Intelsat IV satellites, non-U.S. contractors received 36.3 percent of the hardware business and by 1971, after repeated complaints by foreign Intelsat members, this figure had risen past 40 percent. But of the $382 million spent by Intelsat through the middle of 1971, only 5 percent was spent outside the United States.[20] Meanwhile, non-U.S. ownership in Intelsat had risen from 37 percent in 1964 to more than 60 percent. Intelsat's procurement regulations state that when bids are otherwise equal, "the Committee and the Manager shall also seek to ensure that contracts are so distributed that supplies are procured in the States whose Governments are Parties to the Agreement *in approximate proportion to the respective quotas of their corresponding Signatories to the Special Agreement.*"[21] There is debate about whether NASA's launching bills should be included in the percentages, which would make a significant difference. (The foreign percentage for the first four Intelsat IVs, for example, falls to 14.7 percent if NASA's bills are included.)

Comsat has said that its policy is one "of seeking the best equipment at the best price for the most timely delivery based, to the maximum extent practicable, on public solicitation." It argued that foreign contractors simply have been unable to compete with American companies in submitting bids. In this, the company was supported by Clay T. Whitehead, President Nixon's special assistant for telecommunications. Whitehead said:

> It's mainly the European countries who are bellyaching in the ICSC. They're complaining that they're not getting as much of the production as they want. . . . They're saying, "Ours costs more, but we still have a right to our share." But why should anyone else pay to have your inefficient industry? If Europe wants to subsidize its industry to it can get a share of the Intelsat construction so they can bid at an economic cost, then OK.[22]

But Comsat has created artificial barriers to higher non-U.S. participation in Intelsat, and the Europeans have failed to benefit fully from the sharing of U.S. expertise, which is one of the reasons they joined Intelsat rather than proceeding on their own satellite system as many of them wanted to do in the early sixties. At that time, the United States flatly refused to share technical information about communications satellites until the Europeans joined Intelsat, then for several years afterward made great trouble for any country that tried to start a satellite system outside of Intelsat. (That is, until the United States decided that it wanted to do so itself).[23]

When asked about another frequent charge, "that it overemphasizes technical specifications, thus discouraging innovative bids and bids from foreign manufacturers," Comsat replied:

> We do not believe that any such charge exists or that there would be any basis for it. Our major satellite procurements have been solicited predominantly on the basis of performance specifications, leaving to proposing suppliers the opportunity for innovation reasonably achievable from the present state of the art.[24]

Yet their own private Booz-Allen study of the year before raised this issue clearly.

> A number of major manufacturers interviewed during the course of this study expressed the view that the manager tended to be rigid and restrictive in prescribing the technical approaches in hardware procurement proposals, thereby limiting the ability of the prospective vendors to respond with an alternative technical approach that might enable INTELSAT to derive the benefits of the vendor's own technical expertise.[25]

Booz-Allen discussed the dilemma foreign manufacturers find themselves in.

> A number of the foreign suppliers interviewed felt disadvantaged in competing for INTELSAT contracts due to lack of familiarity and experience in dealing with the complex bidding procedures and relatively short lead time requirements typical of U.S. aerospace industry procurement practices. The term used to describe the situation by one non-U.S. vendor was that of a "hostile environ-

ment." This comment appears typical of the point of view of a number of non-U.S. suppliers."[26]

Another subject of contention among Intelsat members until it was modified by the new agreement in 1971 was Comsat's patent policy for inventions made in the course of satellite contracts. Modeled on U.S. government policy, it insisted that all these new inventions remain the property of Intelsat. ICSC members complained to Booz-Allen and others that this substantially raised the price manufacturers charged to perform Intelsat contracts.[27] Dr. Steiner says that the reason for this restrictive policy "is that Comsat wanted to build for itself a unique monopoly on communication satellite technology," and charged that while patent rights were waived for a dollar for Western military use, Comsat attempted to use them to discourage non-Intelsat commercial systems.[28]

A policy particularly irritating to the small, underdeveloped nations in Intelsat has been Comsat's insistence on achieving a 14 percent annual rate of return on investment in the satellite system. This is what Comsat wants the FCC to allow it as a private company, and what it has aimed to achieve as manager for all the national investors. Trouble is, the investment of these countries is so small that the rate of return makes no difference to them; they are not interested in profit but in increased volume of communication with the outside world. And they feel this policy has led to greatly higher rates and lower usage of the system.[29] (As we have seen, both Comsat and the FCC often ignore the relationship between rates and volume of demand, especially considering the miniscule marginal cost of using extra circuits in already-operating satellites.) Many countries in Intelsat wanted to set rates so that the system merely broke even, but use was maximized. Comsat originally insisted on a 20 to 22 percent annual profit. As a result of the permanent Intelsat agreement of 1971, rates are to be set to generate a profit as close as possible to the cost of money in world markets, plus an allowance for risk.[30]

Comsat's rate-making policy has been a great boon to the older carriers, which dominated it for the first decade of its existence. By maintaining the cost of using satellites at artificially high levels, it allows these carriers to argue that they can build a cable for less than the cost of renting an equivalent number of circuits from Comsat, even though the objective cost of providing the circuits by satellite obviously is less. Thus satellite circuits go empty while more cables are built.

To illustrate why Comsat has been said to have manipulated its role as Intelsat manager for private corporate purposes, we can examine the methods it used to procure the Intelsat IV generation of satellites and to plan for the Intelsat V generation. The same examples illustrate how Comsat's attitude toward foreign members can be said to have clouded the favorable image of American foreign policy that Intelsat was supposed to enhance. We see how, in its attempt to win the domestic satellite race, Comsat broke Intelsat regulations, misled foreign members of the governing board, and cost the consortium several million dollars. Some of this story comes from a detailed chronology submitted to the ICSC by Dr. Steiner late in 1969; some comes from a complaint filed with the FCC in 1972 by one of Comsat's competitors.[30]

The contract for a fourth generation of 4000-circuit satellites went to Hughes Aircraft despite a fierce effort by Lockheed, which had gathered an international group of partners. This was in 1968. Hughes had built the first two successful generations of Intelsat satellites. But since its third, by TRW, had been a failure, Lockheed was worried about being permanently shut out from civilian satellite contracts. Although a decision had to be made on the $73 million contract by October 5, Comsat withheld information about the contract from other ICSC members until September 24 and did not distribute the final text until October 4. Then it demanded a vote the same day. Supposedly because the contract was so controversial, only four satellites were ordered at the time, though it was obvious that more would be needed eventually. Comsat assured the committee that there would be no problem in negotiating favorable options for more satellites. And indeed the next month, November, Hughes submitted to Comsat, as manager of the system, maximum price offers for satellites purchased at various dates before October 1972. Comsat neglected to inform the other ICSC members of Hughes's offers, despite the fact that they expired in 90 days and despite a rule in the Intelsat agreement that any issue involving more than $500,000 must be settled by the entire committee and not by the manager alone. The Hughes options involved more than $20 million. Without informing the committee, Comsat began discussions with Hughes for ordering a modified version of the satellite, rather than more of the same version. Meanwhile the original Hughes offer expired, after two extensions, on June 30, 1969.

The foreign members of the committee knew nothing of this but were getting curious, so when they met in June they voted to place a discussion of "Intelsat IV options" on the agenda of a special meeting in August at Rio de Janeiro. Comsat removed this item from the agenda that was mailed to other members in July, even though only the governing body as a whole is empowered to remove an item it has placed on its own agenda. After protest, the item was reinserted and Comsat announced at the meeting that it had *just received* option proposals from Hughes, which it was still in the process of negotiation. Comsat refused to answer the other members' questions about whether it was considering a modification of the design of the remaining satellites. Instead, it recommended that no new satellites be ordered until December 1970.

The inevitable confrontation came at the ICSC's next bimonthly meeting in October 1969. Late in September, one week before the meeting, Comsat suddenly mailed out a brief proposal to order four satellites from Hughes of a modified version not covered by any contract options. This was the first word non-U.S. members had on what was a major revision of their entire satellite system plans.

ICSC meetings last a week. On the first day of this one, October 2, Comsat suddenly announced that the committee had to decide on this new proposal by October 9, because it expired on October 18. Comsat also announced that regular, unmodified fourth-generation satellites could not be ordered after that date either—exactly one year after the original Intelsat IV contract had been signed—because Hughes's second, third, and fourth year price options were no longer valid. This surprised the committee, since they had first seen these price figures when Comsat had mailed them out the week before, and since Comsat had urged them in August to do nothing for a year and a half. At first, Comsat claimed that the options were not valid because Hughes had not submitted them within a month of the original contract, as specified in that contract. When another ICSC member suggested that Hughes should be sued for breach of contract, Comsat admitted that Hughes actually had submitted the option proposals the previous November—within a month of the October contract—but that it had kept the proposals secret, during which time they had expired. Comsat said it had ignored the options because it felt Hughes's price was too high, but it also admitted that the price Hughes now was asking—even for unmodified satellites—was several million dollars higher than the ones the company had refused to bring before the committee.

Twice, without supplying any of the information the committee asked for, Comsat asked for a vote on its proposal for a modified satellite. Both times, it failed to achieve even the minimum 12.5 percent support needed beyond its own vote. Both times a large majority of the committee voted to purchase four more unmodified Intelsat IV satellites at Hughes's new, higher, bid, and both times Comsat vetoed the proposal. This antagonized not only the foreigners on the ICSC, but members of Comsat's own staff. Why was Comsat so anxious to force its plan through the committee, and why did Comsat feel the need to operate so deceptively? One staff member explains.

> The Intelsat IV was procured from Hughes. It was ordered and everybody knew they hadn't ordered enough satellites. They said this was a way to keep the options open, because there had been a bloody fight between Hughes and Lockheed for the contract. Then a peculiar idea emerged. . . . It came up suddenly in verbal discussion without a prior paper or anything—an unusual procedure. It was called Intelsat IV½ which would change the product by modifying the design to include 24 transponders rather than 12.
> It didn't make much sense to the committee, and Comsat couldn't muster the 12½ percent quota they needed, despite great pressure tactics such as placing a call to Buenos Aires and getting the delegate to Intelsat from Argentina hauled off and replaced by a guy from the Embassy totally unfamiliar with the matters but instructed to vote yes.
> It turns out that Intelsat IV½ was their domestic satellite proposal. Their notion was to get Intelsat to pay for the development expenses—the program with Hughes to develop the necessary changes in the basic Intelsat IV. That was recommended against to management by most of the staff. They thought they were terribly clever and that no one saw through this little ruse. But people did all over the place.[31]

Intelsat eventually purchased four more unmodified Hughes satellites. Two of these were approved at the October meeting, after some ICSC members walked out and called the White House to protest Comsat's behavior as U.S. representative, and two at a meeting in December. Hughes obtained several million dollars more for the same satellites than it had wanted the year before, and charged $100,000 for extending the option at all. Not two years had gone by, however, before Comsat again attempted to force an intermediate generation of satellites on the other Intelsat members—this time successfully.

As satellite generations go, a new one would normally have been scheduled to go up in 1975 or 1976. Comsat proposed in 1971, however, that this new generation, Intelsat V, be delayed until the end of the decade or the beginning of the 1980s. In the interim, Comsat proposed to send up in the middle of this decade another modified version of the Intelsat IV, this time called the IVA. The Intelsat V, whoever builds it, probably will be of vastly different technology and certainly will have far larger circuit capacity. Presumably, the longer the delay, the more advanced it will be, or at least this was the rationale for Comsat's plan. The Intelsat IVA has been built by Hughes. The first of them was launched in July 1975. Some Intelsat members and other satellite manufacturers felt this was another attempt to subsidize Comsat's domestic satellite development costs.

Delaying the fifth generation satellite offered other advantages to Comsat as well. By the permanent accord signed in 1971, Comsat's role as Intelsat manager expires in 1978. But it will be hard for Intelsat to switch managers if it is in the middle of launching a major new generation of satellites. Also, delay may give Comsat enough time to develop the new satellite in its own laboratories rather than ordering it "off-the-shelf" from the manufacturer as it has done in the past. Dr. Steiner pointed out that Comsat had little experience that qualifies it for such an enormous project, and argued that

> it seems obvious that Comsat realizes the building of an experimental Intelsat satellite is the last— if not only—chance ever to have somebody other than it itself pay for this apprenticeship in satellite design and construction.[32]

In-house development would also help justify inclusion of Comsat labs in the company's rate base, a subject of contention before the FCC. Comsat's competitor pointed out in its domestic satellite brief that the delay and in-house development would both "block any cost-sharing advantage that might accrue to one of Comsat's domestic competitors," if the competitor could sell some version of *its* domestic satellite to Intelsat as a fifth-generation international satellite as well.[33]

Late in 1971, Comsat proposed that the controversial Hughes contract be amended once more, to allow Hughes to study a design for a modified Intelsat IV at a price not to exceed $500,000. Before that meeting, however, Lockheed Aircraft had sent the committee an unsolicited proposal for a completely new generation of satellites similar to its own domestic satellite design (later abandoned), which was far more advanced than the latest Comsat/Hughes model intended for both Intelsat IVA and Comsat's domestic system. This would be a so-called "early" Intelsat V—exactly what Comsat was trying to avoid. Comsat delayed action on the Lockheed proposal until the ICSC meeting of February 1972. Meanwhile Hughes asked to broaden its study, presumably to compete with that of Lockheed. Fairchild Industries (another domestic competitor at the time) also submitted a proposal. The ICSC's technical subcommittee, where Comsat did not have veto power, recommended that Lockheed be given a study contract but that the requests by Hughes and Fairchild be turned down. At the February 1972 meeting, a large majority of the members supported this recommendation, but Comsat abstained. Since it is U.S. representative, this killed the measure. Another proposal to give study contracts to everyone *except* Lockheed was voted down by everyone except Comsat, which voted last and abstained once again. Finally a proposal offering contracts to all three companies was passed, with the German and French representatives issuing statements saying they voted for Hughes and Fairchild against their wills, in order to assure that the Lockheed study would be made.

In the end Hughes got the contract for the Intelsat IVAs. They have a capacity of more than 7500 circuits, compared to 4000 on the unmodified Intelsat IVs. Dr. Steiner said in an interview that this "crazy program" could cost Intelsat as much as $120 million.[34] And it will only provide two years of grace between the regular Intelsat IV series and the launching of Intelsat Vs. RFPs (requests for proposals) for Intelsat V were issued in 1974. The first Intelsat IVA was not launched until the last half of 1975, and the fifth generation was to be launched as early as 1977.

Dr. Steiner said that the U.S. representative pursued its goal of a delayed fifth generation and modified Intelsat IV series "with a tenacity that is . . . uncommon even for Comsat." He said, however, that the "very unpleasant episodes" that arose during that controversy

> have made clear, once more, that Comsat does not hesitate to eliminate any and all opposition coming from its international partners, be it through application of its dual role as Manager and interested Signatory or of mere force, culminating in its veto power in the Committee.[35]

When the interim Intelsat agreement came up for permanent re-negotiation in 1969, what was supposed to be resolved in four weeks ended up taking two and a half years. Intelsat operation under the new arrangement, with somewhat reduced power for the U.S. representative, did not begin until 1973. Because of Comsat's poor reputation, the United States found it difficult to retain the degree of domination it obviously wanted in the organization.

As the various parties were preparing for the renegotiations in the summer of 1968, the Soviet Union began one of its periodic promotions of its own satellite system, Intersputnik, in a speech by Premier Kosygin to a United Nations group. This was good timing, and the Russians described their proposed system in a way meant to appeal to discontented members of Intelsat. The Soviets said that in their system decisions would be made by majority rule with one vote per member state. In Intelsat, not only did the United States have complete veto power, but votes were arranged so that together with Britain and either France or Germany it could take actions that all the other members put together could not overrule. The Soviets said their system would be geared to small, less expensive earth stations instead of the elaborate facilities needed in Intelsat, something that would appeal to the poor nations of Africa and Asia. For the Europeans, the Russians promised that members of their system would be allowed to participate in any other satellite system (the United States still insisted on Intelsat exclusivity). This clever proposal came as an international consortium run by Lockheed Aircraft was losing Intelsat IV to Hughes Aircraft and Europeans were especially annoyed at Comsat's chauvinistic procurement policy. Trouble was, the USSR's system was largely on paper; that of the United States was in the air and operating. This fact, and the fact the United States could refuse launchings to any European system, significantly lessened the threat of competition. A greater danger was that America's search for "world peace and understanding" would be made suspect.

The renegotiations began in Washington in March 1969. Under the chairmanship of Washington lawyer Leonard Marks (formerly a Comsat incorporator and later treasurer of Democrats for Nixon), the American delegates initially took a hard line. Comsat would remain as manager, voting power would continue to be related to use and investment, and the United States could continue to own up to 50 percent of the system. In the face of overwhelming opposition by the rest of the participants, however, the State Department began to relent. Mr. Marks left within a month of the beginning of the talks. He was replaced by former Pennsylvania governor William Scranton, and later by a distinguished State Department professional, Abbot Washburn. State and Comsat, the two parts of the U.S. team, began to split on the issues of Comsat's continued management of the system, and the right of system members to join other satellite operations. The negotiation dragged on. The White House's "open skies" memorandum on domestic satellite communication in January 1970 indicated that the United States had abandoned the "single system" idea, but it made Comsat even more insistent—now that its domestic role was circumscribed—that it retain management of the Intelsat system. This position was slowly eroded too, however, under State Department pressure to win an amicable accord. The Europeans were adamant that Comsat's hegemony should not continue. By March 1970 the United States had agreed that Comsat should be replaced by a director general with an international staff, but only after a "transition" period of six years following enforcement of the permanent agreement, during which time Comsat would continue to run the show.

It was not until May 1971 that all the compromises were finally worked out. Any one nation (i.e., the United States) was limited to a 40 percent investment in the system. The votes of at least four countries would be necessary to veto a measure in the Board of Governors, which replaced the ICSC. Two impotent bodies were created above the Board of Governors—one meeting once a year and one meeting once every two years—in which each country has one vote. But in the Board of Governors, voting is by percentage ownership; the United States is dominant. Comsat began the new definitive arrangements with close to the 40 percent maximum interest. But Intelsat has lost its communications business between the Alaska and the "lower 48" to RCA's domestic satellite system. As domestic operations develop, Intelsat probably will lose its business between the United States mainland and Puerto Rico and Hawaii as well. This will reduce Comsat's percentage of Intelsat's total volume, and could knock Comsat's voting power down to as little as 25 percent. Comsat remains system manager until 1978, but in a reduced capacity and subservient to a secretary or director general. Very likely it will lose this job, either to a European consortium or to a decision to let the director general run it himself. There is evidence that Comsat was somewhat chastened by the desertion of the State Department during the renegotiations, and that specifically it is being careful to increase foreign procurement as much as possible.[36]

So the United States has retained dominance, if not control, of the International Telecommunications Satellite Consortium, while making some concessions that were cosmetic in intent, though perhaps not in effect. But to the extent that the permanent Intelsat agreement has succeeded in this purpose, it has failed to achieve "world peace and understanding" because it still makes it impossible for the Soviet Union to join the system. The Russians surprised many people by showing up as observers at the beginning of the renegotiation in 1969. They said they were ready to discuss joining the Intelsat system—presumably along with the rest of Eastern Europe—provided that the system was not dominated by the United States. As of 1973, the Russians were still talking Intersputnik. As of 1973, the only Intelsat stations in the Communist bloc were one in China used to cover President Nixon's visit there, and one being built in Moscow by ITT as part of the White House/Kremlin "hot line." The Russians were having one of their Molniya II stations built at Fort Dietrich, Maryland.[37] American television reception of President Nixon's Russian trip was poorer than that of his China visit because the picture had to be carried by ground transmission methods to an earth station in Western Europe.

By 1975 there were two Intelsat earth stations in China, one in the Soviet Union, one in Yugoslavia, and one under construction in Rumania. But neither these or any other Communist-bloc countries had yet been persuaded to become members of one Intelsat international system.[38]

6

The Domestic Satellite: No Action

In the 1960s, few causes were considered more worthy than educational television. ETV represented America's technological genius at the service of America's future generations. In those days, it was funded almost solely by the Ford Foundation. Ford's $10 million a year was enough to provide a few language lessons and Julia Child, but not enough to do much that was ambitious or controversial.

The New York Times always had a soft spot on page one for educational television. In August 1966, the ETV story was a Ford Foundation proposal for a communications satellite system to facilitate TV broadcasts *within* the United States. The proposal called for using the profits from this satellite to subsidize educational television. Ford said its system, which it called BNS (for Broadcasters' Nonprofit Satellite), would distribute television network shows to affiliated stations around the country for $44 million less than the networks currently were paying for similar service provided by AT&T using traditional equipment. The foundation proposed that the nonprofit BNS corporation could pass $15 million of this savings on to the networks to make it economical for them to terminate arrangements with AT&T, while leaving $30 million for ETV programming as a "people's dividend" from the taxpayers' investment in outer space research. Meanwhile, ETV stations around the country would get to use the satellites for free, thus creating a genuine national public television network. Previously, ETV had had to rely on things like parcel post (what Ford Foundation TV consultant Fred Friendly called the "bicycle method") to send programs from one station to another, because they could not afford AT&T's rates.

Naturally, Ford's plan did not create enthusiasm at the telephone company. Indeed AT&T's lack of enthusiasm, which it had successfully communicated to Congress, to Comsat, and to the FCC, was one reason why the seemingly obvious idea of a domestic satellite system similar to the international one already functioning had been so little discussed. The Ford Foundation plan was an attempt to change this and, by connecting the domestic satellite in the public mind with educational television, to rivet public attention on both. What better reward could we ask for the energies invested in our post-Sputnik lurch into space than a glamorous solution to the dilemma Sputnik had seemed to pose, of why-Johnny-can't-read-when-Ivan-can? Aided by a major publicity drive in honor of McGeorge Bundy's first major project as the foundation's new president, the satellite plan was greeted with attention rarely paid to briefs filed in obscure regulatory proceedings. Editorial writers and television columnists wrote about turning points and breakthroughs. Senator Pastore held hearings. The FCC asked for comments from interested parties. And when the telephone company announced that, according to its own experts, the Ford Foundation's calculations were in error by exactly the $30 million the BNS plan was supposed to save for ETV, Mr. Bundy merely replied, "They're crazy."[1]

Clearly then, we should owe the existence of the U.S. domestic satellite system to the Ford Foundation's clever proposal of August 1966. Except for one thing: almost a decade after the Ford proposal, more than a decade after the first international communications satellite (Early Bird) went into service, more than five years after the FCC's first "final" decision on domestic satellites, three years after its second, and almost two years after its third, the United States had only the rudimentary beginnings of a domestic satellite system. The ultimate shape of that system remained almost completely undetermined. And the tremendous potential impact of such a system had not yet been felt.

Meanwhile Canada's domestic satellite system, launched by the U.S. Space Agency and built by an American company, Hughes Aircraft, had been in commercial operation for almost three years. And the Soviet Union, relieved of the need to deal at all with the United States regulatory process, had been operating an internal communication satellite system since the 1960s.

The Ford Foundation was in no hurry itself back in 1966. Specifically, it urged the FCC to take no precipitate action before the report of the Carnegie Commission on educational television, expected the following spring. Bundy concluded his letter to FCC Chairman Rosel Hyde (reprinted in full in the *New York Times*): "This is a time for due process, and for greatness."[2] Certainly Bundy need not have worried on the former score: the FCC has never shrunk from the challenge of due process, least of all in Docket 16495, "In the Matter of Establishment of Domestic Non-common Carrier Communications Satellite Facilities by Nongovernmental Entities." The FCC is not likely to make any major decision in less than seven months, let alone one that would relieve the telephone company of its monopoly on long-distance communications inside the United States. This decision took more than seven years.

A close examination of FCC Docket 16495 demonstrates many of the problems with government regulation of economic activity. Years went by as various companies took advantage of the rights allowed them in the Administrative Procedures Act to offer, with equal passion and under changing circumstances, contradictory arguments about where the public interest lay—in open competition, in a chosen entity monopoly, in barring vertical integration, in encouraging it. Comsat, for example, which had argued in the past on principle against competition among satellite systems, against participation by manufacturers, and against vertical integration of any sort, ended up enthusiastically supporting all three. Action was delayed twice for more than a year while awaiting two sets of White House recommendations that came to opposite conclusions. The second of these, from Nixon's communications advisor Clay Whitehead, was followed by a threat to go over the FCC's head if the Commission did not ignore all its laborious proceedings up to that date and do what the White House wanted.[3]

The Commission's own statements showed no more consistency over the years than did those of its clients. Months of consideration of a problem were culminated by offering the weakest of reasoning to support their rulings. Toward the end, even AT&T got caught in the FCC's whirligig. Told in March 1970 that the Commission would frown on any attempt by AT&T to put up its own domestic satellite system as being anticompetitive, the company arranged a deal to lease satellite channels from Comsat. Two years and piles of legal briefs later, in June 1972, the Commission announced that AT&T's deal with Comsat was anticompetitive and urged AT&T to put up its own satellite system. After another six months and another avalanche of paper (and after the companies that had most vigorously objected to Comsat's system, supposedly on public interest grounds, had merged with it and withdrawn their objections) the FCC reversed itself again and approved the Comsat/AT&T arrangement. This is not due process, this is a parody of it: undue process.

The Economist said of the original Ford Foundation proposal (with reference to McGeorge Bundy's former academic career), "Like a good Harvard examination question, it will force the Federal Communications Commission to think harder than it had planned to."[4] On the contrary: like a good Harvard student, the FCC knows how to combine an arbitrary smattering of facts with empty but impressive-sounding analysis, and thus has not had to think at all. But three years went by following passage of the Communications Satellite Act before the domestic satellite problem even reached the FCC. This was due primarily to telephone company actions compounded by the shortsightedness of Congress. During the Senate hearings leading up to the floor debate on the Act, AT&T's representatives insisted that if communications satellites had any commercial potential at all, it was in international use. AT&T successfully argued that purely domestic communications enterprises —that is, all domestic carriers except itself—should be excluded from sharing ownership of the proposed corporation, since "the international carriers, by and large, are the ones that have been in the overseas business" and Comsat, of course, would be concerned only with overseas business.[5] Justice Department antitrust chief Lee Loevinger, later in the decade an FCC Commissioner, commented that it was "rather an arid logic" that allowed the South Puerto Rico Sugar Company (operators of a two-way radio between its cane fields and the U.S. mainland) an opportunity to invest in the satellite corporation, but denied the same opportunity to General Telephone & Electronics and other non-Bell phone companies.[6] But this did not deter Loevinger's own superiors at Justice and the White House from making the exclusionary provision part of the final bill. Nor did it deter AT&T from insisting in later years that it was the clear intent of Congress to give Comsat a monopoly on domestic as well as international commercial satellite communication.

Largely because of the insistence of Senator Russell Long that "this whole thing has never been even explored, considered or advocated as a way of providing cheaper telephone service between New York and Chicago, or Chicago and Los Angeles, or Chicago and New Orleans" and that "the big savings and the tremendous profits which could be made, and the great service to the American people, would be the domestic service,"[7] the Comsat Act does contain this provision:

> It is not the intent of Congress by this Act to preclude the use of the communications satellite system for domestic communications services where consistent with the provisions of this Act nor to preclude the creation of additional communications satellite systems.[8]

Senator Maurine Neuberger, in opposing the Act, quoted from an article in the NASA Journal suggesting that communications satellites could reduce transmission costs for educational television, the first known reference to this eventually popular idea.[9] She was ignored, however; to most senators, the exigencies of the Cold War demanded that all emphasis be placed on establishing an international system before the Russians. Senator Pastore, the bill's floor manager, warned that "if we are to pin Russia to the mat at all, we should not delay this any longer."[10] Senator Javits complained that "in the presence of the two space ships that the Russians have in the atmosphere today, the only counterpropaganda we have is Telstar."[11]

AT&Ts basis for arguing that satellites had no application to domestic communication was that a complex nonsynchronous satellite system, though it might someday be cheaper than underwater cables, could never compete economically with the company's ground cable and microwave tower systems used to communicate across land. Further, the much cheaper synchronous satellite system was said to be an impossible dream for the foreseeable future, because of the difficulty of placing a satellite in perfect synchronous orbit.

In 1963, however, after only one failed attempt, NASA successfully launched a Hughes satellite, Synchom II, into synchronous orbit. A disillusioned former employee said that "Comsat was ready to announce a medium altitude [nonsynchronous] satellite system in the fall of 1963 before the Synchom II had been launched, based on AT&T studies."[12] AT&T softened its position, but did not abandon it. As late as 1965 the AT&T representative on Comsat's board said that "there is no need to take a rigid position on a synchronous or medium altitude system since there is undoubtedly a place for each."[13] Telstar, AT&T's 1962 experimental communications satellite, will go down in history as the only nonsynchronous satellite ever used for commercial communication.

In 1962, few legislators were willing to challenge the telephone company's technological self-assurance. "I am not a technician or a scientist," Senator Pastore said,

> I am a Member of Congress who listens to the experts. We have been assured by those who are proficient, conversant and knowledgeable in this particular field that our objective will be realized by a low-altitude system. . . . It must be done expeditiously in order for us to win the race and triumph in this particular field before our adversaries do.[14]

Senator Robert Kerr challenged Senator Long, barely a year before the success of Synchom:

> Is the Senator aware of the fact that the Defense Department, in working on a high-synchronous satellite, has reoriented its program and has temporarily set aside its effort to put a synchronous orbital satellite into orbit? . . . Is the Senator aware of the fact that the reasons the Department took that action is that it had neither the rocket power nor the know-how to put the satellite into orbit?[15]

Domestic communication, far from being an inappropriate area for satellite technology, is the area where potential benefits to be derived from satellite communication are the greatest. The overwhelming part of American communications is domestic, not international (a point that was virtually ignored throughout the Comsat debate of 1962). Furthermore, the particular advantages of satellites over terrestrial communications methods (described in Chapter 2) are particularly applicable to domestic communications needs.

The ability of a satellite to relay a message to several distant points simultaneously ("broadcasting") is relatively unimportant internationally, even though it looms large in the fantasy lives of those in the United States and in the Soviet Union who fear an onslaught of uncontrollable enemy propaganda. But it has many potential applications domestically. It will be especially useful to the television networks in delivering their programs to local stations around the country. Ultimately, it could be used to deliver information of nationwide interest (a Presidential press conference or State of the Union message) direct to people's homes. When we see something on television "live via satellite" now, the program is being sent via satellite from an earth station near the location of the event, to a point somewhere on the East or West Coast. From there it is distributed by AT&T's terrestrial network to local stations, which then broadcast it from a tower several hundred feet high to homes or to a cable TV system.

Satellites also have the advantage over other methods of being "distance-insensitive." This means, as we have seen, that the cost of using it does not increase with distance. (Or, as AT&T has put it, the cost does not go down as the distance decreases.[16]) For example, the cost of connecting Hawaii and Alaska with the mainland does not exceed the cost of connecting two mainland points with each other. The nonmainland states no longer have to suffer the absence of live television and radio broadcasting from the mainland, nor pay for higher charges for telephone calls and other point-to-point services to the mainland. (To some extent the two newest states have benefited from use of satellite technology for several years, Hawaii through the Intelsat international system, and Alaska through use of a NASA, government-owned satellite. These steps were necessary because of the delay in establishing a nationwide domestic system.)

A third reason why domestic satellite communication makes sense is that a satellite's capacity can be allocated, in whole or in part, to any communications routes that need it at any given time, and may be used for communication directly between any two earth stations within its "view." This is also why extensive use of satellite communication within the United States poses more of a threat to AT&T than just the loss of parts, even many parts, of its business. By simplifying long-distance communication and opening it to competition, domestic satellite communication threatens the very justification for a domestic communications monopoly. Routing all calls terrestrially through a maze of wires and microwave paths requires an extremely complex, coordinated national switching system. A satellite message can be sent from any earth station up to the satellite and then be beamed back down to any other earth station, without any more switching arrangements needed. This is one reason why the telephone company fought to keep domestic considerations out of the minds of legislators in 1962, and why it has profited so greatly from the delay ever since.

AT&T's arguments left the 1962 Act ambiguous about Comsat's role in domestic communication. The FCC has decided at various times that this role is total, and that it is virtually nonexistent. Much of the early delay in Docket 16495, between 1966 and 1969, was spent by the commissioners listening to other parties debate about whether the act gave Comsat a monopoly on *all* U.S. commercial satellite communication. The basis for this controversy is obscure, since the portion of the act quoted above specifically denies Comsat such a monopoly. Note, nevertheless, that the distinction between domestic and international communication is an artificial one. Satellites, which are oblivious to national borders and to physical obstructions such as mountains, oceans, and great distances, make it so. Given the enormous, underutilized capacity of communications satellites, simply using the international system for domestic needs might have been the cheapest and quickest way to have gone about things. (Of course AT&T, which was most insistent that economies of scale necessitated a U.S.-wide domestic satellite monopoly, did not pursue the logical extension of such an argument that a single worldwide system, over which it would have little control, would be the most economical of all.) The Comsat Act specifically permits use of the international system for domestic needs, and such use—by the United States and other nations—certainly might have contributed to "world peace and understanding," another goal of the act. But it was unlikely that the world's nations would abandon sovereignty over anything as important as internal communications; and the behavior of Comsat as the American representative and system manager, as we shall see, made certain that no other nation would make such a sacrifice to the Intelsat international consortium. So Nicholas Johnson may have been correct when he predicted, "We are doomed to a world in which every nation must have not only its own airline, merchant marine, and steel mill, but its own domestic satellite system as well."[17]

Certainly it is fortunate for other nations like Canada and the Soviet Union that they went ahead on their own without waiting for the nation that invented communications satellites to decide what it wanted to do with them. Between 1962 and 1965, following the overwhelming defeat of the anti-Comsat filibusterers, the nation left all matters concerning commercial satellite communication to the new corporation and its international carrier owners, none of whom expressed any interest in putting up a domestic satellite. (Western Union, meanwhile, installed an $80 million microwave tower system, which replaced 75 percent of the company's old wires but which itself will largely be replaced by WU's domestic satellite, now in operation.[18] Rate-base regulation makes these enormous investments profitable no matter how soon they become obsolete.)

The only fly in the ointment was an engineer at Hughes Aircraft named Harold Rosen. Rosen was the inventor of the synchronous satellite, and so had good reason to suspect that the carriers might not be as enthusiastic as they seemed about advancing satellite technology. Rosen told *Aviation Week and Space Technology* in February 1965 that a synchronous satellite could be built with current technology for use in television broadcasting, including direct broadcasts to private homes.[19] Rosen attracted the attention of the American Broadcasting Company. In May 1965, armed with information provided by Hughes, ABC informed the FCC of its desire for a private satellite system to deliver network shows to affiliated stations. ABC figured the networks could save substantially on the $50 million a year they currently were paying AT&T.

ABC's satellite plan was partly a battle maneuver in the struggle to prevent the telephone company from raising its rates. The tactic worked then, as it has worked for the networks several times since. In fact, after the Ford Foundation proposal it become apparent that the networks were not all that interested in leaving the reliable Ma Bell, as long as they had the satellite option to hold over her head when needed. Certainly they soon lost any interest they ever had in putting up their own satellite system, both because it looked like they might end up financing themselves a public-network competitor, and because they saw a better deal with less risk in playing hard-to-get among the other satellite competitors. (This is exactly the role that communications lawyer Leonard Marks urged on them in a 1970 speech.[20]) The networks played a greatly reduced role in the domestic satellite controversy after 1966, and NBC wrote in 1971, six and a half years after the original network proposal, that it did not "regard the delay in final authorization as surprising under all the circumstances." NBC called any suggestion that the delay was deliberate "fanciful," with "nothing to support it."[21]

The FCC's response to ABC's plan was to forward it to Comsat for comment. Comsat's response was that the law gave Comsat a monopoly on satellite communication. This is despite the fact that Comsat had no intention at the time of providing the service ABC wanted. Certainly it had made no public statement about domestic service (least of all in competition with its largest stockholder, AT&T), and one former insider has said, "There really wasn't any interest at all at Comsat in the domestic system—at least at the top level—until the ABC filing. When ABC filed, there was the most terrific reaction you ever saw."[22] But despite this original lack of interest, Comsat's claim was almost universally supported at the time. ABC's announcement came just as Early Bird was beginning commercial satellite service, and while this brought the plan great public attention which the network no doubt appreciated if its real purpose was to bring pressure on AT&T, it was ill-timed for a genuine challenge to Comsat. Both the *Washington Post* and the *New York Times* quoted "sources" as saying that only Comsat would be allowed to put up any commercial satellite system in the near future. The *Washington Star* editorialized that "letting competitors in" was like "charging admission for the first ten minutes of a ball game and then opening the gates to anyone," although the paper failed to explain how Comsat intended to compete, or when admission had ever been charged. Even in their news columns, the newspapers interpreted the "unique government needs or . . . the national interest" clause of the Comsat Act to mean that only a system specifically for government use could be established outside the Comsat structure.[23] From this position of total strength, Comsat by 1972 had come very close to losing any right at all to participate in domestic communication.

The telephone company's position on the ABC proposal was that it felt the whole thing was a bit rushed. While conceding for the first time that "we think it will be possible with the advances that are now being made in technology to use satellites for some domestic transmissions," AT&T warned that "there are economic, technical and policy considerations that remain to be resolved."[24] AT&T vice-president and Comsat director Richard Hough said that "we must push ahead on all fronts," suggesting as an example that he still had hopes for a medium-altitude system.[25]

It was not until February 1966 that Comsat got around to officially advising the FCC to dismiss ABC's request to put up a satellite financed by itself to serve its own needs, on the ground that only Comsat was legally authorized to put up commercial communications satellites. At the same time Comsat invited all the networks and communications carriers to a meeting to see what it could do for them.

In March the FCC took Comsat's advice, returning ABC's proposal "without prejudice" and requesting comments on sundry questions by interested parties on August 1. Meanwhile, however, Rosen at Hughes was getting impatient again, so he tried a new approach. "Several things converged all at once in the spring of 1966," according to Lee R. Marks of Ginsberg, Feldman & Bress, the Ford Foundation's Washington law firm.

> Bundy and Friendly and others became aware that their money was not producing dividends. It was keeping public TV alive, but it wasn't growing. Then Fred Friendly met Hal Rosen. Rosen said that satellites could really take care of their problem. Rosen got Friendly and Bundy interested in satellites. They're told that the cost is much less, and figure that somebody is going to save a bundle. So Bundy goes to David Ginsburg, whose name he got from Califano and McNamara because he needed a Washington lawyer to tell him how to make this thing real. We began looking around for what to do, and the first thing we found was the ABC letter to the FCC, which had produced a routine notice of inquiry. . . . We decided to enter the proceeding and use it to float our idea. We got Paul MacEvoy, now at MIT, Abe Katz and Gene Fubini of IBM and started a little group going. Also Paul Visher at Hughes . . .[26]

This is an interesting description of how you go about things if you are the Ford Foundation. The inquiry had been alive for a year and a half, with little attendant publicity, when the Ford Foundation decided to enter it—and it exploded into front-page news. But even Bundy, Friendly, Rosen, Califano, McNamara, and a top Washington law firm cannot always "make things real," and it is sad to note in passing that public television (as ETV came to be called) also has been through some tough times since the Ford Foundation sought to put it on a permanent footing in 1966.

When Fred Friendly came to work for the Ford Foundation, he had just quit as head of CBS News because the network had refused to interrupt regular programming for Senator Fulbright's hearings on the Vietnam war. Friendly and the Ford people saw coverage of public affairs as a major weakness of the commercial networks that public television could remedy. The very first potential public network "service" mentioned in the Ford satellite proposal was "full and live coverage of significant hearings and debates." The second was "interpretation of news."[27] While the domestic satellite lingered in the chambers of the FCC, public television made some early gains. Spurred by the Ford proposal, the Carnegie Commission report, and others, President Johnson proposed, and Congress endorsed, establishment of the Corporation for Public Broadcasting, a Comsat-like semigovernment organization funded by Congress that would bring PTV the advantages of government largesse while protecting it from political influence. As a further protection the Public Broadcast System (PBS) emerged in 1969 to take the money from CPB and produce national programming for distribution to the local public or educational TV stations. Public television also finally got its network interconnections, along with a 10-year contract with the telephone company that may prevent it from taking advantage of satellites when they become available.

As PBS's public affairs programming began to enjoy an impact on viewers, President Nixon became concerned that it was developing a liberal bias. Late in 1971, with the approach of the first national election that public TV had any money to cover, Nixon's communications aide Clay Whitehead suggested to public TV managers that they concentrate on local programming instead of national shows, his reasoning being that if they did not, he would cut off their money. In 1972, Whitehead elaborated that he felt national news and public affairs had no place at all on public TV. This time he gave as his reason his belief that the commercial networks were doing that job well enough.[28]

(Whitehead subsequently accused the commercial network news shows of "ideological plugola" and threatened to have local station licenses taken away unless they did something about it. This action was widely misunderstood. Little attention was paid to Whitehead's proposed gift to the local affiliates; his new legislation would extend license renewals from three to five years, and make it virtually impossible for nonowners to mount a challenge on public interest grounds. Many discussions of this in the press referred to a "carrot and stick" approach. Actually, the local stations are more conservative than the networks and many appreciated having an invitation from the White House to harass the networks politically, as the CBS affiliates did successfully soon afterward, in March 1973, over the antiwar play "Sticks and Bones." One local affiliate called Nixon's bill "as much as any reasonable licensee could hope for."[29])

Barring national public affairs programming from public TV would seem to eliminate what the proponents of large-scale public television saw as its major mission. In the summer of 1972 Nixon vetoed a $155 million two-year appropriation for CPB—the first time public television had managed to get through Congress the large, long-term funding it needed for true independence. Whitehead said: "We have a very strong precedent in this country that you keep the media and the government separate." . Soon after this, Johnson's CPB president resigned along with others, and Nixon replaced him with Henry Loomis, a former director of the United States Information Agency. Loomis told his first CPB press conference that he had "never seen a public TV show," but felt very strongly that "instant analysis" and other national public affairs efforts would have to go, and that long-range financing would not be required for the next few years at least. All that remained was to dispense with PBS, and this was done in January 1973 when it was announced that CPB, under Nixon's men, would take over most of PBS's functions, including all program production. At this press conference it was announced that popular public affairs shows like William Buckley's "Firing Line," Bill Moyers's "Journal," and "Washington Week in Review" would probably get the ax. Nixon's new CPB chairman, a recently defeated congressman named Thomas Curtis, conceded that "I don't know those programs," though he insisted that he was quite familiar with "Sesame Street."[31] In an odd turn of events, Curtis resigned suddenly in April, accusing the White House of "tampering with" his independence. And that summer CPB got its two-year appropriation for a slightly smaller amount, perhaps because Nixon's attack on public TV had been preempted by Watergate. With the demise of the Nixon administration, public television entered another period of tranquility and steady growth.

Obviously, none of this could have gone on if public broadcasting had had a truly independent source of funding, which may be why Whitehead felt so strongly in mid-1971—when his approaching fame was still only imminent—about the Ford Foundation's argument that the public deserved a "dividend" for its investment in outer space, and that an independently funded public television network might be an appropriate way to get it. "I think that's an insidious idea," Whitehead said, going on to condemn the "government imposing its own view of the public interest in opposition to what the corporation would do on its own."[32]

In 1966, when young Tom Whitehead was still a graduate student at MIT, few dared speak out against the insidious idea, and none strongly. Two days after Ford announced its plan, Jack Gould wrote in the *New York Times* that the seeming opposition by AT&T and Comsat "merely underscores how they have totally failed to grasp the real issue."[34] In fact AT&T, at least, grasped the real issue precisely, which was that it stood to lose a great deal of its business—and possibly its justification for existence—unless it moved quickly, and that associating its cause with Comsat would greatly aid it. The previous April, an AT&T Vice President wrote to Comsat Chairman McCormack. Behind the courtly language was a deal: the telephone company would back Comsat in the forthcoming legal dispute in front of the FCC, if Comsat would agree to become a "carrier's carrier" domestically as it had become internationally, selling its services only to the other carriers, which would resell them to customers, thereby leaving AT&T's control over the use of competing technologies complete. Lowell F. Wingert of AT&T wrote of his company's great imaginings:

> we envision a plan to use at least one large-capacity synchronous satellite, with appropriate stand-by, purely for domestic communications service, to supplement our interstate cable and microwave facilities. We recognize there are questions concerning Comsat's position in the domestic satellite field, both under the Communications Satellite Act and the existing international agreements. However, assuming that these are appropriately resolved, we would propose that Comsat launch and own the satellites for which we would assume the responsibility for the carrying charges including a fair return on Comsat's investment, with equitable access to other domestic common carriers upon their bearing their share of Comsat's charges. . . .[35]

Wingert went on that since Comsat would of course be uninterested in selling circuits to anyone except through AT&T and its friends ("satellites to be used exclusively for the many types of services provided by domestic carriers"), and since Comsat could not get very far anyway if AT&T were to withhold land interconnections ("the high degree of coordination required between terrestrial and satellite facilities in domestic service"), the telephone company thought it "especially important that the earth stations needed for the service should be owned and operated by the domestic communications carriers involved."[36] Comsat replied that it would be glad to talk, but that "we view earth stations as an integral and critical part of a satellite communication system which must be planned and operated in concert with the space segment. Accordingly, we feel that this responsibility must be reflected in ownership."[37]

What happened in Docket 16495 for a year following the Ford Foundation proposal in August 1966 looked like activity. There was much extravagant talk about "early" systems planned for 1969 and "advanced" systems planned for 1972, much setting and postponing of deadlines for comments and reply comments by the FCC, much discussion about the public interest by various private interests. But basically nothing happened. The Ford plan, which had electrified Comsat and alarmed AT&T, effectively vaporized the enthusiasm of the networks. The ABC proposal had led the telephone company to back down on its price hike; in determining to its own satisfaction, and announcing to the public, that satellites offered no savings over terrestrial methods for domestic communication users, AT&T ignored its argument that domestic terrestrial costs were rising, thus forcing it to charge the networks higher prices. At first, all three commercial networks praised the Ford plan. The president of the Columbia Broadcast System called it "an imaginative approach to a very vexatious problem,"[38] and ABC called it an expanded version of its own plan. But by the time of Senator Pastore's hearings on it later in the month, President Frank Stanton declared on behalf of CBS that he doubted the plan was consistent with "the free enterprise system."[39] On consideration, the networks weren't excited at the prospect of financing their own competition. Also, as Lee Marks, Bundy's Washington lawyer, ·put it, "AT&T was the bandit they'd been dealing with for years, so even though they knew it was a bandit, they were used to it. . . . And whatever anyone says about AT&T, they are goddamn reliable."[40]

In its August 1, 1966 filing, Comsat said it had a legal right to a monopoly on U.S. commercial satellite communication of all sorts, and that authorizing any other company to spend its own money on its own system would cause the purpose of the Comsat Act to be "eroded beyond any reasonable hope of restoration. Comsat views itself as having been granted a trust of national importance. In addition to being charged with the interest of its stockholders, it considers itself as having been charged also, in the area of its charter, with the best interest of the United States in the broadest sense." AT&T concurred, saying that any authorization of private domestic satellite carriers would slow the development of satellite technology, then went on to warn of the many technical and frequency interference problems that satellites would cause.[41]

Comsat's legal position on the monopoly question was not an enviable one, since section 102(d) of its founding legislation specifically permitted use of satellites for domestic communication and creation of additional satellite systems. Comsat argued that this section meant that Congress was reserving to itself the right to set up additional satellite systems. The Ford Foundation pointed out in its reply legal brief of December 12, 1966 that this would have been superfluous as another section of the Comsat Act reserves for Congress the right to repeal, alter, or amend the act, a right no Congress can deny its successors anyway. Furthermore, the original House version of the bill explicitly reserved for Congress the right to approve additional systems, and this provision was specifically considered and rejected when the Senate dealt with the bill. The House accepted the Senate's amendment.

In the legal dispute over this point, which lasted through the spring of 1967, the Ford Foundation produced quotations from the legislative history to back up its case; Comsat made much of the distinction between an "operative" and a "nonoperative" statutory provision; and the foundation argued that the FCC's power to authorize satellite systems was grounded in the Communications Act of 1934, and that this power emerged from the Satellite Act unscathed. Comsat inevitably abandoned this unsupportable position and began plugging for competition (without ever admitting that it ever had thought otherwise). Another Comsat argument was that NASA was forbidden by Congress to launch any private satellite systems except its own. This position was supported (or rather, it was not supported) by the fact the Comsat Act has nothing to say on the matter. It soon was abandoned as well.[42]

Comsat's public relations position was far stronger than its legal one. With thousands of small stockholders induced to buy shares because of the company's unofficial affiliation with the government (and with nobody being reminded that a few carriers owned a controlling half), the company could argue that any action that damaged it was a betrayal of the voters' trust. But the company had to be careful not to sob itself into a corner. Therefore, actions that it said in August would cause erosion "beyond any reasonable hope of restoration," by December would be "a severe blow."[43] The chairman of the Senate Commerce Committee, Warren Magnuson, was persuaded. He said in November, while touring a Comsat earth station,

> I am hopeful that it [the Ford Foundation plan] won't interfere with the operation of Comsat because we made a commitment to the American people when we passed the bill: that if they put their investment in Comsat and gave it their support, then we would do what was best government-wise and regulation-wise to keep it going. . . . We have that commitment and you can't just say we are going to abolish it overnight because there is some other idea for ETV.[44]

Buoyed by this kind of support, Comsat's attitude toward the Ford

Foundation plan turned from mildly conciliatory to openly hostile. Comsat announced at the end of August an undetailed plan whereby as satellite system manager it would collect a special tax on users to be used to finance educational television.[45] *Variety* declared that this "clearly means that the idea of paying for ETV by satellite revenues is accepted."[46] Yet the company's later specific proposal made no mention of this, and the Ford Foundation complained "that in framing its proposal Comsat consulted neither with us nor with others who have come to believe deeply in this prospect."[47] AT&T was even less enthused with the Ford plan. In one legal brief, according to Jack Gould in the *New York Times,* "the utility took the Ford Foundation's thinking apart on every conceivable ground and maintained that the philanthropic fund should stick to cultural uplift and stay out of communication technology."[48]

Comsat has contended that it had been working on a domestic satellite system since 1964. But company chairman James McCormack admitted on an educational TV program that the system Comsat proposed the same day Ford announced the BNS plan had been completed in a rush so as not to appear as a response to the Ford proposal. This system was not, in fact, a serious proposal, and Comsat came up with two new arrangements between August 1966 and March 1967, when it proposed a $58 million "experimental" domestic satellite system which it would own and manage as a monopoly for at least the first few years. The system was to begin operation in 1970. Chairman McCormack predicted that by that year satellites would be carrying ten times as much business domestically as internationally. This was sophisticated for Comsat, which often did not thrive at regulatory strategy, and which had suffered several times in international communications controversies when the traditional carriers proposed "experimental" or "interim" arrangements that soon became permanent. Although the company reserved the right to rent its telephone and television circuits directly to users, it also was wise enough to concentrate its proposed earth stations in the two western time zones. As a 1968 Comsat internal memo explains,

> Because the bulk of communications traffic in these two western time zones is handled by General Telephone & Electronics and a number of small independents, there is a larger market for long-haul communications available without creating competition for American Telephone & Telegraph. The Comsat filing, incidentally, has been endorsed by AT&T.[49]

General Telephone and the small independents, of course, had been excluded from a role in Comsat on the ground that Comsat never would be concerned with domestic communication. This was AT&T's position for many years, but after the enormous publicity given to Ford's BNS proposal it no longer was tenable. So in December 1966 AT&T produced a satellite proposal of its own, this one costing $340 million. Despite its earlier and later protestations, AT&T said this was about $200 million less than it would cost to provide equivalent service by conventional earth facilities. The proposal, as might be expected, also was clever. Although its enormous system was intended to monopolize all services anyone might want from a domestic satellite, and although it planned to own all the earth stations and land interconnections and to manage the system, the telephone company proposed to let Comsat own the satellites themselves, from which the company would lease all the circuits. Thus the public and Congressional insistence that Comsat should put up all commercial communications satellites would be satisfied, while AT&T would retain essential control over this new technology and protect its monopoly position in the domestic field. Comsat even had $100 million waiting to be invested. Under the telephone company plan, Comsat would end up owning a few satellites floating in the sky, which could be used exclusively by AT&T. To jump ahead a bit, this is essentially the position Comsat found itself in when the smoke had cleared seven years later.

The Ford Foundation hired a consultant to compare the original Ford, Comsat, and AT&T proposed systems. He pointed out the basic inconsistency of AT&T's submissions, which argued that a satellite system would not be economical, then offered to build one. AT&T said that only a multipurpose system that offered both television and telephone service could be made economical, then concluded that such a system would weigh too much to be put in orbit by any available booster rocket. Ford said that a system dedicated exclusively to television transmission would be both economical and technologically possible. AT&T said that the "cost crossover point"—the distance at which satellites become cheaper to use than terrestrial methods—was 1300 miles. Ford pointed out that this neglected the ability of satellites to send messages from one point to several others simultaneously, and that using this for TV distribution would make satellites economical for distances as short as 50 miles, compared with the rates that AT&T was then charging the TV networks for this service. This would mean that satellites were useful in the densely populated East Coast, something AT&T was not anxious to concede because of its especially heavy concentration of terrestrial facilities there. The consultant concluded that "AT&T's estimates of the capital required to set up a satellite system show substantial variation, depending upon whether it is discussing the Ford Foundation proposal or its own proposal."[50] Having abandoned its position that satellites could never be used domestically, AT&T, in its proposal, also tried to bolster its new defensive line by arguing that any domestic satellite system would require extensive terrestrial backup facilities (rather than a single extra satellite that could be used wherever spare circuits were needed), and by raising all sorts of warnings about potential frequency interference with its own terrestrial equipment.

It was now the spring of 1967, two years after ABC's original proposal, but it looked as if the FCC was finally about to act, and that Comsat would be the winner. *Business Week* reported in June that a decision was expected any day permitting Comsat to develop a pilot domestic system "including some educational TV capability . . . in conjunction with domestic communications companies. The ticklish question of who will own the system will be decided later."[51] It seemed obvious to most interested parties that a domestic satellite was a good idea, and that there would be one soon. *Forbes Magazine* said, "It is a mystery why so few in Congress realized that it [satellite communication] would also be the cheapest means of domestic communication."[52] Yet as late as July 1967, in a speech to cable television system owners, President Johnson's Director of Telecommunications Management, a retired general named James D. O'Connell, said he doubted that a domestic satellite offered any real savings over landline communication.[53] And the FCC accepted AT&T's position as late as 1972 that it "disclaims that the satellite technology presently offers any cost savings or other marked advantages over terrestrial facilities in the provision of the switched services that constitute the bulk of its traffic."[54] (In 1967, as we have seen, in response to the Ford Foundation's plan for a TV-only satellite, AT&T had said that satellite television broadcasting would *only* be economical in combination with satellite telephone switching services.) But despite all the signs, the FCC did not approve a domestic satellite system in 1967.

The reason no decision was reached in 1967 was that in August President Johnson decided to appoint an all-star President's Task Force on Communication Policy, chaired by Undersecretary of State Eugene Rostow. The President told Congress he wanted this Task Force because "man's greatest hope for world peace lies in understanding his fellow man. . . . So the challenge is to communicate."[55]

The FCC agreed to postpone any domestic satellite decision until this group could consider the whole question from scratch. The Ford Foundation was anxious that Comsat's pilot program, which it opposed, not be approved in the near future. Comsat hoped that the task force would back its request for a monopoly. AT&T was glad for the delay. The general public was not heard from. The task force was given a year to complete its work. By the time it completed its report in December 1968, Richard Nixon was President-elect. The new administration debated whether the report should be released. When it was released in May 1969, statements to the press made it clear that the Nixon administration felt free to ignore it.

The telephone company made good use of this year-and-a-half hiatus. In January 1968 it filed with the FCC for rate increases for radio and TV transmission service that would have added $25 million to the broadcasters' annual bill, an increase of 44 percent.[56] This is the same service Ford's satellites would have provided them at a $15 million *savings* the year before, while providing enough profit to finance ETV. In October, AT&T warned its stockholders against satellite overenthusiasm.

> Some statements in the press have tended to lead to the impression that satellites might revolutionize the entire communications business. It's an erroneous impression. Satellites, like coaxial cable or radio relay systems, are simply one of several methods of providing communications over great distances, and the benefits of each must be weighed to determine which is better for a particular institution.[57]

The task force's recommendations for domestic satellite policy were largely ignored. With the dismantling of the Johnson administration, the group lacked a constituency in front of the FCC, which had to make the final decision. Basically, the Rostow task force advocated what Comsat wanted and what the FCC had probably intended to do all along——approval of a "pilot" domestic satellite system to be managed by Comsat, with the requisite caveats about its temporary and nonbinding nature, and the need for review by sundry committees. But although Comsat was to own the space segment of the system, what the task force called the "ground environment," presumably meaning the earth stations and local loops, was to be shared by Comsat, the terrestrial common carriers, and "prospective users of wideband services," all of which could "invest as trustees."[58] The report stressed the desirability of broad participation and the dangers of preemptive positions. But the real reason for its position, according to one of the people who wrote the report, was that a deal had been made with AT&T.[59] Another section of the report urged that all U.S. international communication by both cable and satellite be handled by a single "chosen entity," which was not to be AT&T. In exchange for losing its international business, the telephone company was guaranteed a role in the domestic satellite system. The task force's international recommendation had even less impact than its domestic one; AT&T continues to dominate international communication. Meanwhile, the task force prevented FCC approval of a solely Comsat-pilot program, delayed any program at all for at least a year and a half, and led to a situation where AT&T may ultimately dominate domestic as well as satellite communication.

It was now 1969, seven years after the Comsat Act and four years after the launching of Early Bird and the original ABC domestic satellite proposal. The ball was back with the FCC, and FCC Chairman Rosel Hyde promised the Senate Commerce Committee that a pilot domestic satellite program would be approved before the end of the year. He did not promise that Comsat would be picked to run it. But he seemed committed to a single, presumably multipurpose, pilot, and combined with the task force recommendation this left Comsat confident enough to proceed. Comsat contracted with the National Cable Television Association to supply community cable systems with six channels of programming distributed by domestic satellite, and contracted with NASA to use the space agency's communications satellites in combination with Comsat's earth facilities during early domestic service trials. Both of these arrangements were, of course, subject to FCC approval, but this seemed imminent. *Telecommunications Reports* said in June that the Commission required only one more meeting before approving a three-year "interim" Comsat-run system as recommended by the task force.[60]

Even though nothing came of it, Comsat's arrangement with the cable TV system owners was the first public hint of how a domestic satellite system, as it develops, may have its greatest impact. Overnight, one or several new television networks could be created. Until recently any person who might wish to start a new TV network faced two seemingly impossible problems. One is that practically all the established stations already are affiliated with one of the three current commercial networks. To attract national advertisers, the new network would have to somehow set up new broadcasting stations simultaneously in most of the major cities around the country. Even if the money could be found for such an enormous undertaking, there are no empty channels in many of these cities (at least on VHF) that are usable by FCC interference standards. (The FCC created this problem itself during the early days of television when it opted for local television stations in many medium and large cities, rather than a few regional broadcasting centers where every channel could be used because they were too far apart to interfere with one another. The professed purpose was to make television relevant to local communities; the effect was to concentrate programming in the three national networks.)

A second problem facing the aspiring network builder would be the enormous cost of distributing programs by AT&T's long-line system. Without a great deal of money, a new network might be precluded from any live broadcasting. The videotapes on which it would depend would have to be sent around the country (Fred Friendly's "bicycle method"); at best, AT&T's lines could be used during the discount night hours to send shows for taping and later broadcast.

The emergence of mass-subscription cable TV systems and the launching of a communications satellite for domestic use solves both these problems. Cable systems had immediate access by 1973 to 7.25 million U.S. homes with no need for broadcast frequencies or equipment.[61] Dozens of empty channels were on hand, which can be used at practically no added cost. With the addition of a relatively inexpensive earth station, these channels can receive programming to fill as many of these channels as they want. A network center in New York, say, can transmit programming to a satellite which can then broadcast it simultaneously to any cable system in the United States at a cost far less than that of using AT&T's lines. Such networks should greatly stimulate the growth of cable systems and ultimately offer a far wider selection of programming to viewers. They should also stimulate—and discomfort—the established networks and their local affiliates.

Early in 1969 the FCC was about to release the decision that would have made all this possible. In fact, the tentative decision already had been made to authorize a pilot program, and each commissioner had written a tentative expression of his position. (This is according to a statement by Nicholas Johnson two years later.[62] There were only rumors at the time.) Chairman Hyde took a copy of the Commission's opinion to the White House, where the new administration asked him not to release it until the Nixon staff could review the matter. Shortly thereafter, in July

1969—exactly two years after President Johnson had announced his group—the White House announced that it was appointing a "small working group" to look at the domestic satellite question. Once again the FCC deferred all action until the White House's wishes could be made known.

The man behind this group was hitherto unknown White House staff assistant Clay T. Whitehead, who had not yet founded the Office of Telecommunications Policy which he later headed. Whitehead said the group would report in 60 days and was only set up because "we have found the provisions for introducing communications satellites into U.S. domestic communications to be especially important." Whitehead did not specify what he found lacking in the FCC's own decision-making process, but invited the Commission "to participate in any way you deem appropriate."[63] Chairman Hyde said in response that the FCC and the White House clearly were agreed on the need for "a decision without further undue delay, and, at the same time, a full exchange of views so as to assure a result most benefitting the public interest."[64]

Whitehead initiated his study with a definite ideological bias. Despite his declaration that he was concerned with "the general structure and direction of the industry and not with specific applications pending before the Commission" (in an untried field, how was one different from the other?), the White House stepped in this time, unlike two years before, because it suspected that what the FCC was about to decide was not something of which the administration would approve. Even at the time, *Telecommunications Reports* said:

> reports persist that the White House will suggest an entirely "fresh" look at the domestic satellite system question, which has now been a matter before the FCC for about four years. One report being circulated is that the Communications Satellite Corp., which has been considered the likely Commission choice as manager for a "pilot" domestic satellite program, would have its role downgraded, or even eliminated, in any final Commission action authorizing a go-ahead on testing a new system.[65]

This indication that Comsat did not have things sewed up after all set the stage for another period of intense activity with no concrete result. The first one on stage this time was Frank Stanton, president of CBS. The man who had thought three years before that the Ford Foundation's plan was inconsistent with the free enterprise system proposed in October

1969, with maximum publicity fanfare, a plan that was substantially identical to it: a satellite system exclusively for TV network transmissions, unconnected to AT&T or Comsat, which would be financed by the commercial networks and provide equal treatment for public television at no charge. Beyond the free transmission service, PTV (as it had become) would get no actual cash from the system. Times had changed for Mr. Stanton. The networks' profits were down from 1965, and AT&T still was planning to raise its bill to the networks by $20 million a year. The CBS proposal, like that of ABC four years before, was at least in part just one more move in the continuing rate negotiation with the telephone company. Mr. Stanton said the TV satellite system would cost $100 million, while a private terrestrial system duplicating AT&T's facilities used for the networks would cost $700 million to $1 billion. The networks could pay the satellite off in less than two years from what they would save in telephone bills.[66] Stanton did not mention another potential benefit to the networks of his proposal. *Broadcasting* magazine editorialized, "We are not at all sure that a consortium owned by the three existing full-time networks would have the natural incentive to make easy room for newcomers or one-shot competitors."[67] Specifically, it might have made more difficult the kind of satellite-to-cable networks discussed above.

Frank Stanton was not the only one to reverse himself that fall. In a 180-degree move off its 1966 position—which was billed at the time as one based on technological necessity and solemn legal principle—the telephone company announced that it had no objection to the CBS proposal. In fact, it felt that "the widest public policy at this time would be to permit any organization or group interested in establishing a domestic satellite system, including the networks, to apply for a license to establish and operate such a system." It no longer believed that a multipurpose system was essential, and it no longer believed that private operations were a threat to the integrity of its system. (Not that it reminded anyone of its former stance on these issues.) One principle to which AT&T did cling, however, was that satellites were not economical for domestic use. In fact, "Our recent studies indicate that satellite costs currently may be less favorable compared to terrestrial costs than appeared to be the case some years ago." Nevertheless, the company was quick to add that, "Looking to the future, AT&T anticipates that when it makes good technical and economic sense to do so, it will seek authorization to use satellites in its own operations."[68] The reason for AT&T's change of heart became clear shortly.

Meanwhile Comsat also was busy. When Comsat chairman James

McCormack heard one October Wednesday that Stanton was going to make his new proposal that night, he went to the White House and asked Whitehead if he could release a new Comsat domestic satellite plan that the company had submitted to Whitehead's group and promised to keep secret. Whitehead agreed. Under this plan Comsat said it was ready immediately to build a domestic system to serve the networks and any other users, such as cable television systems and the press wire services. The company would build its own earth stations, own the whole system, and sell its services directly to anyone who wanted them, without going through AT&T with its monopoly and middleman profits. Comsat added that any one of its 14 proposed TV channels could handle up to 1800 telephone calls for AT&T, if the telephone company wanted to call Comsat in an emergency. AT&T had no comment on this plan.[69]

About this time, the end of October 1969, rumors were flying that the Whitehead panel was about to release its recommendations. *Telecommunications Reports* said on October 27 that an announcement might be expected within a week,[70] and *Electronics* said in its "Washington Newsletter" of the same date that the Nixon administration, under increasing pressure for a decision, was about to approve that old stand-by, the experimental pilot system, run by Comsat with a program substantially like the one the company had suggested to Whitehead. Comsat, *Electronics* said, not only would own all the earth stations, but was already preparing to let contracts for construction of them.[71]

So the October 30 report in *The New York Times* that Comsat had suddenly come up with yet another domestic satellite plan, "which for the the first time makes no provision for the transmission of telephone calls," was a surprise. This system would have capacity equivalent to 48 television channels, which would be used for the networks and all other customers, but not for telephone calls because of "the recent policy decision of the American Telephone and Telegraph Company to make a further study of the economics of a satellite system before reaching a decision on how airborne relay methods might supplement its present ground transmission facilities."[72]

The reason for AT&T's new position on satellites now was clear. Any decision to set up a monopoly domestic satellite system clearly would give that monopoly to Comsat. Originally this is what AT&T had wanted. AT&T felt that Comsat was controllable, and that therefore it would be assured at least partial control of the earth stations and exclusive wholesaling rights to satellite business. This arrangement had worked out very well for AT&T in international satellite communication; it had kept rates high and protected the telephone company from competition. But now it appeared that Comsat planned to own the earth stations itself, deal directly with users wherever possible (thus competing with AT&T), and even get a toe hold on the telephone business itself. This is why AT&T became an advocate of competition on its own terms. It might lose the network business at first, but it would be assured of retaining control of its telephone business. And with all this business to share the cost, it would be in a good position to get the networks back if it ever decided to put up a satellite of its own—something it expressly reserved the right to do, while insisting that it would never want to because satellite circuits were so expensive compared to terrestrial ones, and getting more so all the time.

The telephone company culminated this particular line of argument, and this particular period of domestic satellite inaction, in January 1970 with testimony by Vice-President Richard R. Hough (also one of AT&T's Comsat directors) in front of a House subcommittee. Once again, as in 1962, AT&T was preaching calm. Hough said that all the excitement was unnecessary and that any domestic communication satellite system should be postponed indefinitely because developments in cables had made satellites comparatively uneconomical. Hough then said that a few satellites might be useful at some future date, primarily as back-up for terrestrial facilities, "if the cost disadvantage can be minimized," and that in this case AT&T would insist on owning them. As Katherine Johnsen pointed out in *Aviation Week & Space Technology,* these both were reversals of AT&T's earlier position. In 1966 the telephone company had wanted to build a $340 million satellite system, which it said would save $200 million over equivalent terrestrial equipment. It had wanted to let Comsat own the satellite portion of the system because it believed Comsat was entitled to this under the law. Hough now said, "We perceive no barriers, legal or otherwise, which would prevent us from owning and operating a satellite system for domestic communication."[73] Not that they wanted to, of course. But they might. In fact, within a year they had proposed another huge telephone satellite system just like the earlier one.

7

Action of a Sort

The White House produced its recommendations on January 23, 1970, in the form of a memorandum for Dean Burch, Nixon's new FCC Chairman, from Peter M. Flanigan, President Nixon's assistant in charge of relations with big business.[1] There was no attempt to hide the real author. It is known among Docket 16495 buffs as the Whitehead memorandum. Overnight, it wiped out five years of laborious public proceedings by coming to a conclusion exactly the opposite of the one the FCC already had reached. Just because he disagreed with the FCC certainly does not mean that Whitehead was in the wrong when he rejected a "chosen entity" or "pilot project" or some other name for what would essentially be a new, closely regulated monopoly, and urged instead a situation that would be as competitive and unregulated as possible. Whitehead's "open skies" recommendation was a current of fresh air blowing through the stuffy, tight room where the commissioners and their carrier clients had been enjoying their privacy for almost 40 years. It took the FCC three more years to make its own final decision. This time was spent turning Whitehead's clear-cut policy, for good or bad, into the usual regulatory goulash of dubious economics and timely compromise.

Mr. Whitehead wrote:

In the absence of clear economies of scale and overriding public

156

interest considerations to the contrary, the American economy has relied upon competitive private enterprise rather than regulated monopoly to assure technical and market innovation, long-run optimum use of resources, and industry flexibility.[2]

He found neither of these necessary preconditions to market interference present in domestic satellite communication.

The historical development of telecommunications policy, regulation, and industry structure has resulted in a blurred distinction between public and private interests. A confusing patchwork of cross-subsidization between public message and specialized service offerings has become the norm rather than the exception. Therefore, it is possible that satellite services could, through cost-reducing innovation and competition, cause some existing services now surviving on a cross-subsidized basis to become uneconomic. Even if the benefits of such cross-subsidization accrue to the public users rather than to private service offerings, however, there seems to be no merit in protecting suppliers of such services from fair competition. The primary impact of such competition should be the provision of those services through lower-cost alternatives. Should such competition result in curtailment of some public services that are necessary as a matter of public policy, however, a direct public subsidy would in most cases be less costly to the public than forced cross-subsidization and restraint of competition.[3]

Whitehead also said that technical barriers to greater competition had been exaggerated.

Applying his Adam Smith viewpoint to the domestic satellite situation, Whitehead said "we find no reason to call for the immediate establishment of a domestic satellite system as a matter of public policy." He added, however:

Subject to appropriate conditions to preclude harmful interference and anti-competitive practices, any financially qualified public or private entity, including Government corporations, should be permitted to establish and operate domestic satellite facilities for its own needs; join with related entities in common-user, cooperative facilities; establish facilities for lease to prospective users; or establish facilities to be used in providing specialized carrier services on a competitive basis. Within the constraints outlined below, common-carriers should be free to establish facilities for either switched public message or specialized services, or both.[4]

Whitehead specifically warned against the frequent Washington regulatory practice of protecting established industries from newcomers. He said that the potential economic impact of new satellite systems on the terrestrial common carriers or specialized carriers should not be considered in approving them and that owners of these systems should be able to sell circuits directly to users without having to give the established carriers a wholesale cut. Whitehead suggested a few minimal restrictions. Applicants would have to prove they had enough money to establish a system. Those who might want to share a system (like the networks) would have to agree to include any potential user of similar services (like a new network) without discrimination. Common carriers would have to prove that any satellite system they might wish to put up was not being cross-subsidized by services in which they had a monopoly, and they would have to supply ground interconnections for competitive systems without prejudice. But aside from these, and various warnings about frequency problems and honoring international commitments, Whitehead's attitude was that anything goes.

(Whitehead's memo contained no reference to free connections for public television or any other kind of "people's dividend" from space. As we know, he found this "an insidious idea.")

Comsat's stock dropped $6.75, 13 percent of its value, the day Whitehead's memo was published. Anonymous company employees were quoted in the trade journals calling it "arbitrary" and "capricious."[5] In an official statement, Comsat offered once again its contention that Congress had the exclusive right to authorize commercial satellite systems and that so far it had shared this right only with Comsat. But the fact was that after five years of unassailable but unusable dominance in the domestic satellite field, Comsat had been outfoxed. *Forbes* said, "There is unrestrained joy at American Telephone & Telegraph," and quoted Comsat president Joseph Charyk explaining why.

Since they can route as much of their existing traffic via satellite as they wish, they should certainly be in a position to offer incremental capacity to other users at a lower price than a fellow like us who has the same total investment but no initial set of customers. We are prohibited by law from dealing directly with users, you see. So the question of "competition" becomes a very interesting one indeed.[6]

Interesting indeed that Charyk should automatically assume that the FCC's "authorized users" policy, which forbade Comsat from dealing directly with users of international circuits, would apply to domestic business as well. Especially when the Whitehead memo specifically said it should not apply.

In January 1970 AT&T had asked for an indefinite postponement of any domestic satellite system on the ground that there was no need for one in the foreseeable future. On February 2, three days after the Whitehead report was released, AT&T announced its intention to apply as soon as possible for a domestic satellite to use as an integral part of the nationwide phone network. Board Chairman H. I. Romnes said that AT&T had been studying the domestic satellite question for "a good many years," and that while "there appears to be no current economic advantage in using satellite systems in place of terrestrial systems," satellites could "enhance the usefulness" of the telephone network and "add a new dimension of flexibility" to it.[7]

At the FCC, Chairman Burch, who had not participated in any of the deliberations of past years which had resulted in an opposite conclusion, welcomed "receipt of the Executive's views" and promised to give the domestic satellite "highest priority before the Commission."[8] Commissioner Kenneth Cox said that the White House policy "underrated the virtues of regulation and overstated the virtues of competition." He complained about "blithely putting everyone on the same footing and not protecting the rights of the owners of existing terrestrial microwave systems."[9] After leaving the Commission, Cox became president of MCI, the leading terrestrial microwave company.

On March 24, 1970 Burch brought the first half-decade of Docket 16495 to a close by producing the Commission's *First Report and Order* in the matter of domestic satellites.[10] Although it was about three-quarters of an inch thick, what it announced in essence was that the Commission felt it could not create an overall domestic satellite policy without having specific applications before it to consider. It therefore urged anyone interested in putting up a satellite to apply for one. In 1965, we recall, the Commission had rejected ABC's application to put up its own satellite on the grounds that it could not rule on any specific applications before it had created an overall domestic satellite policy.

The Commission ordered applicants to submit their opinions on a number of public interest issues relating to domestic satellites. This is one of the most puzzling aspects of Federal regulation. Why should these private interests have insights on the public interest superior to those of the FCC members and staff? And why would the private interests offer these insights freely if they were in conflict with their own self-interest? In this case, the FCC wanted to have everyone's opinion on whether it should limit the initial role of AT&T in domestic satellites, in order to prevent the giant monopoly either from competing unfairly by means of cross-subsidization or from discouraging satellite development to protect its terrestrial investment. The Commission indicated that it might limit AT&T to using satellites only for its monopoly public message service, or even force AT&T to lease channels on a system owned by someone else for some initial period. Commissioner Cox wrote a partial dissent attached to this *Report and Order.* He thought the other commissioners "unwisely and unnecessarily question the role of the Bell System in satellite communications," and exaggerated the danger of cross-subsidization.

The *Report and Order* did say clearly that to foster competition, the "authorized users" doctrine of international communication, which limited Comsat to selling only through the other carriers, would not apply, and that the terrestrial carriers would not be allowed to thwart satellite competition by making trouble for ground interconnections. It did not take a clear position on free circuits for public television or any other "people's dividend" from satellite revenues, but merely asked applicants to state whether they intended to provide either of these. Obviously no applicant would want to pay out a "people's dividend" if the others did not have to, yet any one would be willing to do so as a price for getting the Commission's approval. This clearly was a matter of public policy, one way or another, for all the systems concerned, yet the FCC by its refusal to take a stand turned it into a sort of bluffing exercise.

On September 23, six months after its first report, the FCC amended it in a *Further Notice of Inquiry,* asking applicants to discuss the possibility of using radio frequencies higher than the four to six GHz (gigahertz) bands to which communications satellites currently were assigned.[11] The current frequencies had to be shared with terrestrial microwave systems and this meant, according to the terrestrial carriers, that to avoid interference earth stations had to be located 40 to 80 miles away from city centers. Sharing frequencies with terrestrial microwave lines gave the terrestrial carriers influence in deciding what kinds of satellite systems would be developed. Distant earth stations raised the cost of such systems compared to the terrestrial lines, which is why AT&T and Western Union both argued that the public interest would be damaged in sundry ways by use of higher frequencies. The aerospace firms that already had designed satellites using the lower frequencies used the same argument, as did Comsat. This is just one example of the subsidiary issues that arose during the next year, and of how the various companies reacted to them.

By the time of the FCC's September revision of its March report, only one company, Western Union, had filed an application for a satellite. Western Union's previous application in the fall of 1966 had been considered premature. The company continued to be quick with the legal brief, and became the first company with a domestic communications satellite in orbit.

Western Union applied in July for a $100 million domestic satellite system including three relatively small capacity satellites (12 transponders) and six major transmit-and-receive earth stations scattered around the country.[12] (One transponder equals one television channel or about 1000 telephone circuits.[13]) The company said it could make $28 million a year from this system when it was fully operative, which would be 32 months after the FCC approved it. Though many corporations were busy looking for partners in such an enormous enterprise, and some had sounded out Western Union, Western Union said its system was intended as a "sole-company undertaking." But it added that

> if in the course of the Commission's proceeding relative to the establishment of such services, the Commission determines that a joint undertaking with other applicants would better serve the public interest, Western Union will cooperate in working out arrangements for such an undertaking.[13]

As a common carrier, Western Union knew that the Commission might not truly be committed to unregulated competition in domestic satellites. If the commissioners ended up returning to a sharing-the-pie policy (as in the Earth Stations controversy), Western Union wanted to be sure it got a piece.

Western Union planned to use one satellite for its own message and data transmission business, one for new business it hoped to attract, and one as a spare. It figured to break even if its capacity was half used. The company said one advantage of a large multipurpose system was that one spare could be used for both satellites. The new business for which the company intended to use at least 10 of the 12 channels in its second satellite was television network business. Under Western Union's plan, the local stations would own their own inexpensive receive-only earth stations and rent space on the satellite to relay network transmissions from New York or Los Angeles.

Western Union was not the only prospective satellite owner with an eye on the television and radio networks, and the economics of the situation made the attraction mutual. The telegraph company, for example, estimated it would charge the broadcasters about $1,260,000 a year for each channel they used. The broadcasters determined, meanwhile, that if they gave their business to satellites, they would need 11 channels most of the time and as many as 22 on football weekends.[14] Even if they rented 22 full-time channels at Western Union's rates, their annual bill would be only $27,720,000 compared to the $70 million they were paying AT&T at the time. The receive-only earth stations, less than $100,000 each, would be a one-time only investment. And for this price they would get unlimited "real time" (live) transmissions to Alaska and Hawaii for the first time. The networks were much sought after because they represented the only really large chunk of business except for that of the telephone companies and Western Union. The networks were so important to any prospective satellite system, Chairman Burch said in October 1970, that "it may be that some or even all of the applicants—apart from AT&T and possibly Western Union—are not in a position to proceed without the large volume television program transmission business."[15]

At first the networks still considered having a system of their own. A study they commissioned concluded that either a satellite or microwave system, network-owned, could save them up to 35 percent on their annual AT&T bills. But it soon appeared they could save far more by renting channels from someone else. In March 1971, the affiliates applied for permission to build receive-only earth stations; the networks announced their intention to play the field. Their business was so sought after, they said in their brief, that they had negotiated with every single system applicant.[16]

Hughes Aircraft was one of several aerospace firms that saw the White House recommendation and the FCC *Report and Order* as an opportunity to get in on the communications satellite action from which Congress had excluded them in 1962. Hughes wanted to take advantage of its position as the dominant commercial communications satellite manufacturer, while other companies wanted to use the domestic field to remove Hughes from dominance. Hughes applied to put up two 12-transponder satellites similar to the ones it was selling to the Canadian domestic satellite company and to Intelsat, for international communication. Hughes said in an advertisement that its satellite tubes had spent "more than a million hours in space without a failure."[17]

Hughes had become interested in creating a satellite-to-cable television network. It wanted to supply community cable systems with full-time channels of special interest programming, such as children's shows and theater, which the mass-oriented national networks could not offer. Hughes was part owner of a cable system in Manhattan, and a large stockholder of TelePrompTer Corporation, the largest cable system owner (800,000 subscribers in 1973). But it had talked to all the cable owners, and wanted to supply programming to all comers. Hughes applied for two large transmitting earth stations and seven receive-only stations near the headends of CATV systems, worth a total of about $75 million. It planned eventually to have hundreds of receiving stations at cable systems around the country.

Hughes's real coup was signing up General Telephone & Electronics, the second largest U.S. telephone company. GT&E saw satellites as a way of participating in long-distance business, for which it was completely at the mercy of AT&T. With satellites, the company could connect long-distance calls between its own noncontiguous phone systems and route intercompany calls at least part of the way through its own equipment. GT&E signed a $50 million contract with Hughes and applied for four large earth stations of its own, worth $26 million, to begin with.

Originally Comsat had hoped to sign up GT&E, which decided early not to risk putting up a system of its own. But Hughes made a better deal. While Comsat was asking about $1 million a year for each satellite channel, and wanted to make the price contingent on the "fill factor" (how many other channels it could sell), Hughes offered a flat guaranteed rate of $900,000 and clinched the deal. When AT&T heard of the price GT&E had gotten from Hughes, it forced Comsat to reopen its contract and settle for a lower price.[18]

Lockheed was another aerospace firm that wanted to build satellites. Like Hughes, it anticipated great profit if it could build a domestic satellite and sell the same model to Intelsat, and it had a model it thought was superior to Hughes's. Lockheed teamed up with MCI (Microwave Communications Incorporated), one of the canniest companies around. In

1969, after six years of dispute and by a four-to-three majority, the FCC gave MCI permission to build a microwave communication line between Chicago and St. Louis, and to sell circuits to large users who needed them full time. This was a precedent-shattering decision. Together with a general policy decree in 1971, it created a whole new industry of so-called specialized common carriers set up to compete with AT&T for the business of leased line users on selected routes around the country. MCI now has a coast-to-coast microwave network. The 1969 MCI decision was cited as an important precedent in both the Whitehead memo on opening satellites to competition and the 1970 FCC *Report and Order*. While MCI was busy lobbying this through, Comsat was still arguing protectionism for itself and making deals with AT&T.

MCI was quick to realize that satellites were even more advantageous than microwave towers for its own type of large-user, major-route business, and it realized that it had more experience than anyone in finding these users and attracting them away from AT&T. It was convinced that Lockheed's larger and more sophisticated satellites would give it an additional edge. So a new company was formed—MCI Lockheed Satellite Corporation. MCI Lockheed applied to launch two 48-transponder satellites—four times the capacity of the Hughes model—and to build earth stations in the major cities, all costing $169 million and producing annual revenue of $68 million. MCIL had an eye on the networks but did not really need them. It figured to break even with as few as 20 transponders leased. (One satellite was an in-orbit spare.) Perhaps the most interesting thing about the MCIL application was that it proposed to reflect the economic advantages of satellites by charging distance-insensitive rates. Because it cost the same to communicate from one earth station, through a satellite, to another no matter how far apart the two stations are, MCIL proposed to charge the same. No other domestic satellite applicant, including the one that specializes in satellites, Comsat, was willing to be so competitive.

Another specialized common carrier, Western Telecommunications, Inc., teamed up with another aerospace firm, North American Rockwell, for a $67 million two-satellite system after Hughes told WTCI there was no more room in the Hughes deal.

The most imaginative application came from yet another aerospace firm, Fairchild Industries. Fairchild proposed an enormous, $220 million system involving two satellites with 120 transponders each and more than 100 earth stations. Fairchild's satellite was similar to one it had designed for NASA's Applications Technology Satellite Program. Because it was so large, its proposed rates were very low. But it needed AT&T's business if it ever was to be filled up. The proposal was based on the assumption that the FCC would go back to the idea of a monopoly "chosen entity" satellite. Fairchild argued that its proposal demonstrated how economies of scale made a monopoly advantageous, and hoped that the Commission would choose it and force AT&T to use it. Because this seemed far-fetched, and because the decision to apply came somewhat late, Fairchild's application was regarded in the trade as quixotic.

Another interesting idea from a manufacturer never became a formal proposal. In 1969, General Electric suggested a satellite system specializing in nonvoice communication (sometimes called "record carrying"), including computer communication, video services, and—most interesting—mail. The Post Office filed a comment on the GE proposal saying that up to 56 percent of the U.S mail might possibly be sent electronically in this way. AT&T said the GE proposal "rests on an erroneous assumption of a national policy in favor of competition in the common carrier field.[19] GE decided not to risk its money.

The Commission had indicated in its *Report and Order* that it would require any applicant wishing to service the 48 contiguous states to provide similar service to Alaska and Hawaii. Most of the applicants said they were willing to do this to win approval of their systems. But RCA applied to build a system intended, at first, primarily to service Alaska, with five transmit-receive earth stations in that state. RCA had purchased Alaska's internal communication system, such as it was, from the government the year before. Alaska stood to gain much from the advent of communications satellites; some of its communities have virtually no communication with one another, let alone with the "lower forty-eight." Alaska Senator Mike Gravel was a bitter critic of the FCC and Comsat, which he blamed for the delay in establishing a system to service his state.[20]

RCA proposed eventually to expand into a $200 million system with three satellites, 27 receive-transmit earth stations, and 300 receive-only earth stations. The company had its eye on the network business, but the fact that it owns NBC may be a disadvantage, making the other networks reluctant to have to depend on a competitor to supply an important service. One interesting piece of business RCA bid for was the distribution of movies by satellite from major film distribution points to local theaters around the country, which would then show them by closed-circuit TV. In the 1930s, during the early days of talkies, RCA's sound-on-film system beat out AT&T's sound-on-disc arrangement for the talking picture business. RCA hoped to repeat this coup. It said it was also willing to service public television at a substantial discount.

Meanwhile, Comsat, which had thought it had the field to itself, suddenly found it had at least six serious competitors, including its own satellite supplier, Hughes, and several companies it had hoped to have as customers. AT&T, which had been hoping to postpone any domestic satellite development indefinitely, found that events were no longer subject to its control.

The two corporations had been talking with each other in a leisurely fashion until July 1970, when Western Union filed for its system and the FCC gave everyone else one month to express interest in filing an application. A December deadline for formal applications later was moved to March 1, then to March 15, but beginning the previous July, with Western Union's application, there was a need for haste. On October 15, AT&T and Comsat announced that they would apply for a joint system. The plan was prepared in such a rush that the FCC rejected it one week later as "incomplete and unacceptable." It was revised and resubmitted. Under this plan, Comsat would own two satellites, worth some $110 million (later increased to three, worth $145 million), and the telephone company would own all the earth stations—of which there would be only five, costing $96 million. AT&T also would be manager of the system and handle all sales to customers.[21] AT&T's Hough said that satellite sales would be completely integrated into their terrestrial network and that "there will be no satellite-only services." Hough accompanied his announcement with another declaration that, in fact, satellites were more expensive to use for all purposes than terrestrial methods. AT&T was applying to use satellites because,

> In spite of the unfavorable economics . . . it is possible that a domestic satellite system closely integrated with the terrestrial network could provide offsetting advantages by providing circuits on a time-shared basis to relieve peak traffic demands or as a backup facility.[22]

But in spite of this, Hough made clear that AT&T intended to keep the network business and use its satellite system for it if necessary.

This plan was perfect for AT&T. As the *Wall Street Journal* pointed out, if approved it would extend the controversial "authorized users" doctrine of international satellite communication into the domestic field, giving

AT&T control over the new technology and preventing the relative economics of the different technologies from manifesting themselves through competition—at least in the telephone switching business and possibly in other areas.[23] This domestic arrangement was even better because internationally Bell had to share earth station ownership with Comsat. Comsat had completely abandoned its 1966 position that, "as an integral and critical part of a satellite communication system," earth stations must be controlled by the satellite operator. This deal would give AT&T the appearance of using satellites—and of deferring to Comsat—while it actually pursued a far less ambitious program, and at a much higher cost, than any of the other applicants.

In their later official comments, the other applicants tried to insist that there was something fishy about the AT&T–Comsat agreement, and they got the Commission to agree with them up to a point. This was the cause of great confusion for the next two years. It does not take conspiracy or conflict of interest theories, such as those offered by some of the other companies, to understand why Comsat wanted to get AT&T's business. Any domestic system operator would want AT&T's business, simply because it was by far the biggest volume of business around. Similarly, some charged that AT&T wanted to deal with Comsat only because its 29 percent ownership would provide it with a sort of legal kickback on Comsat's domestic satellite profits from AT&T's business. But AT&T may instead simply have decided on the basis of the *First Report and Order* that the FCC was not going to let it put up a system of its own, yet might require AT&T to use satellite circuits leased on a system owned by someone else. There is no telling where something like that might have led. Comsat was willing to make a deal that no one else would make to let AT&T into satellites on its own terms.

The more controversial aspect of the joint Comsat/AT&T proposal was not the *fact* that the two companies decided to work together, but the arrangement they agreed to. And the potential detriment was not to the other competitors, but to Comsat itself. Comsat was left as nothing more than a source of capital and good will for the telephone company, owning the pieces of metal in the sky but having no control over their use or nonuse. Furthermore, AT&T made clear from the start that this association was disposable any time it was no longer needed.[24]

The fact that Comsat would agree to an arrangement like this was widely regarded, even by the FCC, as proof of AT&T's anticompetitive influence with Comsat. To look ahead a bit, the commissioners dealt with this evidence in a somewhat typical way, by making approval of the Comsat/AT&T deal contingent upon the telephone company's divesting itself of its Comsat stock and giving up its seats on the Comsat board. Worse than shutting the barn door after the horse has escaped, this is allowing her to escape, so long as she agrees to shut the door on her way out.

At the very last moment, on March 1, 1971, Comsat applied for a second system of its own, involving three orbiting satellites and 132 earth stations, costing about $250 million. Comsat said this was intended as a high-capacity, multipurpose system to serve the needs of all communications users except AT&T, which was already taken care of. It also was intended to revive the notion of Comsat as a "chosen entity" for all commercial satellite communication. "The Corporation emphasized," said a press release accompanying the application, "that only a single multi-user system of high capacity such as it proposed—rather than a proliferation of separate systems—would result in proper conservation of limited frequency space and bring the full economies of scale to all users, large and small."[25] Comsat President Dr. Charyk told a press conference that the Comsat II system, as it became known, could cut the network communication bills in half.[26] Several people who worked for Comsat at the time or were close to industry scuttlebutt have said that this second application had not been planned originally, and that it only emerged the previous fall after Comsat staff members showed great discontent at the proposed relationship with AT&T. When the FCC asked prospective domestic satellite applicants in August 1970 how long they would need to complete their applications, Comsat general counsel David Acheson wrote back that Comsat would be ready by October 23. This indicates that during 1970 Comsat envisioned the applications necessary for the AT&T system, which it submitted October 15, but not those for its own system,which turned up more than four months later. AT&T made no secret of its opposition to Comsat's independent application; Comsat had to complain to the FCC that its largest shareholder was making trouble for its efforts to obtain land interconnections for its second system.[27]

The timing was not the only unusual aspect of Comsat's second domestic satellite proposal. It seemed to have little idea of whom it was going to sell all those circuits to. One economist said of the proposal that Comsat "seems to prefer to be a carrier's carrier even when it doesn't know who the marketing carriers are going to be.[28] This statement, made in 1971, is especially interesting in light of subsequent events. Unless the FCC supported its demand for a monopoly, Comsat had already lost to Hughes the volume business of General Telephone and the cable systems, and also faced Western Union's intention to put up its own system. Dr. Charyk admitted at his briefing that the Comsat II system needed the networks to be viable, yet Comsat knew that AT&T intended to keep this business if it could through its Comsat-owned satellites. Comsat's notion that it could somehow compete with itself for this and other business was somewhat bizarre, especially accompanied by the simultaneous notion that its two systems deserved a share monopoly because competition was inefficient. As the economist quoted above, William Melody, said:

> Comsat's economic rationale for its proposal and its plea for an exclusive monopoly borders on the incredible. In the interest of single-system economies of scale, the FCC is supposed to approve the two separate systems that involve Comsat and reject all other proposals. One of the systems is supposed to provide some kind of competition between the satellite and the landline transmission technologies [while the other, he might have added, is proposed on the basis that such competition is unnecessary]. Obviously, if the FCC were to adopt the principle of a chosen entity in a single system, it should simply reserve the technology for Bell. And since Comsat seems to identify capacity size with economies of scale and efficiency, regardless of the specialization trade-offs and the market conditions, it would seem that it would now have to recommend that the FCC grant an exclusive monopoly to Fairchild-Hiller, which has proposed a system of much greater capacity than Comsat's proposed system.[29]

And at much cheaper rates, too. The comparison with Fairchild points out a fundamental fact about both of Comsat's proposed systems: neither was particularly innovative. Both proposed to use a slightly revised model of the satellite Comsat already had built for Intelsat, and one that also was intended for Intelsat use. The company that had been created to specialize in commercial satellite communication—the one that invoked special expertise and claimed privileged treatment on this basis—had come up with the least imaginative and advanced of all the proposals.

The passing of the March 1971 deadline for domestic system applications left many questions unanswered. It was clear there was nowhere near enough traffic to fill all the satellites companies proposed to launch.

Which applicants were sincere in saying they were ready to go it alone, and which were ready to deal? Or would the FCC yet go against the White House recommendation and choose only one company, Comsat or Fairchild or AT&T, to have a domestic satellite monopoly? What limitations would the Commission place on AT&T, or on the other companies? Would it, for example, approve the deals at set prices that some system applicants had made with large customers (Hughes with GT&E, Comsat with AT&T), or would it require any system owner to be a common carrier—selling circuits to all comers at the same price?

It took five years for the FCC to decide to accept applications and another year for the applications to be prepared. Despite Chairman Burch's declaration after the applications were in that a decision would be made by the end of 1971, it took another year for the FCC Common Carrier Bureau staff to prepare its recommendations, three more months for the commissioners to decide to overrule these recommendations, and another six months for the losing corporations to persuade them to change their minds and overrule themselves. Of all the corporate filings and commission rulings included in Docket 16495, following the rules prescribed by the Administrative Procedures Act, the ones filed during the spring and summer of 1971 are perhaps the most interesting. This is when the corporate applicants and other interested parties had the opportunity to submit comments on the various system applications, and then to submit "reply comments" on everyone else's initial comments. These call into question most seriously the value of the "public interest" regulatory proceeding. We find frequent repetition of the words "public interest" but little evidence of true concern for it.

Take, for example, the comments filed by Comsat on May 12, 1971.[30] They were the longest and most elaborately packaged of the 33 comments by various parties filed with the Commission on that day. They were signed by David Acheson, Comsat's general counsel and son of the late secretary of state, and by four other Comsat lawyers and four outside lawyers listed as "of counsel." These latter included the distinguished Washington lawyer Lloyd Cutler and Donald F. Turner, a Harvard Law School professor who was assistant Attorney General for antitrust under President Johnson. The burden of Comsat's comments was still that only Comsat should be allowed to launch satellites for use in domestic commercial communication. But, with the help of all those lawyers, the issue was approached obliquely. Comsat did not attempt to repeat the argument that Congress had given it by law a monopoly on all commercial satellite communication. It had long since abandoned this as hopeless, along with the question of NASA's authority to launch anyone else's private satellites. The company did not even dwell on the economies of scale that it previously had argued would justify a monopolistic, multipurpose domestic satellite system. Instead, Comsat launched into a new and detailed discussion of the dangers of conflicts of interest, and "numerous anticompetitive questions."

Comsat said it saw serious anticompetitive problems arising from three different types of applicants, and urged the FCC to deny applications from any company that fit one of these three categories. Applications from manufacturers of satellite equipment, Comsat said, "carry with them a most serious anticompetitive potential" by giving those firms an unfair advantage in finding a market for their equipment. On this ground, Comsat would have prevented RCA, Fairchild Industries, Hughes, and MCI from putting up a domestic satellite. Similarly, Comsat wanted the FCC to forbid "user applicants." If Hughes could sell circuits to its own proposed cable network or RCA could sell them to its own television affiliate (NBC), Comsat suggested, this would give them an unfair competitive advantage over other satellite circuit sellers and over other satellite circuit buyers. In fact, Comsat wanted to exclude *any* "entities that have an interest in an activity other than the transmission of a message or signal." Finally, Comsat wanted to disqualify anyone involved in a terrestrially communications system, because "to the extent that an applicant has a major stake in terrestrial facilities, it may be reluctant to participate aggressively and innovatively in the development of satellite technology and service."[31] To Comsat, this eliminated the proposed systems of MCI Lockheed, RCA, WTCI, and Western Union.

To encourage competition in domestic satellite communication, therefore, Comsat wanted the Commission to ban *all* of its potential competitors from the field. This is the same conclusion Comsat reached in earlier years when it was urging the FCC to forbid competition. Comsat said that all of these anticompetitive dangers could be avoided "by entrusting the operation of a domestic satellite system to an entity that does not have a special interest of its own."[32]

Comsat's new antitrust standards were very strict. So strict, in fact, that if they really were to be applied, the FCC would have had to reject not only the applications of all six of Comsat's competitors, but both of Comsat's applications as well. As many opposing applicants pointed out in their reply comments, this is simply because Comsat was 29 percent owned by

AT&T, which is by far the largest terrestrial common carrier and, in the case of the joint proposal, was intended to be both manager of the system and its *only* user. (MCI and Lockheed noted that in their own joint proposal, neither company could act without the approval of the other, while the telephone company faced no such countervailing power within Comsat.[33]) Did this flaw in their argument never occur to the lawyers who wrote Comsat's brief?

Comsat's suggested exclusion of the manufacturers was reminiscent of the arguments AT&T used so successfully in getting Congress to cut manufacturers out of Comsat ownership back in 1962. And it was invalid for the very same reason that AT&T *is* a major manufacturer of communications satellite equipment, through its wholly-owned subsidiary Western Electric. As a matter of fact AT&T, in *its* comments filed with the FCC the same day, said that its own application had to be approved "to encourage continued research and development by AT&T in the use of advanced satellite technology.[34] Bell's presumption in offering this argument is especially impressive because at the same time, in the TAT-6 international cable dispute, the company was insisting that the FCC had to continue approving its undersea cables to prevent it from abandoning research and development of *cable* technology.

At various times since 1971, Comsat's second domestic satellite system also has been attached to several other large corporations, all of which ought to have been disqualified by Comsat's own strict antitrust standards.

In its discourse on the dangers of vertical integration, Comsat stumbled into an unfortunate comparison with the domestic airline industry, mentioning "interlocking directors, officers or stockholders with controlling interests, between air carriers, other common carriers and any company engaged in any other phase of aeronautics" and suggesting that "it is appropriate for the Commission, in resolving the problems before it in these proceedings, to give serious consideration to the regulatory pattern designed to avoid restraints on competition that has been followed in the domestic air transportation industry." This passage indicates the main theoretical weakness in Comsat's argument against vertical integration, besides the fact that it would have eliminated all the applicants. Economists are of many minds about vertical integration. As the Justice Department pointed out in its *Comments:*

> In evaluating the entry of suppliers, it must be realized that here, unlike some markets, each operator will be effectively committed to

a single supplier during the system's life so that the maximum diversity of actual manufacturers is limited by the number of independent systems. A regulatory scheme which divorces operators from suppliers thus will not at this time increase the diversity of satellite technologies in use. In fact it may do the opposite my making it more likely that Comsat will be the sole domestic operator.[35]

In its *Reply Comments,* the Justice Department accused Comsat, in the company's *Comments,* of willfully misinterpreting Justice's regulations on the subject of vertical integration.[36]

The dangers of vertical integration are disputed. But there is little dispute among economists about the dangers of *horizontal* integration (combinations between competitors) in a free market economy. *This* is why interlocking directorates are forbidden among common carriers, as in the airline industry. Of course, Comsat was at that time one of the major examples of horizontal integration in the United States. To have followed the regulatory pattern of the airline industry would have been to ban Comsat from any involvement in domestic satellites at all.

Comsat was not the only company that felt strongly that, to encourage competition, certain competitive applications must be rejected. MCI Lockheed, for example, said that the AT&T/Comsat application should be denied because "AT&T proposes no new services and offers no reduction in rates for existing services. In fact, AT&T asserts that it can provide equivalent services at lower cost through existing terrestrial facilities than it could by satellite.[37] The company added that AT&T's interest in Comsat created a conflict of interest that should not be allowed to penetrate the domestic field. It suggested coyly that instead, "in view of the real public benefits which will accrue from the use of satellite transmission for long distance communications (although, as yet, AT&T is reluctant to recognize the fact)," AT&T should be encouraged to lease circuits on "satellite systems owned by carriers with whom it has no affiliation." Several applicants wanted to ban AT&T. MCI's unique angle was that it felt the FCC "should not be inhibited" from banning Comsat too, on the ground that Comsat's role as manager of the Intelsat international system created "conflicts of interest of potentially serious proportions." MCI argued that the FCC's publicized concern not to interfere with the Intelsat system gave Comsat influence over the Commission's decisions on whether to approve its competitors' applications, and that Comsat's ability to use the same satellite models for international and domestic services gave it an unfair economic edge over these competitors. MCIL advanced this argument strenuously, with variations, for the next year.[38] This did not stop it from accepting Comsat as part-owner of its own system shortly thereafter and withdrawing all objections to Comsat's role, as well as that of AT&T. Nor did it prevent Lockheed from trying to sell its own domestic satellite model to Intelsat.

Western Union also began by saying that there was no need for a monopoly, and then went on to suggest guidelines that excluded all of its competition. The telegraph company said the FCC should approve applications only from companies wishing to use satellites for their own existing business—either the terrestrial common carriers or private users such as the networks (two groups Comsat would have *banned* for similar "public interest" reasons). Then it went on to say that AT&T had to be an exception because it was so big it "might well tend to hinder other satellite grantees," that MCIL's proposal was "too risky," and that the proposal of Western Telecommunications was "wasteful of orbit spectrum." Since the networks had not applied, this cleared the field.

In what *Fortune* called a demonstration of "noblesse oblige," AT&T commented that so far as it was concerned the FCC should approve as many domestic satellite "as can reasonably be found in the public interest." But AT&T Vice-President Richard Hough was quoted as saying, "You don't put your cards on the table before the hand is played."[39] (AT&T later decided that General Telephone's satellite plans threatened the public interest in any number of ways, then still later dropped its objections and merged.) Beyond this, the company merely repeated its declaration that satellites were not economical and would not result in lower rates but that it wanted some anyway. Several of the other applicants pointed out that the estimated cost of satellite circuits in both of Comsat's proposals was higher than that of any other applicant except RCA. The Justice Department suggested that this might be why AT&T was so anxious to help Comsat dominate the field.[40]

Justice was the most important of the nonapplicants that entered comments at this point. The government antitrust lawyers endorsed the White House recommendations for completely open competition, except for some initial restrictions on AT&T to give other satellite systems a chance to gear up for competition.

With a couple dozen other domestic satellite applicants and other interested parties filing comments of similar length to the ones cited above, the trade journal *Telecommunications Reports* remarked when the filing date had passed that the "deluge of comments . . . suggested that there should be little left for anyone to say when reply statements come due June 9."[41] *Telecommunications Reports* was wrong. The reply deadline was delayed for more than a month until July 12, and everyone had lots more to say. Comsat, for example, was very upset with the Justice Department. The company wrote:

> The central question before the Commission in this proceeding is whether it will accept the superficially appealing thesis of the Justice Department that if the domestic satellite market is permitted to grow like Topsy the end result will somehow be beneficial, or whether the Commission will recognize what we conceive to be its statutory responsibility to provide regulatory leadership and guidance in the creation of an essential communications service.[42]

Comsat said generously that it found the Justice Department's error "understandable" but reaffirmed its belief that "the Commission should license only those qualified operators who lack debilitating conflicts of interest and whose proposals offer the optimum in economies of scale, efficiency, reliability, and the assurance that the needs of all users—large and small—will be handled in a non-discriminatory manner." Comsat also devoted much space in its 74-page document to denying that there was anything "improper," "illegal," or "sinister" about its relationship with AT&T.

By the summer of 1971, all of the interested parties except one had made known—at great length—their reactions to the various applications and suggestions as to how the FCC should deal with them. That one was the White House. Whitehead apparently did not feel constrained by the Commission's deadlines, however often they were postponed. His Office of Telecommunications Policy sent a stern memo to Chairman Burch in November, laying down the White House line and also labeling the long delay "a source of serious concern to the Administration." Whitehead's letter was consistent with his recommendations of 22 months before: he urged the FCC to approve all eight applications without conditions and without delay. The OTP estimated that the market for domestic satellite services "would support a capacity of 100 television equivalent channels and involve an investment of about $450 million." It said the eight proposed systems, if they all went through, would have a total of 600 channels and cost more than $1.2 billion. "Even so, there is no evidence to indicate that selection of the successful operator(s) by the government is either necessary or preferable on public interest grounds to a marketplace determination." Whitehead said that those who were thinking of investing such huge amounts of money were in the best position to decide whether the investment would pay off. Despite all the sniping in the applicants' comments and reply comments, the OTP concluded that the cost per channel of all the applicants' proposals were approximately the same, except that of Fairchild, which was too uncertain to estimate.[43]

Despite this clear-cut and not unassuming reassertion of the White House position, there were signs that the FCC was slipping away from a completely competitive, "open skies" solution as 1971 came to a close and Docket 16495 approached its seventh birthday. The FCC Common Carrier Bureau's staff recommendations had been promised by the end of the year, but had not surfaced by February 7, 1972, when Chairman Burch testified in front of the Commerce Committee's hearings on Phase 2 of President Nixon's economic policy. Burch told the committee that the "big problem is a question of disqualification, not qualification" and that "open entry sounds wonderful, but it does not answer such questions as who it is open to."[44] Thus the man who managed Barry Goldwater's presidential campaign revealed that even he had lost his taste for laissez-faire economics after a brief stint in a federal regulatory agency.

On March 22, 1972, the FCC Common Carrier Bureau published its recommendations in the form of a "Proposed Rule Making" taking up 41 finely printed pages of the *Federal Register*. The staff described their recommendation, diplomatically, as one of "limited open entry." Completely open entry, which the White House had suggested, they said, "presents a real danger . . . of fragmenting the market . . . to such an extent that most carrier entrants would fail to come even remotely close to covering their costs." Having described an unfortunate situation that might result from having too many competitors, the staff concluded that this might lead to having no competitors at all, because all those except AT&T would be scared away by the risk of losing money. "This would defeat the situation the Commission is seeking to create where competition would determine how the most efficient survive."[45]

To encourage competition, therefore, the staff wanted to force applicants proposing to use similar technologies to merge with one another, as "the best course, both from the point of view of the using public and the applicants themselves." (As the OTP later pointed out, the FCC staff seemed intent on assuming a condition of "mass irrationality" on the part of the giant communications corporations.[46]) They suggested authorizing Western Union and Hughes/GTE to put up three Hughes satellites, and inviting RCA and Western Telecommunications to join in if they wanted. This kind of grouping requirement, replacing business judgment by government dictate, would have been advantageous for smaller firms like WTCI, which would have been forced onto larger systems and given a chunk of the action simply because they had the foresight to submit an application of their own. If other companies had suspected that this would be the FCC's final word on the subject (which it was not), they undoubtedly would have flooded the agency with applications.

Since MCIL and Fairchild both were proposing to use substantially different technologies, the staff suggested that both applications be approved. To prevent "overcapacity," however, the Commission was supposed to authorize "minimum facilities" for these and all other systems, and both companies would be encouraged to share ownership with other companies that might be interested.

As for AT&T and Comsat, the staff proposed to place severe but somewhat peculiar restrictions on both. AT&T would be limited for at least the first few years to using satellites only for noncompetitive services such as long-distance telephone calls. This was, in keeping with the Commission's recent decisions concerning the new microwave carriers, in order to give competitors a chance to gain a foothold in the market for leased lines and other specialized services. The staff also wanted to forbid AT&T from leasing its space segment from Comsat, unless it could prove that this would be cheaper than sharing ownership or putting up a satellite of its own.

In a long discussion of the relative potential benefits to AT&T of leasing and owning satellite equipment, the staff overlooked a couple of fundamental points. Under normal circumstances, the benefits of ownership always are more attractive to a rate-base regulated company than are those of leasing similar equipment or hiring services from others; the company is entitled to earn a profit on ownership investment, whereas leasing costs are merely deductible as expenses (the Averch-Johnson effect). A regulator frequently can have reason to want proof that an ownership interest is the cheapest method of providing some service to customers. AT&T's reason for wanting to *rent* circuits from Comsat rather than owning them had less to do with immediate economic considerations than with public relations, a desire to keep Comsat's aspirations under control. It also had to do with the FCC's own strong indication in its first *Report and Order* that it might actually *forbid* AT&T to own its own satellites and *require* it to lease circuits from someone else. And who better to deal with, if forced, than Comsat? Not, as AT&T claimed, because of its great satellite expertise, but because of its demonstrated willingness to follow AT&T's wishes and its favorable public image.

The staff also suggested that Comsat should be required to choose between serving AT&T exclusively and being a common carrier serving all comers. This was the strangest provision of all. This was in part a response to charges by Comsat's competitors that the guarantee of AT&T business would give Comsat an unfair advantage in competing against others. As Comsat pointed out in its reply, it was never made clear whether the staff feared that users of the Comsat II system would subsidize AT&T or the other way around. Furthermore, as Comsat pointed out in a later response to the Commission, most of the other applicants were large, diversified corporations with unrelated divisions that could cross-subsidize satellite operations during periods of fierce competition at least as easily as Comsat could.

The FCC staff made its recommendation based on exactly the opposite fear: that the association with AT&T would cause Comsat to be *uncompetitive* in its other system, for fear of antagonizing its largest customer. The staff reviewed the close relationships of ownership and international business dealings that already bound Comsat to AT&T, and concluded that therefore "it is only natural to expect that it would seek to maximize its opportunity to retain AT&T as its domestic customer," and "it is not realistic to expect Comsat to compete vigorously in the development of specialized services and thereby challenge AT&T's terrestrial domination in this field."[47] The Commmon Carrier Bureau did not reflect, at least in its report, that *any* domestic satellite owner would want very badly to retain AT&T as a customer, if it could get AT&T as a customer. This would be true regardless of any other relationship it might have with AT&T, and whether it used its AT&T arrangement to compete unfairly for other business or, to pacify AT&T, went easy on competing for other business. And even assuming that Comsat was under strong pressure not to make things difficult for the telephone company—which certainly was the case—it is strange logic that concludes that the best way to deal with a company that might be reticent to compete is to forbid it to compete at all.

The bureau took an ambivalent stance toward free or cheaper circuits for public television and radio, saying that the Commission should not require such circuits, but that those who had offered to provide them should be told to do so (which was an ironic result for those who had thought that offering to help PTV would bring them some sort of special favors). Likewise with the question of Hawaii and Alaska, they said that *some* system should serve those states, that anyone who wanted to should have to indicate in detail what services were to be offered, but that Comsat should in fact be forbidden to serve them because this would conflict with its role as manager of the Intelsat system, which served them already. This was the staff's only concession to MCI Lockheed's argument that Comsat's international role precluded a domestic one.

Chairman Burch said that the FCC would make a final domestic satellite decision based on the staff's proposals by the end of May. The staff recommendations, of course, opened the flood gates for another wave of comments by interested parties. AT&T did not even wait for the official deadline to issue comments notable for the repeated use of the adjective "eventual" to modify words such as "savings" and "economy." The company used these and many other terms to explain the disaster that would affect the telephone-using public if AT&T were restricted even in the limited way suggested by the staff from using a technology the company earlier had said should be delayed indefinitely.[48]

AT&T also had a new angle. At this point the Defense Department wrote the FCC saying that the restrictions on AT&T "would unduly restrict the purchase and/or configuration of vital and necessary military communications services."[49] The Pentagon said the proposed rules would prevent it from using domestic satellites, without having "to forego the ability to be able to hold one carrier responsible for the integrity of the service." This was a bit thin, especially since the one responsible carrier claimed there was currently no advantage to using satellites. To prevent the Commission from making an exception for the military without fundamentally changing their rule excluding AT&T from competitive satellite services, DOD added that it did not think AT&T would bother to "duplicate its landline facilities" with satellites at all "if it cannot use them in the competitive private line market."[50] There was never the least indication that this was AT&T's official position, as the Pentagon must have realized.

In its official comments of April 21, 1972, the telephone company merely noted that the "proposed restriction would significantly impair the Bell System's ability to be fully responsive to the communications requirements of the U.S. government."[51] Like all of the companies on which the staff had suggested to place restrictions, AT&T spent most of its brief in praise of competition in its most rigorous and uninhibited form, something the company had not been too enthusiastic about in the past. "The staff's plan . . . imposes artificial and unnecessary constraints on the applicants which could well prove to be unworkable for reasons which neither the staff, nor the Commission, nor even the applicants now foresee." AT&T did make one exception: it agreed with the staff that General Telephone should be prevented from using satellites for its own long-distance connections unless it could prove this would not damage the interstate switching system. Like the other applicants, AT&T said it believed in competition, but that other competitors would have to be restricted.

The most interesting version in this particular round of filings of a request for restriction inserted in a general discussion of the benefits of unrestricted competition was that of Hughes Aircraft. Hughes said that while in principle it saw no need to prevent Comsat from serving both AT&T and the general market, it "concedes the Commission's expertise with regard to these particular parties" and "accordingly defers to the Commission's judgment on this particular point."

Comsat—which for years had been Docket 16495's resident expert on, alternatively, the illegality, diseconomy, and futility of a competitive domestic satellite situation—became at this point competition's most enthusiastic supporter. Criticizing the staff proposals as "unfair and anti-competitive" and "complicated and repressive," Comsat said it wanted "a truly open-entry approach." In oral arguments before the Commission during May 1972, Comsat general counsel David Acheson said the staff proposal suffered from "a fundamental defect . . ., that of substituting the regulator's judgment for the market judgments of the parties concerned." Acheson also said that "if the FCC decides to go the super-regulation route, then at least wait until round two. Round one should go to a fully competitive policy."[52] This was exactly the opposite of Comsat's previous defense of its request for a monopoly, on the grounds that it would be a "pilot" system that could be followed after several years by a more competitive arrangement.

Within hours after the FCC staff proposal was released, the White House Office of Telecommunications Policy released three studies which, they said, supported their position of completely open entry. The next month, April, Clay Whitehead told the *Washington Star* that if the FCC's final decision was "sufficiently out of step" with the White House position, the White House would go to Congress with legislation to have the Commission overruled.[53] Whitehead did not repeat his reassurance of 1970, when he first made his proposals, that they were only recommendations and not intended to override the FCC's decision-making power in any way.

On June 16, 1972, more than two years after its *First Report and Order* and more than seven years after the docket had first been opened, the FCC released its *Second Report and Order* on domestic satellites.[54] It was a four-to-three decision with Chairman Burch leading the dissent. It rejected the staff's proposal to force the applicants into consortiums, which the staff had called "limited open entry," and said the Commission would approve most applications under certain conditions different from any that had been considered before, a situation it called "multiple entry," in contrast with the White House's proposed "open entry." The Commission agreed with the staff that both AT&T and Comsat needed to be restricted, but disagreed as to why and how.

The Commission's main concern was cross-subsidization. To prevent AT&T from overwhelming competitors in the new market for specialized and lease-line services, and to provide an opportunity for realistic cost comparisons between satellites and terrestrial methods for these services, AT&T was to be prevented for an initial period of up to three years from using satellites for anything but long-distance calls, military needs, and emergency restoration. The decision went on that "the same considerations" had led the commissioners to forbid the AT&T/Comsat arrangement. In one remarkable paragraph, the FCC endorsed both the view of Comsat's competitors that this arrangement would give Comsat an unfair competitive advantage, and the view of the staff that it would lead Comsat not to behave competitively.

First, since AT&T is a principal source of the domestic service revenue that Comsat would seek to obtain, it is not realistic to expect Comsat to compete vigorously in the provision of specialized services on an end-to-end or "retail" basis and thereby challenge AT&T's terrestrial domination in this field. Secondly, if Comsat should proceed in the dual capacities proposed in its two pending system applications, the revenues that would be guaranteed to Comsat from the AT&T contractual arrangement would give it an extraordinary advantage and head start over all other potential domestic satellite entrants seeking to develop specialized services in competition with Comsat as well as with AT&T's terrestrial services.[55]

If Comsat wanted to serve AT&T, the Commission said, it would be *required* to serve other communications companies on an equal basis as a "carrier's carrier," but *forbidden* to compete with them in the provision of end-to-end communication services for user customers. A "carrier's carrier" was exactly what the FCC had said it intended *not* to make Comsat, in its original *Report and Order* of 1970. Meanwhile the AT&T/Comsat contract was invalidated and AT&T was given the option of putting up satellites of its own, or renegotiating a deal with Comsat or with "any other carrier who elects to proceed solely as a carrier's carrier."[56] If Comsat decided not to settle for the guaranteed volume of AT&T (or if AT&T decided to go it alone), Comsat was free to compete with everyone else for end-to-end customers, such as the television networks.

In other conclusions favorable to AT&T, the Commission placed rigorous demands for proof of public benefit on GT&E's request to use satellites to get a piece of the long-distance switching action, and it gave AT&T the right to provide long-distance connections by satellite to Alaska, Hawaii, and Puerto Rico. It also said that the only companies it would require to provide free or reduced services to public broadcasting were the ones that had offered to do so in their applications.

The *Second Report and Order* contained major advantages for AT&T. The telephone company was explicitly permitted to own and operate its own domestic satellite system if it wanted to. Furthermore, if it opted for the Comsat "carrier's carrier" arrangement, Comsat would be even more at its mercy than under their proposed contract, because the telephone company would be able to threaten at any time to pull out its business and either give it to someone else or put up a satellite itself. Still, from the viewpoint of AT&T, the logic of the *Report and Order* was frustrating. The arrangement to lease satellite circuits from Comsat had resulted from the Commission's suggestion in its *First Report and Order* that it probably would not permit AT&T to own its own satellites—a situation AT&T probably would have preferred—in order to encourage competition. Yet the *Second Report and Order* said the Commission would not allow the AT&T/Comsat match for the very same reason—competition—and it encouraged AT&T to put up a system of its own.

For Comsat, the decision represented the nadir of the company's hopes. In the four days following its release, Comsat's stock dropped from $68 to below $54. Two and a half years before, Comsat had been on the verge of a monopoly of domestic satellite communication. Now it was faced with the likelihood that AT&T might decide to put up its own system. As a Comsat source admitted to Robert Samuelson of the *Washington Post,* any attempt to build an independent system might be doomed unless Comsat could get the network transmission business, for which it was competing against five other companies while also facing the networks' increasing reluctance to leave AT&T.[57] And this was not all. The Commission had agreed with the staff that any Comsat domestic system should not be allowed to serve any area served by the Intelsat system—meaning Alaska, Hawaii, and Puerto Rico. This was somehow related to the commitment of the United States not to do anything that would damage the international system, of which Comsat was manager. But the other domestic system applicants were allowed and indeed strongly encouraged to provide communication service between these points and the U.S. mainland. This represented almost all of Intelsat's business to and from these points, and 40 percent of the international system's total volume. Because Intelsat has a policy, for political reasons, of averaging costs between high- and low-volume routes throughout the world, a domestic satellite owner has an excellent chance to underbid Intelsat for these few overseas domestic routes. So Comsat suddenly stood not only to be shut out completely from a role in domestic communication, but to lose almost half its international business as well.

Chairman Burch wrote a testy dissent. He accused the majority of "failing to discipline itself against the temptation to piggyback . . . its favorite regulatory schemes and hangups (for example, the desire to 'get a handle on AT&T')" on a controversy he felt contained not only complexity but "even subtlety." He said the *Second Report and Order* "leaves reality behind and takes off into the blue sky of academic abstraction." He condemned the majority for excessive concern to create a comparison between satellite and terrestrial costs for communications services, "most of which services are not unique to satellite technology anyway."[58] Of course if they were unique to satellites, a cost comparison would be both pointless and impossible. But he scored some telling points off his colleagues on the subject of Comsat's restriction from serving domestic overseas areas, and pointed out wisely that the advantage given to Comsat by its association with AT&T might not really be "unfair" as the other applicants had suggested, but a realistic result of legitimate economies of scale. (Not that these economies were reflected in Comsat's proposed rates, which were higher than almost everybody else's.) Anyway, some of those competitors were soon to change their minds once again about what was "unfair" and what was not.

The *Second Report and Order* set off yet another round of filings and delayed deadlines. A U.S. commercial domestic satellite system was still one more report, and two more years, away. Meanwhile, certain parties unencumbered by the need to deal with the FCC were showing the impact a domestic satellite system could have. Impatient at the delay in establishment of a commercial system, the Department of Health, Education, and Welfare arranged with NASA to establish satellite communication with 300 receiving stations in or near schoolhouses in isolated areas of Alaska and the Rocky Mountains, bringing children in these communities, for the first time, educational opportunity equivalent to that available in more densely inhabited parts of the country.[59] And before 1972 was out, Canada had a domestic satellite launched, operating, and filled to capacity.

The entire process, from legislation to operation, took less than four years in Canada, as opposed to twelve in the United States. Canada's parliament first passed a communications satellite bill in March 1969 (when the Nixon administration was examining the Johnson administration's U.S. satellite recommendations and was about to ask for further delay while it prepared more of its own). This bill set up Telesat Canada, a semipublic corporation similar to Comsat except that the government retained partial ownership and the corporation was instructed specifically to build a domestic system.

By November 9, 1972, when Telesat launched its first satellite—called "Anik," the Eskimo word for brother—almost all the U.S. domestic satellite applicants had inquired about renting capacity on the Canadian satellite for use with U.S. earth stations, to get themselves a head start on acquiring business for their own satellites whenever the FCC got around to approving them. Several U.S. users, such as the cable TV system owners, also made inquiries. Ultimately, a change in Telesat's chartering legislation, an FCC waiver, and an agreement between the governments of the United States and Canada cleared the way for two U.S. system hopefuls to rent space on Anik II, the Canadian back-up satellite launched in April 1973. In 1973, RCA instituted communication between earth stations in New York and California, and between Alaska and the "lower 48, and Canada" using Anik II, but even this was delayed waiting for FCC final approval. The embarrassment of getting this country's first domestic satellite communication service from a Canadian spare part is compounded by the fact that the Canadian technology is borrowed almost entirely from the United States. The satellites were built by Hughes Aircraft in California, and launched under contract by NASA at Cape Kennedy.

As in 1970 following the FCC's *First Report and Order,* Western Union was first to file after the *Second Report and Order* in 1972. By ordering three Anik-type satellites (one fewer than it previously had intended) from Hughes in August, just as Hughes was completing its Canadian contract, the company obtained a favorable price.[60] On January 4, 1973, Western Union's domestic satellite system became the first to be approved by the FCC and in July 1974 it became the first to begin operation. Only a quarter of the satellite system's circuits were intended for business Western Union already had. To attract business for the rest of its channels, the company announced tentative rates in March 1973 that were dramatically lower than current rates for similar services using a terrestrial means. This provided hard evidence of the savings competition from satellites might have provided the consumer for the past decade. For example, Western Union wanted to charge $1000 a month for a coast-to-coast voice-grade circuit, one-third of AT&T's current rate of $3000 for the same service.[61]

Hughes and GT&E continued with their plans to put up a satellite system, despite a strong challenge by AT&T, which began filing briefs contesting General Telephone's right to compete for the long-distance telephone business. These were the cards Hough had said AT&T was not putting on the table back in 1971. It was not a strong hand. Among other items, the GT&E system was criticized because it "would simply be included in the overall network of interstate facilities," so that "the costs of its system would be obscured by their inclusion in prevailing settlement arrangements, and wasteful diseconomies would be encouraged."[62] This of course was exactly what AT&T itself intended to do with its own satellite system.

Fairchild Industries, which had entered the domestic satellite race only because it happened to have a highly advanced satellite it had designed for the government, came to realize that it lacked both the commercial communications expertise and the business volume necessary to make such a system profitable. So after the *Second Report and Order* it teamed up with Western Union International—an overseas cable company not connected to the domestic Western Union—to form American Satellite Corporation. In 1973, Amsat purchased three ordinary 12-channel satellites from Hughes (as opposed to the 120 channels in the satellite Fairchild proposed originally), with plans for Fairchild to build a 24-channel model later on. The new company hired away one of Comsat's top engineers to be their vice-president in charge of communications system development. The man who held the equivalent post at Comsat, Wilbur Pritchard, was quoted at the time by the *Washington Star-News* as saying, "I certainly was not surprised that American Satellite would turn to us to fill a key job. . . . I'm sure other people will [leave] before we're done."[63] Ten days later, Pritchard left Comsat to become president of Fairchild's space satellite subsidiary.[64]

Despite the lack of progress at the Commission and the losses from its staff, things were by no means as bleak for Comsat as they had seemed the previous June. Six months after the *Second Report and Order,* the FCC completely reversed itself once again on the question of domestic satellites.

Within a month after the June decision, Comsat and the telephone company both filed a long *Petition for Reconsideration.* AT&T protested the part of the ruling prohibiting it from using satellites to provide competitive specialized services. It repeated its insistence that since satellites offered no cost advantage, AT&T's use of them would not result in lower prices. Then it said that its commitment ahead of time not to lower prices proved it did not intend to indulge in unfair cross-subsidization. Therefore, AT&T argued, it should be allowed to use satellites for whatever it wanted—for the very reason, essentially, that there was no advantage to doing so. In discussing service to Hawaii, Alaska, and Puerto Rico, AT&T gave another example of its approach to economics. "The Commission attaches too much significance to the fact that satellite costs are distance insensitive," AT&T said.

> Indeed, from one perspective, satellite costs do not decline as distances become shorter—a fact which is particularly pertinent with respect to service between the Mainland and Puerto Rico, the cost of which would be no less than for service between the Mainland and points of Europe.[65]

An effective Commission would hold the telephone company to this analysis, and see to it that AT&T reduces its rates to Europe to equal those on calls to Puerto Rico—especially after the new domestic satellite industry brings competition to the Puerto Rican route. Comsat's petition pointed out many of the anomalies in the _Report and Order_ already discussed above.[66]

Comsat found a better angle. On September 6, it announced that it had agreed with MCI Lockheed to merge their two proposals and form a new corporation (soon dubbed CML) of which Comsat, MCI, and Lockheed would each initially own one-third. The surviving satellite system—and this was not emphasized in the subsequent publicity—was not Comsat's but MCIL's. The deal was made contingent upon the FCC's reversing itself on the original AT&T/Comsat proposal. This was for Comsat's benefit. And it was made contingent upon the FCC's _not_ reversing itself on preventing AT&T from competing for specialized services. This was for MCI. The companies' lawyers declared that this deal would solve all the problems the FCC was worried about. The FCC agreed.

The CML arrangement was just as economically sound as any other corporate grouping that emerged from the FCC's seven years of equivocating. What is enlightening about it is how it stands in contrast to everything both parties had been declaiming for so many years until the previous week. Comsat had commented repeatedly about the danger of letting equipment manufacturers or terrestrial carriers have an interest in satellites, and had wanted the FCC to ban MCIL on both grounds. MCIL, alone among the applicants, had wanted Comsat excluded from domestic communication because of irremedial conflicts with its international role.

The strangest aspect of the CML deal was MCIL's commitment to urge the FCC to reverse itself and approve the AT&T/Comsat deal. This company had been AT&T's most vociferous opponent on the very same issues for two and a half years, and MCI was AT&T's most aggressive competitor. What possible pro-AT&T argument could it offer, and why should the Commission accept any argument from a company that had so recently argued exactly the opposite? After all, what is the purpose of all the comments and reply comments and petitions for reconsideration allowed to interested parties under the Administrative Procedures Act? Supposedly, it is to let them aid the Commission in making good decisions by supplying persuasive arguments—not simply by staking themselves down on one side or another of the question at hand. The validity of MCI's former arguments against AT&T and Comsat—most of which the FCC had accepted—should not rely on MCI's continuing support if the whole process is to have any meaning, and MCI's withdrawal of endorsement for them should not change the FCC's view.

But MCI Lockheed was a master regulatory game player. Having raised fictional issues for years in its attempt to disqualify Comsat, it dispatched them with equal dexterity. For example, it previously had endorsed the view that AT&T's minority interest in Comsat might inhibit the company from competing effectively. Now it said that Comsat's reduction to a minority interest in the independent satellite system would eliminate this danger. Indeed the company that had seen conflict of interest in every liaison now saw it all in terms of balance of power.

> While MCIL to some extent may be in competition with MCI in the retail specialized services market, neither Lockheed nor Comsat suffers any restraint or inhibitions in vigorously competing in that market. And Lockheed, a space hardware supplier, cannot control the hardware acquisition of MCIL. The understanding proposes a structure for MCIL that blends the know-how, expertise, and vigor of its owners in a manner that at the same time removes or neutralizes institutional restraints and inhibitions.[67]

Likewise, it now advocated that Comsat be allowed to service domestic points also served by Intelsat because "the suggested Comsat conflicts would be diluted to insignificance" under the new arrangement. The company that was labeling Comsat's 33 percent interest in CML as "insignificance" was the same one that had identified AT&T's 29 percent of Comsat as "domination" the previous April.[68] Comsat's contribution to this new argument was to suggest that the factors it previously said made for an unfair competitor were now, in its opinion, those of a "stronger applicant."[69]

The other competitors suddenly found themselves taking Comsat's former position that the FCC should disallow arrangements that might lead to dangerous conflicts of interest. Comsat replied that "it would be incongruous to disqualify a particular consolidation on the ground that the participants have potentially conflicting outside business interests."[70] Incongruous, yes. Also a perfectly concise summary of Comsat's previous position. The competitors seized on the illogic of MCI Lockheed's attempting to justify the CML arrangement almost solely on the grounds that Comsat would have absolutely no influence in the new company. But they were forced into the equally questionable opposite position. Western Union International said there was only one possible conclusion to be drawn from the deal: "It is clear that Comsat will inevitably dominate the joint venture."[71] But was it clear? Comsat Chairman Joseph McConnell said shortly after the deal was announced that one advantage to Comsat would be that MCI had the marketing experience which Comsat, as a carrier's carrier in the past, did not. McConnell, whose company only the week before had been intending to spend $250 million on a system of its own, said, "I don't know where the business is going to come from."[72] With MCI doing the marketing, Lockheed in all probability building the satellite, and Comsat abandoning its own system plans in favor of the MCIL model, Comsat was left performing essentially the same function for these two companies as it wanted to perform for AT&T: public relations.

In its final domestic satellite *Report and Order* of December 22, 1972, the FCC virtually abandoned all its restrictions on Comsat.[73] This was done not by admitting that its former reasoning had been bogus, but by coming up with new reasoning to argue that the previous reasoning no longer applied. The decision was unanimous. The commissioners accepted MCI's and Comsat's new notion that conglomerate enterprises somehow represented a subtractive process of power and influence rather than an additive one. Why Comsat was less dangerous as an applicant now that it had teamed up with the leading microwave carrier and a leading satellite manufacturer was never spelled out. The wording of the decision was an exercise in justifying an arrangement that had been agreed to by the participants completely outside the Commission's control. Even AT&T had more or less agreed not to fight the provision against its competing for specialized services, in exchange for MCI's support of its deal with Comsat. Once this was agreed upon, the reasons were easy for the lawyers to manufacture and pass on to the FCC.

In approving the Comsat/MCI/Lockheed arrangement, the commissioners accepted the parties' balance of power theory, having been especially impressed by an elaborate multiclass board of directors system that they had created. They said this eliminated the fears they previously had held of letting Comsat simultaneously serve AT&T and compete for other business, and of letting Comsat serve U.S. points also served by Intelsat. But the Commission had invalidated the specific AT&T/Comsat contract in any event. It had said that even if Comsat decided to serve AT&T, it would have to do so as a carrier's carrier and provide circuits to all other communications firms on an equal basis. Six months later, it said this was no longer necessary because other carriers had many options to rent space on similar satellites. Of course this was just as true before the

June decision as it was the following December. In fact the only real change in the situation facing other carriers was that the satellite option most similar to the service Comsat intended for AT&T—Comsat's own second proposal—had been eliminated. In another concession to AT&T, the FCC said the telephone company could provide private line service by satellite to all parts of the federal government and not just the military, and committed itself firmly to remove all competitive shackles within three years.

The biggest surprise of the third report and order (called a *Memorandum Opinion and Order*) was the Commission's decision to make all its concessions to Comsat and AT&T contingent upon AT&T's selling out its 29 percent interest in Comsat. Since the logical basis for its other reversals was not strong, a large portion of its 50-page decision was spent discussing the reasons for this. As pointed out above, if the FCC felt AT&T's arrangement with Comsat had emerged because of undue influence by AT&T within Comsat, it made little sense to eliminate the influence but approve the arrangement anyway. The Commission listed many sensible reasons why AT&T should not be allowed to own such a large part of a company like Comsat. What it could not explain was why it had ignored all of them for so many years, only to insist on them in its third reversal of itself at the end of an eight-year controversy. The best it could do was to suggest at one point that, given the new Comsat arrangement with MCI, AT&T might now, through its ownership of Comsat and Comsat's shared ownership of a system with MCI, somehow dampen the enthusiasm of its fiercest competitor.

The FCC's second and third domestic satellite pronouncements of 1973 cleared the way for Western Union to launch two satellites and begin operation of its system, Westar, in 1974. But in the years that followed there were renewed delays, the situation continued to evolve, and a decade after ABC's original application for a domestic satellite system significant use of satellites for domestic communication still seemed several years away. Even the ultimate structure of the industry remained quite uncertain.

Two major corporate realignments had taken place, both somewhat surprising given the previous positions of the companies involved. Early in 1974 AT&T persuaded GT&E to lease independent capacity in AT&T's proposed satellite system, for use with General Telephone's own earth stations for the connection of long-distance calls between General Telephone's scattered local telephone systems. Since 1971, AT&T had argued that independent satellite long-distance service by its largest competitor—which has always been dependent upon AT&T's Long Lines division for long-distance service—would threaten the "integrity" of the long-distance network. GT&E, meanwhile, had been insisting on the great advantages of complete independence from the Bell System. Sensing that General Telephone's use of satellites was, at last, inevitable, AT&T made a deal to reassert at least partial control, and GT&E went along. At any rate, at the time of the deal the AT&T system still was several years off.

In July 1974 Comsat announced that MCI and Lockheed were selling out their interests in its own second proposed domestic satellite and that IBM, the giant computer company, wished to purchase a 55 percent interest in it. Computer data transmission will be one of the major uses for domestic satellites. IBM thus became the first major communications user with no previous stake in the industry to invest in satellite communication. This was one of the classes of parties that Comsat had insisted in 1971 should not be permitted to have a role in domestic satellite communication. As with MCI and Lockheed two years earlier, these objections were long forgotten. Comsat's competitors revived them, of course, and the FCC soon was inundated by briefs, counterbriefs, and demands for delay and reconsideration. Even without any substantial regulatory delay, the Comsat-IBM system was not planned to be operational until "late in the 1970s."[74]

Not only have the delays continued, but the promise of a competitive new industry has diminished. GT&E's desertion, and a series of FCC decisions and reversals that clouded the cable television picture, deprived the Hughes Aircraft system of its two major customers, and this plan was abandoned. Fairchild's proposal, known as Amsat (for American Satellite Corporation), was converted from an independent system to a lease of space on a Western Union Westar satellite. RCA leased space in the Canadian domestic system, though it retained plans for eventually launching its own satellite.

The threat of satellite competition was a major factor in AT&T's 1973 decision to lower its rates to the television networks by $18 million a year.[75] But this aside, the benefits of domestic satellite communication remained in 1975—a decade after technology had made them possible—purely speculative. In the interim, hundreds of millions of dollars have been spent on landlines, microwave towers, and switching centers, much of which might have been unnecessary if commercial satellite communication had been available. By the rules of rate-base regulation, the telephone company will be entitled to set its phone rates so as to make a profit on these investments even after satellites begin operating.

Whether further benefits appear and multiply—now that domestic satellite communication has begun—depends on the strength of the FCC's determination to foster competition and prevent AT&T from hiding satellite economies in a thicket of unnecessary terrestrial investments. If the telephone company is able to apply domestically some of the regulatory techniques it has learned in the international area, the FCC's long-overdue approval of commercial communications satellites for domestic use may be just the beginning.

8

Regulatory Innovations: The Corporate Eunuch, The Presidential Directors, and the White House Staff

June 1973 is a good vantage point from which to compare the corporation that resulted from the Communications Satellite Act to the one supporters and opponents of the Act had in mind during the 1962 debate. That was the month AT&T sold its 2,895,750 shares of Comsat; thus it was the last time Comsat closely resembled the entity Congress had created 11 years before. Furthermore, the prospectus prepared for the sale provides a thorough, objective description of the company and its activities.[1]

Comsat emerges from the prospectus as a fairly healthy young company. It was earning money (net income) in mid-1973 at a rate of almost $3 a share per year. (By mid-1974 the rate was approaching $4.) These were the shares it sold for $20 in 1964. Its profit had increased steadily since it first turned the profit corner in 1967 and seemed likely to continue doing so. The profits came from the 3000 circuits Comsat leased in the international system. But the company was involved in several promising ventures for future profit. These included two domestic satellite systems, one with AT&T and one with MCI and Lockheed; a proposed satellite system for communication between ships at sea (nicknamed "marisat"); and another for communications between airplanes and ground controllers ("aerosat"). Comsat also was helping to build an Intelsat earth station in Nicaragua, and investing $3.6 million in it. The company ran an ambitious research and development program, on which it spent $8.8 million in 1972.

Public confidence in the company continued high, and its price per share seemed to have little connection to its current financial condition. Released at $20 a share, the stock soon climbed past $60. In 1968, the year after its first profit, Comsat's stock had the highest price/earnings ratio of any profitable stock on the New York Exchange. After dipping to its all-time postissue low of $25 in 1970, the stock reached its peak of $84 in 1971, shortly after the launching of the first Intelsat IV, which contained more circuit capacity than all the other satellites and cables then in operation put together. When AT&T sold out, the stock was at $44, its lowest point in two and a half years, but still a healthy fifteen times earnings. (The stock continued to plunge, along with the rest of the market.)

Under "Selling Shareholder," the prospectus points out that "AT&T is the Corporation's largest customer. In 1972, service to AT&T provided 54% of the Corporation's total operating revenues." It went on that AT&T "has major interests in undersea communications cables which provide significant competition to the corporation." Also, "AT&T, the Corporation, and certain other communications common carriers are co-owners of four United States earth stations pursuant to an interim FCC policy." And, "AT&T and the Corporation are the parties to an agreement" to put up a domestic satellite system. This brief, frank collection of facts about their relationship was something neither AT&T nor Comsat had emphasized during the previous decade.

The Communications Satellite Act was a unique experiment, and it left an inherent ambiguity in the institution it created. Was Comsat supposed to be a private corporation like any other, or was it supposed to have some attributes of a government agency? Had its chartering by Congress given it an exclusive franchise on commercial satellite communication, or had it been nurtured with the intention of merely placing it on an equal footing with other private enterprises? As we have seen, this inherent ambiguity has been the source of great contention before the FCC, which has yet to clarify the situation. Comsat clearly has evolved further toward becoming a purely private company than its creators intended. This is the impression given by the 1973 prospectus—which mentions almost nothing about Comsat's unusual origins—and in discussions I had with officers of the company. The impression is supported by the changes that have taken place in the company since 1962.

Yet Comsat also has been willing to exploit its uniqueness. When requesting a monopoly on domestic satellite communication in 1966, Comsat wrote that it "views itself as having been granted a trust of national importance. In addition to being charged with the interest of its stockholders, it considers itself as having been charged also in the area of its charter, with the best interests of the United States in the broadest sense."[2] When the General Accounting Office discovered that the Space Agency was selling launches to Comsat at less than half their true cost, and the State Department argued that this was justified because Comsat's management of Intelsat was an important part of our foreign policy, Comsat encouraged this interpretation.[3]

Certainly the press and the public do not regard Comsat as a private corporation like any other. The *Wall Street Journal* led off a 1963 article about Comsat's stock offering by saying, "Americans with a bent for speculative investment will have an opportunity early next year. . .to buy shares in a company that has no earnings and no operating history, but has the U.S. Government squarely behind it."[4] News reports that Comsat is "a semi-government agency"[5] or that Congress gave half of it "to the companies" and half "to the public" foster in the public mind the idea that Comsat is something special.[6]

Of course the public/private ambiguity of Comsat's structure was intentional. In satellite communication, swift development and application of high technology was desired; the government and public at large had a tremendous stake in the outcome. Comsat was supposed to provide the genius and efficiency of private enterprise combined with the wider perspective and concern for the public interest of a government agency. Has it done so? This chapter—along with the discussion in earlier chapters of this book—presents good evidence that it has not. Comsat's officials, although they enjoy emoluments equivalent to those of other corporate executives, have not performed as fully competitively as a private company might ordinarily expect. In fact, many more of them come from backgrounds in government—especially the military—than from private enterprise.

Comsat's headquarters is in L'Enfant Plaza, a redevelopment area in the southwest section of Washington. (The two other major buildings in L'Enfant Plaza are occupied by Amtrak, the passenger railroad organization, and the U.S. Postal Service. Both are semipublic corporations modeled in part on Comsat.) It is a beautiful, luxurious building, an island of corporate splendor in a sea of sterile government architecture. Such a building is part of the corporate, rather than the government, life style, and in this respect Comsat is thoroughly the private company. The fact that it is located in Washington rather than New York reflects its close government ties.

So many former Pentagon officials are employed on Comsat's upper floors that the company is known in the communications industry as "The Old Soldiers Home." The Space Agency and other divisions of the government also contributed generously of their personnel. Of the four senior officers listed in the 1973 prospectus, the president, Dr. Charyk, had been assistant secretary of the Air Force; the general counsel, David Acheson, came from the Treasury Department; John A. Johnson, senior vice-president, came from NASA; and George P. Sampson, senior vice-president, was a retired general who once ran the defense communications system. Another vice-president, Lucius Battle, who later left briefly and then returned in 1974 as a senior vice-president, came from the State Department. In 1969, 25 percent of Comsat's top 130 officers came from the civil service, and 13 percent came from the military. By comparison, only 22 percent came from the communications industry, and 11 percent from electronics.[7] Compared to the top civil service salary of $36,000, Comsat paid General Sampson $69,074 in 1971, according to information on file at the SEC. Dr. Charyk got $116,383, up from $80,000 when he first went to work there in 1963. Comsat also pays membership fees for its executives at several Washington clubs.[8]

Comsat went through three chairmen between 1962 and 1975. Dr. Charyk was never promoted to that spot. Nor was he named chief executive officer, even though the third chairman, Joseph H. McConnell, retired president of Reynolds Aluminum, unlike his predecessors, was part-time. The first chairman was Leo D. Welch, retired chairman of Standard Oil of New Jersey (now Exxon). He got $125,000 a year from Comsat, and retired before the company made a penny. When Welch announced his retirement from Comsat in 1965, the *Wall Street Journal* said the search for a replacement was being kept quiet "to avoid embarrassing Joseph V. Charyk . . . who apparently isn't being considered."[9] There are various conspiracy theories about why Charyk has not become chairman. One person we interviewed believed it was because Charyk once bucked AT&T on some issue, and AT&T has never trusted him completely. Another said it was just the opposite—that Hough of Long Lines completely controlled Charyk, but that they wanted someone with a more independent image as chairman. Opinions also differ concerning Dr. Charyk's ability. One former Comsat executive interviewed for this book said that he "may be a good scientist, but couldn't run a carry-out as far as business in concerned." Another said that "the person who gets his way with Charyk is the last one he talks to." According to the *New York Times*, on the other hand, Dr. Charyk "might be the prototype of the bright young space scientist-executive."[10]

Comsat's chairman after Welch and before McConnell was James McCormack. McCormack, a retired two-star general in the Air Force, came to Comsat following jobs as vice-president of MIT and chairman of the Metropolitan Boston Transit Authority, and was paid $125,000 a year.[11] He retired in 1970 to go to work for Aerospace Corporation, a consulting firm located in another building at L'Enfant Plaza. That same year, Comsat gave Aerospace Corporation a research and development contract for $120,935. The next year, 1971, Comsat awarded Aerospace another contract for $60,468.[12] Immediately upon his retirement as chairman, McCormack himself got a consulting contract from Comsat for $30,000 a year plus an annual premium of $2,924.50 on a $50,000 life insurance policy plus "travel and living costs where appropriate." Here is a quotation from a copy of the contract filed with the SEC.

> WHEREAS, James McCormack was Comsat's chairman and chief executive officer for approximately four and a half years; and
>
> WHEREAS, James McCormack has acquired an expertise in the field of communications via satellite which is of unique and substantial value to Comsat; and
>
> WHEREAS, Comsat is of the view that its best interest would be served if appropriate arrangements were made to assure that James McCormack would be available to provide advisory and consultive services from time to time, as required, so that Comsat would have exclusive rights to his knowledge and experience in the field of satellite communication for a period of years. . .[13]

The contract ran for five years, which is half a year longer than McCormack spent as chairman, acquiring the expertise that was of such "unique and substantial value." McCormack also remained on the Comsat board, and received $200 for each board meeting he attended. This amounted to $3000 in 1971.[14]

Comsat employed 1222 people at the end of 1971, of whom 237 were officials or managers and 476 were professional or semiprofessional employees.[15] All doing what? Whether through their own fault, that of the FCC, or that of the terrestrial carriers, Comsat employees have very little to do. This was the opinion expressed repeatedly in my interviews of past and present Comsat employees; it is borne out by an examination of its activities. One former employee said, "That company could be run out of a telephone booth." Another, perhaps more sensitive to the impropriety of operating out of property owned by AT&T, expressed the same thought but suggested a room at the Mayflower Hotel. Several suggested that a lot of energy is expended on internal politicking. This indicates that despite the luxurious surroundings and generous remuneration, Comsat's executives have brought the culture of bureaucracy with them from their former Federal haunts.

The list of activities under "Business of the Corporation" in the 1973 Comsat prospectus is more impressive than it is substantial. For example, take the international satellite communication business which in 1973—and 1975—still supplied all of Comsat's operating revenues. Comsat is manager of the system on behalf of the Intelsat consortium, and it leases the system's circuits in the United States. It simply buys the circuit time from the consortium, then resells it to the four big terrestrial carriers—AT&T, Western Union International, RCA Globcom, and ITT Worldcom. This is almost entirely a bookkeeping operation. Comsat has little power to affect the volume of its own business. As a result, the volume is low. According to the prospectus, Comsat leased the equivalent of fewer than 3000 half-circuits in 1972. This is less than half the capacity of a single Intelsat IV satellite. All the empty circuits in the satellites Comsat had sent aloft could have been used at practically no additional cost. But because of the policy of the FCC and the attitude of the other carriers, these channels remained empty. Of course, we have seen that Comsat's own sluggish management and timid behavior helped to bring about the unfavorable FCC decisions in question.

As for the other side of Comsat's international business—its management of the international consortium—it has lost its policy-making role to an international secretariat, as we have seen, and has had its voting power in the deliberative body greatly reduced. In 1978, when its contract runs out, it may very likely lose its management role completely. This, too, would be at least partially its own fault. With the international body making its own decisions on future satellite configurations, and with the other international carriers doing all the marketing of whatever circuits Intelsat makes available to U.S. customers, Comsat's international job almost disappears.

Then there are the two proposed domestic systems, assuming that they both materialize. Comsat's role in these also is something of a facade. In one of them, Comsat will arrange for the launch of three satellites similar in design to the Intelsat IV, and construction of one more to be kept for emergencies. The entire capacity of these will be leased by AT&T at a preset fee of $1.25 million a satellite per month. The telephone company will build, own, and operate five earth stations around the country. Hughes Aircraft had designed and will build the satellites. The Space Agency, of course, will launch them. If we didn't know about the extended and complex evolution of the domestic satellite situation, under the supervision of the FCC, it would be difficult to understand what exactly is Comsat's contribution to this arrangement.

When Comsat teamed up with MCI and Lockheed to build a domestic satellite system to compete for non-AT&T business, it abandoned its own oft-revised plans for an independent system. The intended system of the CML Satellite Corporation—the ranking of the initials in the corporation's name notwithstanding—was identical to the one MCI and Lockheed were planning before they teamed up with Comsat. Once again, Comsat had nothing to offer its partners beyond some possible cash and a good reputation. MCI was the world's expert at marketing communications services in competition with AT&T, and Lockheed was one of the major communications satellite manufacturers. Comsat had nothing to do with the running of the short-lived company, which was run out of MCI's headquarters in Washington's downtown section, and shared many of MCI's executives. Comsat's later arrangement with IBM promised to require more of the company's satellite and communications expertise. But IBM retained a 55 percent interest, and the constant changing of plans delayed any actual operating system until the end of the decade.

The prospectus said Comsat was seeking FCC approval for a proposed satellite system ("marisat") for use by the U.S. Navy (until it could put up its own system in 1976) and by commercial shipping interests. Its evolution will sound familiar to those who have read earlier chapters of this book. The contract for the permanent system, which the Navy will share with the Air Force, was won by TRW Systems Corp. in 1972.[16] It may be worth as much as $140 million before it is concluded. The Navy needed something to serve its communications needs in the interim, and so requested bids from Comsat, ITT Worldcom, RCA Globcom, Western Union International, and a smaller firm involved in maritime communications. Comsat won the contract in March 1973; it was the only one that submitted a bid. Comsat immediately announced plans for a $70 million system to serve both the Navy and the commercial maritime market. This was the first time Comsat made any attempt to serve this potentially lucrative market.[17]

All the record carriers immediately filed comments with the FCC opposing Comsat's proposal, even though they had failed to produce any of their own. As usual, they said Comsat's proposed maritime service would be cream skimming. By appealing primarily to the larger ships, RCA said, Comsat would deprive the existing maritime communications industry of this business. This might cause these firms to fail, thus depriving all the small ships of necessary communications services. Western Union International said, "Comsat is seeking an obvious competitive advantage and a disruption of the Commission's authorized user policy" and suggested that "Comsat should operate the proposed satellite system as a carrier's carrier." Another firm complained that "the Comsat showing of 'urgent' need is really little more at this point than a repetition that there is great urgency."[18]

The FCC resolved the dilemma by giving Comsat permission to purchase the necessary satellites from Hughes (a modification of the Canadian Anik model), only if it turned its proposal into a consortium and shared ownership with the companies that had refused to compete with it. Comsat owns 80 percent and is the consortium manager.[19] By the time all the comtroversies had been settled, the system was planned for operation in 1975, making it of little use to the Navy.

The proposed "aerosat"—a satellite system for communication with airplanes in flight and another obvious application of satellite technology— remained under discussion for years after it could have been put into operation. It not only will reduce the cost of such communication, but will greatly reduce the likelihood of midair collisions, by allowing ground controllers to pinpoint plane locations with far greater accuracy, especially over oceans. Successful experiments with this type of communication were conducted as early as 1964, using NASA's Syncom satellite. In 1965, the U.S. airlines that belong to the Air Transport Association applied to be considered authorized users of any future Comsat system. They were, of course, rebuffed when the FCC decided to restrict authorized usership to the four international communications common carriers. But the airlines were so enthusiastic that they convinced the Federal Aviation Agency to drop its plans for an interim radio communication set-up for transoceanic flights, which would have cost $18,000 per plane.[20] Ironically, the FAA had wanted the interim system because it felt that an aeronautical satellite system would not be possible until the 1970s. The agency decided in 1965 that technology had proved it wrong. It did not realize that bureaucracy would prove it right after all.

The international aerosat proposal soon got bogged down in a dispute between Americans and Europeans over which part of the spectrum it should use. The Americans wanted to go with a VHF system, using technology which was already proven and which, not incidentally, the U.S. dominated. The Europeans wanted a UHF system, using an area of the spectrum more reliable over long distances, less crowded, and less dominated by American know-how. A disillusioned former Comsat executive said that Comsat's insistence on the more conservative technology in 1966 ruined an opportunity to win Intelsat approval for an aerosat as part of the consortium. "They backed a dead horse too late," he said. "There were arguments for years and eventually Comsat lost out. They wasted a lot of time that could have been bringing them a lot of money."[21]

In 1970, Comsat (having abandoned its attempts within Intelsat) formally applied to the FAA for exclusive rights to operate an aeronautical satellite using both the contested spectrum bands experimentally. This proposal was not considered promptly; nor was another from Boeing Aircraft. In 1971, the FAA announced that it had reached an agreement with the European Space Research Organization, negotiating for the European government-owned airlines, whereby the FAA and ESRO would put up a system owned half by the FAA and half by the ESRO. The Europeans were promised half the construction contracts. This proposal was endorsed by Secretary of Transportation John Volpe and Secretary of State William Rogers. But it was not pleasing to Clay Whitehead, director of the White House's Office of Telecommunications Policy. Whitehead had put out a statement earlier in the year saying that an aerosat system should be developed by a private corporation from which the FAA should lease its services. In this case, there also was heavy pressure on him from private enterprise itself to do something about the

FAA decision. In February 1972, Whitehead and Henry Kissinger both put out statements that the arrangement negotiated by the FAA, and approved by two cabinet departments, was unacceptable because it was not in accord with White House policy.[22] (This approach to government decision-making is examined more closely later in this chapter.)

The Europeans, having won the spectrum controversy, agreed to share an aerosat system with an American private company rather than with the FAA. In 1973, after various negotiations, the choice was down to either Comsat or RCA Globcom.[23] But there were still many major diplomatic and bureaucratic hurdles facing the increasingly impatient Europeans. Meanwhile, just as in the case of the domestic satellite, a decade had gone by since a major communications breakthrough was technologically possible, and it still had not become a reality. The Europeans hoped an experimental system would be in operation by late 1976. Comsat had spent $1.5 million in development costs and had nothing to show for it.

Comsat's other international venture is a joint effort with the government of Nicaragua to set up an Intelsat earth station in that country. According to the prospectus, Comsat had $3.6 million invested in this effort, a nominally private company called Nicatelsat. The prospectus says that Comsat "may seek similar joint venture opportunities . . . in those areas of the world where political and economic conditions would justify investment by the Corporation." But in 1973, Nicaragua was the only place outside the United States where Comsat had attempted to invest in satellite communication equipment. A former member of Comsat's International Development Division, whose job was to recruit new member countries for Intelsat, said middle-level Comsat executives made repeated efforts to encourage this kind of investment—all of which were blocked by the board of directors, which was dominated by the terrestrial carriers. The Comsat staffers saw several advantages to this kind of investment. By sharing Comsat's expertise and financial resources with underdeveloped countries that were short of both, it would be helping to fulfill the promise of the Comsat Act to bring the benefits of satellite communications to all parts of the world. It would be good for the company by increasing the potential volume of business on the Intelsat system. And it would create a profitable, satellite-related investment opportunity for the $100 million Comsat had in the bank because it had raised twice as much money as it needed back in 1964.

But the carriers on Comsat's board were not interested in any of these benefits for Comsat or the people of the world. They had their cables to worry about. ITT was especially uninterested; the company owned the communications systems of several underdeveloped countries, mostly in South America. ITT made clear from the beginning that if earth stations were to be built in these countries, ITT would build and run them, and perhaps some in other countries as well. Not suprisingly, Comsat's first tentative venture in Nicaragua came in 1970, two years after ITT sold its interest in the company. In 1974, a year after AT&T sold out, Comsat purchased a 40 percent interest in the international satellite communications system of Panama.[24]

Comsat's "temporary cash investments" are the clearest symbol of the company's sluggish management, and the comparison to ITT is appropriate. As one former Comsat employee put it, "Imagine what Harold Geneen would have done with that $200 million." Of the money Comsat raised from its stock offering in 1964, $145 million—almost three-quarters—was sitting in the bank in 1968. In 1972, $92 million—almost half—was still there.[25] Under normal circumstances, any company with such extreme liquidity and no debt would be ripe for takeover by a conglomerate. But Comsat's special legal status scared away prospective buyers.

The former middle-level executives we talked to, many of whom had come to the company thinking they were in on the beginning of a truly exciting experiment, used words like "stupid" and "complacent" and "lazy" to describe the general attitude on the upper floors of the Comsat Building, and to explain why they left. They described a company full of retired soldiers and former bureaucrats looking for a soft life, wracked by petty infighting, wasteful, and unambitious. A logical conclusion is that the Comsat solution—then unique, now common—does not bring to government decision-making the ruthless efficiency often attributed to private enterprise. Just the opposite: it places on supposedly private organizations the stultifying influence of government bureaucracy.

And yet this listless enterprise enjoyed, during its formative years, the consultative services on its board of directors of three men from the company that dominates American communications, AT&T, and of two men from the company that has a reputation for the sharpest management in the world, ITT. It seems hard to believe that Comsat's performance would have been so uninspired had these companies wanted it any other way. ITT made its position clear when it sold its stock in 1968 for three times what it had paid in 1964 (when it had been careful *not* to make its position clear). ITT said it was "in basic disagreement" with Comsat's attempts to "extend its role in the international communications field" beyond that of "the U.S. 'carriers' carrier' for the global satellite system."[25] One former Comsat insider complained, in a vein similar to that of several persons we talked to, "How could any of the others argue with the carrier directors? They think communications 24 hours a day. What these six common carrier people did was help Comsat stay out of the communications business." This is the carriers' lasting contribution to Comsat, now that they have left its board. Certainly it is not what the supporters of the Comsat Act in 1962 professed to intend.

Opponents of the Comsat Act predicted that having representatives of the terrestrial carriers on its board would put Comsat at an extreme disadvantage in situations where it might compete with these carriers. Not only would they be able to influence Comsat policy, but they would be able to gain private company information that would help the other carriers competitively. This seems obvious. We asked Comsat how this problem was handled in the many situations—of which it was so proud—when it competed against the carriers for some kind of business. This was in 1971, when AT&T was the only carrier with representatives remaining on Comsat's board. Comsat answered:

> The AT&T-elected directors have abstained from discussion and voting with respect to contracts between Comsat and AT&T . . . and often have withdrawn from Board meetings when such agreements have been considered. Moreover, when a discussion of adversary matters, or of matters directly affecting AT&T, has occurred (*e.g.*, the reduction in rates for satellite services in the Atlantic region), the AT&T-elected directors have either abstained from participating in the discussion or have withdrawn from the meeting.[26]

In at least one instance, however, a carrier clearly used inside information gained at a Comsat board meeting to Comsat's competitive disadvantage. In this case, the carrier was ITT. It involved the so-called "30-circuits" dispute, discussed in Chapter 5, in which the Pentagon decided, despite the FCC's Authorized Users doctrine, to lease 30 circuits across the Pacific directly from Comsat, rather than dealing through the other carriers. The reason was that Comsat was offering a lower price. In the middle of this complicated proceeding, ITT went to the U.S. Court of Appeals in the District of Columbia with an emergency petition for an injunction to prevent the Defense Communications Agency from signing with Comsat for the 30 circuits.[27] ITT said it had discovered ("petitioner is informed and believes") that Comsat had offered DCA a rate $3000 a year less per circuit than what it had offered to ITT (which, of course, planned to turn around and sell it to DCA). ITT said that the differential rate violated a section of the Comsat Act providing for "nondiscriminatory access" to the satellite system for all "authorized users." The company neglected to mention that what it concurrently was seeking, and eventually got, from the FCC was a reverse differential, forcing all users including the Pentagon to pay a *higher* rate to the carriers themselves than they were paying Comsat. What is interesting is how ITT found out about Comsat's offer to the DCA. "Petitioner's information and belief," the petition said, "is derived from the Memorandum of the Chairman of the Board of Directors of Comsat for the Directors relating to the Board Meeting of June 17, 1966." Of course, AT&T had access to Comsat's internal memos all those years, too.

The President of the United States is entitled to appoint three directors to Comsat's board, with the advice and consent of the Senate. This aspect of Comsat's structure is at the core of the creative ambiguity inherent in the Communications Satellite Act of 1962. These directors are presented as proof that the interests of the American people are being protected in this government-chartered corporation and that domination by the private carriers is being prevented. Yet any attempt to investigate their effectiveness in representing the public meets the response that they are ordinary directors with ordinary responsibilities like any others, except that their method of appointment is a little unusual. In fact, so far as can be determined, this is exactly how they have approached their duties. The only difference between the presidential directors and the privately appointed ones seems to be that the former have little knowledge of communications and a wider range of outside duties, and therefore are far less influential within the corporation.

In July 1971, while trying to arrange interviews with people at Comsat, we asked Comsat general counsel David Acheson about the duties of the various directors. He said, "The Series I directors represent the investors, the carrier directors represent the carriers, and the presidential directors represent all the shareholders." When we asked whether the presidential directors were not supposed to represent the public, Acheson replied in a patronizing tone, "Most books on corporate law will tell you that corporate directors represent the stockholders."[28] Barely a week before, however, Comsat had filed comments in the domestic satellite docket attempting to refute charges of AT&T domination, saying that the presidential directors were meant "to act as a counterbalancing public influence both to the carrier interests and noncarrier stockholder interests."[29] These comments were signed, on behalf of Comsat, by Acheson.

Comsat's 1971 written comment is a good summary of the view expressed repeatedly during the 1962 debate by members of the Kennedy Administration and other supporters of the Comsat Act. The provision for presidential directors was used to deflate both the contention that expensive technology developed at government expense was being turned over free of charge, and the prediction that AT&T and other carriers would control the company. At various times it was suggested that the presidential directors would exert a positive public-interest influence within the company, or at the very least serve as a communications link, letting the President know what the company was up to and letting the company know the President's views on important matters. Attorney General Robert Kennedy suggested more vaguely that the presidential directors' job would be "protecting the interests of the public at large, as distinguished from the Government." But as Herman Schwartz pointed out in the *Harvard Law Review,* neither the Comsat Act itself nor the committee reports that preceded it discuss the specific duties of presidential directors, beyond their method of appointment and term limit of three years.[30]

Comsat's articles of incorporation say specifically that "Each director, regardless of the method of his appointment or election, shall have the same fiduciary duty to the Corporation and its shareholders."[31] In its written comments to me, Comsat was careful to define this section to mean that the duties of directors are identical *"so far as the Corporation and the shareholders are concerned."* It insisted further on, however, that "any conflict that might be seen in the duties of the Presidentially appointed directors to the the President and the Corporation . . . we would characterize as more theoretical than real." Asked what benefit the presidential directors had brought to the company, Comsat mentioned not the benefit of the government's viewpoint (which would have been difficult to support considering the directors the Presidents have appointed) but "their individual and collective business experience and maturity of judgment."[32]

President Johnson announced the names of his first three representatives to the board of what he called "this great adventure between government and free enterprise" in September 1964: Frederic Donner, Clark Kerr, and George Meany. These were the heads, respectively, of General Motors (retired), the University of California, and the AFL-CIO.[33] Drew Pearson quoted Johnson as saying to friends about his selections, "We've just got to have good men running the government, and I am proud of some of the men who have been willing to join me." According to Pearson, Johnson told Donner, "The President of the United States can't run the country all by himself. He's got to have help."[34]

Johnson's original appointments established a tradition that continued for several years. Presidential directors would represent the three great constituencies of business, labor, and education. There were at least two other approaches Johnson might have taken. He might have appointed actual high-ranking members of the government, such as cabinet officials, to the Comsat board. This would have established Comsat far more clearly as a company with a special relationship to the government. Or he might at least have appointed men with expertise in communications. Men with full-time duties and overriding interests elsewhere, no knowledge of communications, and no mandate to behave otherwise than as ordinary directors of a private company hardly were likely to provide the kind of public interest protection they were used as a guarantee of during the 1962 debate.

We wrote all three of the original presidential directors asking them how they interpreted and exercised their duties under the act. We also asked for interviews. Neither Meany nor Donner answered our letters. Kerr wrote that he could not shed any light on the role of presidentially appointed directors in semipublic corporations, because "it was never possible for me to attend a [Comsat] meeting."[35] Several people we interviewed said that most presidential directors rarely attended board meetings, and that they certainly attended less often than directors who had been privately appointed. We asked Comsat to supply us attendance figures so we could check out this charge. The company responded with a list of the average percentage of *all* directors attending board meetings during each year since its founding. This, of course, was useless information. There was no need for Comsat to be so disingenuous, because information on file with the Securities and Exchange Commission indicates that the attendance records of presidential directors are only moderately below average. Between the years 1965 and 1971, Frederic Donner attended 76 board meetings; George Meany attended 62. Clark Kerr resigned in the middle of 1965. He was replaced by William A. Hagerty, president of the Drexel Institute in Philadelphia. Hagerty and *his* successor attended 82 meetings during those years. By comparison, Dr. Charyk attended 91 meetings between 1965 and 1971, more than Meany but not as many as James Dingman, head of AT&T's Long Lines division. The best attendance record—104 meetings—was that of Bruce Sundlun, a Washington lawyer and one of Comsat's original incorporators.[36]

The ineffectiveness of the presidential directors is no doubt a result less of low attendance (all directors, except for executives of the company, get $200 for each board meeting they attend) than of their lack of expertise. Comsat declined to discuss the individual contributions or duties of various directors and said it had made no public statements on the matter. One former Comsat executive told us "George Meany doesn't know squat about the communications industry" and "all Hagerty did for Comsat was to play golf with Joe Charyk." Another interviewee said that Meany did help design Comsat's pension plan. Donner, however, was credited by several people we talked to with a very active role in the company. But apparently he has acted less as a "counterbalancing public influence . . . to the carrier interests" than as a general advocate of financial conservatism. One man who had prepared a detailed report urging that Comsat use some of its enormous reserve of cash to invest in an earth station for a certain South American country was told the plan had been vetoed by the board primarily at the insistence of Donner, who had said that GM once put money into that country and lost it. This kind of influence would make Donner a valuable asset within Comsat for both ITT and AT&T. Certainly as the retired chairman of the second largest corporation in the world, he must have felt more at home than his two fellow appointees, sharing a board table with three representatives of the largest corporation, AT&T, a former chairman of Jersey Standard (now Exxon), Leo Welch, and the two representatives from ITT.

President Nixon disrupted the business/labor/education symmetry of Comsat's presidential directors in July 1970 when he gave the putative education seat to Rudolph Peterson, retired chairman of the Bank of America. The reason, openly announced, for Peterson's appointment is a telling antidote to any claim that presidential directors offer any unusual public interest protection within Comsat. Peterson had been a regular Series I or public stockholder director until Comsat's annual meeting the previous May, when he had resigned. Hagerty, who had been a presidential director, was elected to replace him. Then President Nixon appointed

Peterson to replace Hagerty in one of the three government seats. The purpose of all this? Peterson, who had joined Comsat's board only the year before (1969), also was a director of Time, Inc. This, it turned out, was against Comsat's bylaws, because Time owns some television stations and cable TV outlets. The bylaws forbid interlocking directorates with other communications interests because of potential conflicts of interest. But the company's bylaws clearly do not restrict the President of the United States, over whose selections for its board Comsat ostensibly had no influence. So Peterson and Hagerty switched places. And Peterson, far from being a countervailing public influence to balance the communications interests, was made a presidential director precisely *because* his involvement with another communications common carrier disqualified him as a private director. Hagerty, meanwhile, was able to be elected privately.[37]

Peterson is an interesting example of the closed circle of business connections that had far more influence within Comsat than, say, the President of the United States. In the résumé he submitted to the Senate Commerce Committee when it was considering his fitness for its advice and consent as a presidential director, Peterson listed no fewer than five corporations of which he was a director, all of whose names began with "Kaiser." (Besides these, he was a director of ten other companies.) Edgar Kaiser, son of the late Henry and present-day head of the California-based Kaiser empire, was one of Comsat's original thirteen incorporators. Kaiser's Washington lawyer is Lloyd Cutler, and Cutler's law firm is "of counsel" in all of Comsat's domestic satellite filings. In 1971, Comsat paid Cutler's law firm $71,996. In more recent years, Cutler's bill has been somewhat lower, but in 1966 it was $134,000.[38] Another man listed as "of counsel" in Comsat's filings is Donald Turner, a professor at Harvard Law School. Turner and Cutler went to the same law school, Yale, and once worked for the same law firm.[39] Turner was assistant attorney general for antitrust under President Johnson. His successor under President Nixon, Richard McLaren, said in 1971 that the Comsat arrangement was "contrary to the normal antitrust prohibitions against anticompetitive stock acquisition and director interlocks" in the Clayton Act. By that time, Turner was working for Comsat. Another Comsat incorporator, and a director until he left to join the Nixon cabinet in 1969, was David Kennedy, chairman of Continental Illinois Bank. Continental Illinois received $313,062 from Comsat in 1971 as its stock transfer agent, making it the company's third largest outside contractor. Continental Illinois also held $17.5 million of Comsat's "temporary" cash reserves.[40] The incorporators, like the presidential directors, all were appointed by the President and approved by the Senate.

In 1973, Peterson resigned as a presidential director and became a Series II or carrier-appointed member of the board. This, too, was a technicality. AT&T had already announced its plan to sell its stock, and so offered to give its board seats to whomever the other board members recommended.[41] Strangely, Peterson remained on the board of Time, Inc. as well. Meanwhile, George Meany also had submitted a request to President Nixon that he be allowed to retire from the board of "this extraordinary corporation."[42] To replace him as guardian of the public interest, President Nixon nominated Frank Fitzsimmons, president of the Teamsters Union.[43] Two months before this White House announcement in May 1972, Fitzsimmons had been the only union representative to remain on the President's Pay Board, after Mr. Meany and two others had quit in a huff.

In 1975 these two vacancies among the three Presidential directors had yet to be filled. Fitzsimmons's scheduled hearing before the Senate Communications subcommittee in June 1972 was postponed when he became ill. The nomination officially died at the end of that session of Congress. According to Nicholas Zapple, who runs the Communications subcommittee for Chairman Pastore, the White House never resubmitted Fitzsimmons's nomination. Nor did it rush to nominate someone to replace Rudolph Peterson. This job would have fallen to Clay Whitehead, director of the White House Office of Telecommunications Policy, who was not enthusiastic about presidential directors. He told us in 1971 that so far as he was concerned, "they are custodians of the stockholder interest and the public interest only where the public interest is similar." He said they would resent taking orders from the government on how to vote within the company, and even could "find themselves subject to suit if they ever voted the public interest over stockholder interest." He added, "I don't see much sense in having presidentially appointed directors on a private corporation."[44]

In March 1973 the Office of Management and Budget circulated some proposed amendments to the Communications Satellite Act. The amendments had been written by Whitehead's OTP. Among other changes, the bill would have removed provisions in the Comsat Act providing for presidential directors, along with those referring to carrier directors (reflecting AT&T's decision to sell its stock). It would have provided that Comsat be "treated, insofar as possible, as any other stock corporation would be under the laws of the District of Columbia."[45] The OTP's proposed revision of the Comsat Act, officially introduced in both houses early in 1974, was one of many issues that got sidetracked in the subsequent rush of Watergate events.[46] By the opening of the new Congress in 1975 no official changes had been made, even though two of the President's three seats had been vacant for up to three years. Still, it seemed likely this particular regulatory innovation, so widely hailed in the early sixties, was doomed.

Whitehead's dislike of ambiguous policies that encourage hypocrisy and confusion was one of the admirable influences he had on government communication policy during his controversial tenure at the OTP. His position during the domestic satellite controversy was one example, and his belittling of the concept of presidential directors is another. He professed a desire to prevent the government from muddying the waters of competition. Unfortunately, his real contribution was to supervise the abandonment of the FCC's regulatory power—not to the market system, but to the White House. Whitehead's Office of Telecommunications Policy, like Kissinger's expanded National Security Council and Nixon's Office of Management and Budget, represented an effort to remove government power from departments and agencies at least partially subject to popular and congressional supervision, and place it in the hands of presidential aides. If the corporate eunuch and the presidential directors were President Kennedy's and President Johnson's contributions to the art of government regulation of economic activity, the enlarged role of the White House staff was President Nixon's.

Clay Whitehead was a 30-year-old MIT Ph.D. from Neodesha, Kansas who volunteered his services to the Nixon Campaign in 1968. After the campaign he got a job as an aide to Peter Flanigan, President Nixon's assistant in charge of relations with the business world. Whitehead wrote "Reorganization Plan No. 1 of 1970," which created the Office of Telecommunications Policy to replace the Office of Telecommunications Management. President Nixon then nominated him to be the first director of the OTP, after several other people refused the job. Whitehead represented a type of presidential aide that has since become associated in the public mind with the Nixon administration—serious, somewhat arrogant, outspoken but humorless and unflamboyant compared to the style associated with Presidents Kennedy and Johnson. He puzzled *Broadcasting Magazine* when it first profiled him in 1970. "He does not come on as the whiz-kid type familiar to Washington,"*Broadcasting* wrote.

> And he expresses a respectful, almost old-fashioned feeling for those older than he with whom he deals—which is almost everyone—although he is not intimidated in talking to industry senior vice presidents or high government officials. "I respect their experience and knowledge. I don't have 30 years experience," he says, "but I can organize information, find out what is needed and get it.". . .
>
> In the briefing he gave reporters, he surprised them with the candor with which he discussed the broad powers that are vested in OTP as the President's arm in telecommunications matters—powers that he intended to use. There was no tone of aggressiveness in his recital; rather one of considerable self-confidence.[47]

Broadcasting quoted a participant who was present when some FCC officials went to the White House to talk to Whitehead about the domestic satellite issue. "We explained our position for 20 minutes, and got absolutely no reaction in all that time—not a word, no change in expression. When we finally stopped talking, there was a pause, then he said, 'Is that all?'"[48]

Whitehead's OTP replaced the Office of Telecommunications Management, which was part of the Office of Emergency Preparedness and concerned itself primarily with spectrum management for the government's own communications needs. The OTP was entirely different. President Nixon said its purpose was to "enable the executive branch to speak with a clearer voice and to act as a more effective partner in discussions of communications policy with both the Congress and the Federal Communications Commission." He added that the OTP "would take away none of the prerogatives or functions assigned to the Federal Communications Commission."[49]

Whitehead, however, was quoted as saying that "the White House has no qualms about seeking to influence the Commission or any other so-called independent agencies."[50] There was good reason to believe Whitehead, as this was one month after his memo that totally reversed FCC policy concerning the domestic satellite.

Despite these advance storm warnings, the new office was praised in almost all quarters. The FCC voiced no objection. The *New York Times* editorialized that the reorganization "gives belated recognition to the complexities of Government-regulated broadcasting."[51] Senator Pastore praised it. As late as July 1971, RCA Chairman Robert Sarnoff joined Whitehead in warning the American Bar Association that government regulatory techniques had not kept pace with technology in the communications field. Sarnoff said these techniques were "relics of the age of Marconi" and "hopelessly ill-adapted to the age of the satellite." Whitehead said a new approach was needed "of a less detailed, more flexible character," which he called "regulation by policy."[52] I interviewed Mr. Whitehead the next month, August 1971, and he expressed much the same opinion.

Shortly thereafter he began to gain notoriety. The "policy" by which he wished to regulate came into sharper focus, and broadcast executives like Mr. Sarnoff regained some of their enthusiasm for Marconi-age relics. In November 1971, Whitehead began his attack on liberal bias in public television. The following summer President Nixon vetoed government funding of the Corporation for Public Broadcasting. Then Whitehead gutted the structures that had been created to protect PTV programming from political influence and filled various posts with Nixon loyalists. During this time, he also challenged the FCC's rule-making authority concerning cable TV by summoning all the parties to the dispute to his office and browbeating them into an agreement more to his liking than what the FCC was inclined toward. Whitehead's notoriety peaked in the fall of 1972 with his famous "ideological plugola" attack on the commercial networks, and his challenge to the local stations to censor them. In 1973 silence descended on Whitehead as suddenly as it had left him in 1971. He returned quietly to academia the next year, following the Watergate denouement.

Before he became more widely known through his attacks on television, Whitehead demonstrated his theory of government "regulation by policy" in action when he squelched an effort by the Justice Department and a member of the Senate to amend the Communications Satellite Act. Although in other circumstances he claimed to favor competition and disdain government interference with private enterprise, he used his power to defend the antitrust exemption granted to the terrestrial carriers by the Comsat Act and the FCC decisions that followed it.

As we have seen, Senator Mike Gravel of Alaska felt that the presence of the carriers on Comsat's board led to abnormally high prices for

Intelsat circuits and delay in introduction of domestic satellite communication, which were especially detrimental to his constituents, isolated as they are from one another and the rest of the country. Gravel made an attack on Comsat's structure one of his major issues almost from the beginning of his Senate term. In September 1969 Gravel wrote President Nixon urging new legislation to make Comsat independent both of the carriers and of foreign interests, which preferred cables to satellites. In October he got a letter from Peter Flanigan saying that "the communications industry is very complex," and that a review of satellite communications was "entirely appropriate." "We are giving your views serious consideration," Flanigan added.[53] Correctly believing that these were empty phrases, Gravel wrote directly to Richard McLaren, assistant attorney general for antitrust, asking "whether a de facto antitrust situation has developed in the Comsat Act of 1962 as now written" and asking for McLaren's opinion of a proposed bill to get the carriers out of Comsat.[54] McLaren responded in January 1971, almost a year later. But surprisingly, he endorsed Gravel's views and even went beyond them. McLaren said the Justice Department

> would favor enactment of legislation along these lines to eliminate direct carrier control or influence over Comsat. Such a step, combined hopefully with some modification of regulatory constraints on Comsat's activities (discussed below), would significantly enhance Comsat's competitive potential.[55]

Below, McLaren said that the FCC's Earth Station and Authorized Users decisions "have been at least as significant a factor in limiting Comsat's competitive potential vis-à-vis existing carriers," though he was vague about whether he saw a legislative or regulatory solution to this dilemma. He was clear in saying that the act itself was inconsistent with the provisions of the Clayton Antitrust Act, and that in practice the carriers had been able to exercise anticompetitive influence over Comsat. In one paragraph, McLaren pointed out that his position was consistent with the original position of the Justice Department during the 1961–1962 debate, ignoring Attorney General Kennedy's crucial role in compromising that very position. Then he said it was consistent as well with the Nixon Administration's policy of "placing 'more reliance on economic incentives and market mechanisms in regulated industries.'" McLaren later accepted a Federal judgeship. Unfortunately, this was not before he had made decisions in the famous antitrust case against ITT, decisions that would come back to haunt him.[56]

McLaren's principled stand over Comsat got him into a considerable muddle. Immediately on receiving McLaren's letter, Gravel put out a press release saying, "The Nixon Administration has endorsed Senator Mike Gravel's . . . contention that communications carriers should be 'eliminated' from the Board of Directors of the Communications Satellite Corporation (Comsat)."[57] The story was picked up this way by the press. The *Washington Star,* for example, reported:

> The Justice Department—presumably with White House backing—has called for legislation that would force American Telephone & Telegraph Co. and other major communications firms out of ownership and management of Communications Satellite Corp.[58]

Within hours, Whitehead put out a statement saying that the McLaren letter did *not* represent the official position of the Nixon administration. He said, "The administration has formulated no specific views regarding this policy area and has no plans for the submission of legislation on this subject." Whitehead implicitly chided McLaren for forgetting that he was a bureaucrat, unable, like those in the White House, to consider the larger picture.

> This is a particularly important and complex area of communications policy that goes beyond antitrust concerns alone. The OTP will take into account all pertinent considerations before deciding what, if any, policy recommendations and legislative proposals will best serve the national interest.[59]

So it appeared that Senator Gravel had willfully misinterpreted and deviously publicized the McLaren letter, and the Nixon Administration had been a victim of its own freewheeling openness. But in fact the White House *had* approved the Justice Department position before it had been passed on to Gravel. This is one reason why the whole process took almost a year. (McLaren also sent a copy to the FCC, which drafted—but never sent—a reply disagreeing with the Justice Department. Typically, the Commission said Gravel's bill was inappropriate because it was considering all these issues in its TAT-6 docket. Needless to say, none of them were resolved there.) A young McLaren assistant who dealt with communications matters, Joseph Bell, told us that not only had the OTP seen the letter, but the person who had written it later took a job with the OTP. Certainly the philosophy behind the McLaren letter would seem to be in keeping with Whitehead's own laissez-faire attitude.[60]

When we asked Whitehead about the McLaren letter episode, only several months after it occurred, his explanation was vague and contradictory. At first he said the problem was that Gravel's query had been misdirected. "We would probably take a position if the bill was submitted to us," he said. But Gravel's complaint, at least, *had* been submitted to the White House, and had been brushed off by Peter Flanigan, Whitehead's superior. It seems unlikely Whitehead had not known of this. Asked what position he would take if the bill were submitted to him, Whitehead said, "I suppose we would conclude that the bill was premature pending our proposals for the international communications industry." Whitehead had promised these proposals to Senator Pastore at his confirmation hearing in 1970. In 1973, after repeated prodding, his office produced ten typed pages of vague comments, but no legislation. When we told Mr. Whitehead earlier in the interview that the Senate Commerce Committee had told us Gravel's bill was being held up pending the OTP's international recommendations, he said, "I hadn't heard of that one."[61] So much for "regulation by policy."

9

The Old Frontier

P resident Kennedy chose the metaphor of the frontier to symbolize
his administration because frontier imagery has a traditional
appeal to Americans. The American adventure in outer space gave a lit-
eral legitimacy to Kennedy's appropriation of the phrase "New Frontier." As we saw in Chapter 1, he used it to good advantage. The Comsat
arrangement was Kennedy's major institutional contribution to development of outer space. But although the Comsat arrangement—both in
its failures and its successes—may seem a singular product of twentieth
century corporate America, and thus far removed from the frontier
spirit of individualism and roughhewn honesty, a comparison of development of America's two frontiers a century apart reveals striking paral-
lels. It not only suggests how Comsat came about, but even may explain
what might come next.

In the 1960s friends and foes alike saw Comsat as a unique enterprise.
Vice President Hubert Humphrey called it "an amazing new devel-
opment . . . the partnership of government and private enterprise."[1]
Estes Kefauver saw it as an aberration in the flow of U.S. economic history.

Mr. President, this is the first time in the history of the United States
that one type of carrier would be allowed to control another. . . .
I cannot recall any time in the history of our Nation in which the

217

Government has carved out an exception in the antitrust laws for the purpose of itself creating a monopoly. I had always thought that the purpose of the Government was to foster free and competitive enterprise and to prevent monopolies from growing up.[2]

But the Comsat phenomenon is isolated from neither the American past nor the American future.

Take, for example, the role of the railroads in the development of the American West, what a historian calls "the greatest . . . of all the publicly supported improvements of the nineteenth century."[3] As in the case of development of outer space, popular clamor and national pride required a large investment for exploration and development that private business *appeared* unwilling to undertake. In both centuries, alienation of public domain and financial support from government made development possible, even though government ownership was rejected for ideological reasons, to the benefit of powerful private interests. Various kinds of government supervision were concocted, but this supervision served less to protect the public investment than to consolidate and heighten the economic power of a small part of the private sector.

Many reasons were given to justify government aid to railroad development in the nineteenth century; most of them will sound familiar. Construction of a railroad to the Pacific was a manifestation of patriotism, a reflection of "the spirit of public improvement."[4] The finished product would be the "nation's pride."[5] The railroad would be a financial boon to all the nation's citizens in many ways—among others, "by enlarging trade, creating new demand for labor, raising greatly the value of land in all directions, rewarding industry by large profits."[6] As with Comsat and many similar projects, the final argument lay in defense and foreign policy considerations. By encouraging Western settlement, the railroads would secure United States control over the continent once and for all, and prevent a foreign invasion.[7] (It also was hoped they would unite the economies of North and South and make a split more difficult.[8]) They would also give the nation an edge in international commerce, according to one of Senator Pastore's distinguished predecessors.

Commerce is power and empire. Its conquests are greater, more universal and enduring, than those of arms. . . . Give us, as this railroad would, the permanent control of the commerce and exchanges of the world, and in the progress of time and the advance of

civilization, we would command the institutions of the world. . . .
Either England or the United States must in the end control that
commerce. . . . We have not a day or an hour to lose. . . . Shall we . . .
wait until England shall have secured the monopoly of this commerce for herself? Is this a British Parliament, or is it a Congress of
American statesmen and patriots to whom such an appeal shall be
made in vain?[9]

(Rhetorical devices have changed little in a hundred years. Ralph Yarborough asked on the Senate floor in 1962, "Is this the council hall of the
states, or has the Senate become the council hall of the corporations?"[10])

Federal subsidies of railroad construction took two main forms: land
grants and loan guarantees. There was also extensive state and local aid,
and there were other minor forms of federal subsidy.

Before 1860, most government aid to railroads came from or through
the states. "Railroads were not considered as purely business ventures but
rather as public works benefiting the state and nation," writes historian
Robert Riegel, and it was not considered unnatural for one man to be
head of both the state railroad line and the state senate internal improvement committee.[11] Just as few people saw a conflict of interest in the FCC's
appointing a committee of terrestrial communications carriers in 1961 to
decide public policy for communications satellites, few people saw any
conflict of interest here. Most local aid was given for less ostensibly
altruistic reasons: to entice a railroad terminal to one's city, lest it be built
elsewhere, dooming a place to obscurity.

State aid, naturally, began in the East. Massachusetts voters defeated a
plan for a state-owned road in 1830 and other plans for state stock
subscriptions to private companies were never executed. Nevertheless,
the state used its chartering prerogative to nurture certain lines with
monopoly status. By the time of the Civil War, Massachusetts had invested
$7,350,000 in railroad promotion.[12] In the West, beginning in 1849,
Missouri loaned $25 million and Minnesota $5 million in state bonds to
private railroad companies for railroad construction. Other frontier legis-
latures and town councils passed similar plans, often following heavy
lobbying of their members, or actual financial involvement. Texas offered
to lend any railroad company $6000 per mile from the public school fund.
State and local direct monetary subsidies of transportation construction
before 1860, mostly to railroads, totaled more than $400 million.[13]

Despite these subsidies, such was the celebration and power of private enterprise that none of these states developed the railroads themselves, as was done in Europe. Nevertheless, many states were left with millions in debts when panics drove bond prices below par, funds became insufficient for construction, firms went bankrupt, and private owners fled.

> Excessive debts were created in a spirit of buoyant optimism, with little thought as to their amount, their probable effect, or their repayment. Many of the schemes were ill-advised and predestined to failure. Lack of supervision, insufficient knowledge, waste, incompetence, and corruption played their parts. . . . The whole experience constituted one of the important causes of a revulsion in feeling and the creation of the later anti-railroad movement.[14]

Federal aid mainly took the form of massive giveaways of public land. These began in 1850 with a grant to the Illinois Central Railroad, engineered by an ambitious young senator named Stephen Douglas. Alienation of public domain to private companies—whether it is land, areas of outer space, or parts of the crowded radio spectrum—is the equivalent to giving them money. (The areas of outer space we have given away are valuable because there is a limited number of them suitable for synchronous satellites.) These kinds of subsidies have a great advantage for the government and the companies involved, however, because they are "hidden." Their value is never computed, and they never appear on the government's balance sheets to arouse the curiosity and anger of taxpayers. In the 1850s, Congress authorized grants of land to every state along the west bank of the Mississippi, which in turn gave the land to railroad developers. After 1862, the federal government began making direct land grants to the railroads. Ultimately, Congress authorized grants directly to railroads of 180 million acres, of which 100 million were used. In all, historian Riegel figures the U.S. government gave away 129 million acres for railroad construction, and this does not include autonomous state grants, which in Texas alone totaled 32 million acres.[15]

These huge grants, of course, were intended only incidentally to provide room for railroad tracks and stations. Primarily they were intended to be, and were, sold to finance the corporations. As we know, Comsat's executive suites are filled with former Air Force officers and NASA officials. Many of the corporate beneficiaries of federal grants for railroad development were run by former Civil War generals. Sometimes the railroad companies sold land to immigrants and other new settlers, many of whom were no different except for their late arrival from the squatters and homesteaders who had earlier received federal land for free. More often the land was sold to speculators; or a railroad would form its own land speculation subsidiary to resell the land or to hold it for development. Some railroads hold substantial western acreage to this day; this may be their only valuable asset.

Many railroads received indirect Federal subsidy through lucrative mail-carrying contracts. The government later used these contracts to justify sending U.S. soldiers to help the railroad companies break strikes. The railroads also were possibly the first U.S. developing industry to benefit from earlier government research. Government-sponsored exploration and surveying, beginning with Lewis and Clark, expedited railroad construction.[16] Private satellite developers, of course, have benefited far more from this doubly hidden type of subsidy.

In 1862, exactly 100 years before the Comsat Act, Congress passed an act establishing the Union Pacific Railroad, a government-chartered corporation meant to construct a railroad system to the Pacific. The considerations leading up to the act, and its provisions, are breathtakingly similar to those in the Comsat Act. And yet none of those involved in creating Comsat expressed any awareness of the Union Pacific episode, which was one of the seamiest in American history.

All the considerations of national prestige and profit discussed above helped forge a belief in the necessity of a transcontinental railroad. As with Comsat and the FCC's ad hoc carrier committee, it appeared at first that the road would be developed privately. A New York merchant, Asa Whitney, volunteered to build a transcontinental railroad to be owned by himself; all he asked for in return was that the government give him a 60-mile-wide strip of land extending from Lake Michigan to the Pacific Ocean, a total area approximately equal to the State of Illinois. The House of Representatives committee that reported favorably on the Whitney plan ignored this massive public contribution and praised it for being based on "the principle of private enterprise and private responsibility," just as the communications carriers later won praise from the FCC for their suggestion that they be given complete control of satellite communication.[17] (They "express a willingness and indicate a capability to marshall their respective resources," the FCC said in 1961, ignoring the massive Federal investment they would be getting free of charge.[18]) Whitney at one point offered to pay 16 cents an acre for the land, but the favorable House committee recommended in 1850 that 10 cents would be sufficient.[19]

As with Comsat, a majority of legislators would have been content to turn the project completely over to private hands. But the Whitney plan eventually was dropped, like that of the ad hoc carrier committee, because of stiff opposition by a few staunch advocates of national ownership. Further delay was caused by regional rivalry over the railroad's route (not unlike the jurisdictional dispute between the communications interests and the aerospace lobby over who should control satellites). But secession solved this particular problem and a "chosen instrument" corporation called the Union Pacific Railroad was chartered by Congress in 1862.

In addition to the gift of considerable land holdings along the railroad's route, the Union Pacific Act of 1862 provided for a loan of $60 million in 30-year five-percent United States bonds to become available as construction progressed. Sale of the bonds—at par, by law—would provide the railroad with about half the total estimated construction cost. The other half, plus start-up costs, would be raised by a stock issue, specified in detail in the chartering legislation. There were to be 100,000 shares at $1000 each, of which no more than 200 could be held by a single person. Like the similar details written into the Comsat Act, the purpose was to insure widespread distribution of stock holdings and a chance for the "little people" to invest in the nation's future.[20] Because of the government investment, and to prevent the road from falling into the hands of monopolists or speculators, supposedly strict government controls were instituted. These included a review commission. Also, two seats on the 15-member board of directors were reserved for government representatives as, according to historian Riegel, "a small enough concession . . . to those who favored a government road."[21] The Union Pacific began construction from the East while another company with whom similar arrangements had been made, the California Pacific, began from the West. When the two lines were joined in 1869,

> the blows of the sledge, as well as the speeches marking the occasion, were carried to the East by the telegraph. All over the country whistles were blown, bells were rung, guns were fired, processions were formed, and speeches became the order of the day. Congratulations were showered upon the officials of the successful companies. Editors joined in a paean of praise. In truth, the completion of the first transcontinental road marked an epoch.[22]

Editors offered similar sentiments for Comsat's first success. The *New York Times,* on its front page, called Early Bird "the first link in a global electronic network that is expected to alter economic, social and political patterns."[23] British Prime Minister Harold Wilson spoke to President Johnson by satellite and quoted to him from Isaiah: "Nations shall speak to nations, neither shall they learn war anymore."

The seamier side of the Union Pacific story is well known, and its similarity to some of Comsat's problems is startling. The railroad spent one-quarter of the first $2 million it raised from selling stock in a lobbying effort to weaken the act. In 1864 the act was amended to double the land grant and to reduce the government lien on the company to a second mortgage, allowing it to float its own bonds as well. The inside ring of distinguished businessmen, who were supposed to bring the new project the efficiency of private enterprise, set up a corporation of their own, called the Credit Mobilier of America, to which they let all of the Union Pacific construction contracts. The best that can be said about the Credit Mobilier is that it got the railroad built by evading a requirement in the Union Pacific charter that all stocks and bonds be sold by the company at par. The Credit Mobilier would sink all its construction income from the railroad into Union Pacific securities, which it would then turn around and sell at depreciated market prices. Construction payments were established high enough not only to make up for this depreciation, but to assure the Credit Mobilier a tidy profit. In 1867, with UP shares selling at 30 percent of their original offering price and no dividends in sight, the Credit Mobilier declared a dividend worth $3 million, or 100 percent on capital invested. The official congressional investigation in 1873 concluded that Credit Mobilier members made a profit of $23,366,319 over the years. More recent scholarly studies have suggested that a mere $16 million is more like it.[24]

Even after the 100 percent dividend in 1867, congressmen were able and even encouraged to buy Credit Mobilier stock at original value. In fact, a congressman and a former Vice-President were among the founders of the enterprise, which eventually produced a scandal "becoming a major issue in four Presidential elections, and involving a dozen Congressmen, a Secretary of the Treasury, two Vice Presidents, a leading Presidential contender, and one man who was later to become President."[25]

The Credit Mobilier group's relationship with the Union Pacific was meant like that of the international carriers with Comsat to provide initiative and business experience and to "avoid the profligacy associated with government enterprise." It was similarly claustrophobic. During Comsat's first decade, AT&T was its largest customer, largest stockholder and largest competitor. A critic complained at the time of the Credit Mobilier:

> Under one name or another a ring of some seventy persons is struck at whatever point the Union Pacific is approached. As stockholders they own the road, as mortgagees they have a lien upon it, as directors they contract for its construction, and as members of the Credit Mobilier they build it.[26]

Apologists for the Credit Mobilier arrangement have pointed out that "at least the road was being built," while "the only parties who had any complaint were the small stockholders and the government."[27] But as with satellites, building a system is one thing, building and using it correctly is another. Mobilier members were more interested in their own short-term profits than in the long-term viability of the road. This, as well as haste resulting from the race between the Union Pacific and the Central Pacific to deprive each other of government-subsidized miles, caused shoddy construction which left the road, when E. H. Harriman bought it in 1897 after several financial struggles and turnovers, "two dirt ballasted streaks of rust . . . most of the equipment fit only for the scrap pile." Meanwhile, however, a powerful new economic interest had been established, whose political power not only was strong in Washington, but in some Western states was "practically supreme."[28] Later official amendments to and reinterpretations of the chartering legislation, like the series of FCC decisions through the late 1960s concerning use of cables and satellites for international traffic, served to debilitate the public interest provisions and to benefit the insider group.

As for the government-appointed members of the board of directors, many "were clearly political appointees with no particular qualifications for the position."[29] This too, of course, was repeated a century later. Although the company officials claimed that the government directors were an unfair burden on a private company, these men never objected in principle to the Credit Mobilier arrangement, and in fact one Union Pacific official described them as "the most squeamish men that ever lived about taking any responsibility."[30]

The Union Pacific was a major issue in the presidential campaign of

1872, a year that marked the turning point in public attitude toward the railroads. "What Horace Greeley had proclaimed the 'grandest and noblest enterprise of our age' was transformed into an object of national shame."[31] Not just the Union Pacific, but the entire railroad experience seemed to turn sour.

> People became resentful of the failure of the railroads to bring a utopia, and began to fear large aggregations of capital and absentee ownership. Political corruption and demoralization, which were frequently linked with the railroads, served to advance the feeling still further. In popular fancy the railroads were transformed from gifts of a beneficent providence to dreadful vampires, the product of Satan, sucking the life blood of the country.[32]

The growing antirailroad feeling had many causes. Western citizens who were supposed to reap the benefits of these enterprises, and who felt a proprietary interest in them because of their public subsidy, found that the roads had been taken over by Eastern monied interests without knowledge of or interest in local sentiments; schedules, employment practices, and so forth were decided without regard for them. State governments were left holding large bonded debts, and bankrupt and incomplete rail lines. Farmers found themselves mortgaged up to the neck to railroad companies for land the railroads had received free from the government, and also often had to go into debt to pay railroad freight rates many Westerners considered exorbitant. Special resentment was felt by those who paid higher rates for shorter distances because they were not on competitive routes and by those small shippers on the wrong end of price discrimination practices. Corruption of local and national officials continued to create antirailroad feelings not only among honest citizens and reformers but, in one state at least, among politicians who failed to get on the dole.[33] Another disgruntled group was the small stockholders who had invested in the railroads for the same sorts of economic-romantic reasons that led people to snap up all of Comsat's stock in 1964. Heavy profit-taking in construction contracts had left the roads grossly overcapitalized and wiped out many shareholders' life savings.

The sum total of this resentment was known as the "granger movement," and it led not only to repudiation of state loan guarantees, but to state attempts to regulate the railroads. In the 1870s five Midwestern states followed the lead of Massachusetts in founding commissions with power to set and, it was hoped, to enforce maximum rates. The railroads fought these efforts by means foul and fair not because they were so troublesome—usually they were gotten around—but because they created the possibility of strict regulation in the future.[34]

The idea of national regulation of railroads was not unheard of before 1887. Provisions in the land-grant legislation said that railroad rates could be controlled by Congress. A Congressional committee report in 1874 urged a law requiring public filing of rates, strict antitrust regulations, and government-owned competing lines to keep railroad rates down. An 1878 report urged a law prohibiting discrimination, rebates, combinations, and higher rates for shorter hauls. The proposals were defeated; both Congress and the Supreme Court ruled that regulation was a state matter.[35] Several other proposals appeared and one even passed the House in 1884. After the Supreme Court ruled in 1886 that state commissions could not regulate interstate commerce, Congress moved with relative dispatch and the Interstate Commerce Act was signed into law April 5, 1887. It forbade pooling, rate discrimination, and kickbacks. It also forbade the practice of charging more money to go shorter distances along routes where there was competition between the end points but not between other cities along the line. It required public notice ten days in advance of all rate changes. And it established the Interstate Commerce Commission, the first of the major U.S. regulatory agencies and the conventional model for government regulation of business for the next 75 years.

Meanwhile, the railroads were facing other problems besides their growing unpopularity. Attempts to prevent fierce competition had resulted in formation of the rate-making and traffic-sharing associations that the Interstate Commerce Act ostensibly outlawed. In the first of these, the "Omaha Pool" of 1870, the roads serving the Chicago to Omaha route agreed to split receipts evenly after deducting half for expenses. More sophisticated arrangements followed—the Tripartate Agreement, the Colorado Traffic Agreement, the Transcontinental Traffic Association, the Southwestern Railway Rate Association, the Iowa Trunk Lines Association—culminating in establishment of the Western Traffic Association in 1887, the year of the Interstate Commerce Act.[36] But two problems plagued the pools. First, new construction was constantly opening alternative routes and competitive lines that bypassed the pooling area; emerging competition from water carriers was also a difficulty on many routes. (No one suggested at the time, however, that the railroads should be given control over the water carriers because of their great transportation experience and ability to raise capital, as the carriers later argued in the case of communications satellites.) Second, the pools could not prevent secret rebates to large shippers, a form of price discrimination from which all but the smallest shippers benefited to varying degrees. New pooling arrangements and backsliding caused fairly constant turmoil in the railroad industry through the middle 1880s.

The historian Gabriel Kolko has convinced most of his colleagues that the Interstate Commerce Act was passed with the complete support of the railroads and not over their opposition. He argues, with considerable supporting evidence, that following the failure of the pools, the railroad companies saw government regulation as the best means of institutionalizing and enforcing rate agreements and legally avoiding competition. "The railroads realized they needed the protection of the Federal government, and they became the leading advocates of Federal regulation on their own terms," Kolko writes. The ICC Act was not a concession to, but rather a false front against, popular resentment and the granger movement; and it was not so much a culmination of as a check to growing state regulatory measures.

> The hostility of workers and farmers, many of whom controlled state politics, pointed to the possibility of local attacks which threatened to dislocate railroad systems that were regional, if not national, in their scope. Federal railroad regulation appeared to many railroad leaders as a safe shield behind which to hide from the consequences of local democracy, as well as a means of solving their own internal problems. . . . If the public could be led in a direction compatible with their interests, many railroad men realized, much more serious attacks could be avoided in the future.[37]

Sometimes the buffer imagery emerged in railroad statements, such as one by the president of Michigan Central in 1883 that, "When there are commissioners to stand between the railroads and the public much dissatisfaction can be avoided and many things made plain."[38]

Kolko's 1962 study of the emergence of the ICC was a major force in the modern reinterpretation of the role of regulatory agencies. The traditional view was that the purpose of Federal regulation is to protect the public from unavoidably powerful economic interests such as natural monopolists, oligopolists, and holders of scarce government franchises.

The increasingly accepted modern view is that the historic purpose of regulatory agencies often had been to protect powerful established interests from the public and from the scourge of competition, and that beyond political influence there is no logical reason why some industries are regulated and some are not. Agencies treat the companies they are supposed to regulate as "clients," a favorite term of regulatory critics.

The early development of the ICC fulfilled the railroads' hopes. Commissioners chosen by President Cleveland and his successors were highly sympathetic to the companies, interpreting the vague law as much as possible in their favor, encouraging further prorailroad legislation, nurturing the formation of railroad associations and other institutional arrangements to reflect the Commission's role as den mother to a cartel. As a result of Commission rulings, court decisions, new legislation, and the general convergence of expectations between the railroads and the government, a regulatory system emerged from World War I that exempted the railroads from the antitrust laws, permitted pooling, and gave the Commission a positive role in *encouraging* railroad mergers. The system also assigned the Commission power to set minimum rates, and guaranteed the railroads a fair return on invested capital. A series of Supreme Court decisions and a 1920 law removed virtually all danger of nettlesome state regulation. And new legislation and official statements continued to provide a useful outlet for public antagonism against the railroads without damaging the companies' dividend rates, which doubled between 1888 and 1910. Theodore Roosevelt campaigned on his reputation for being tough with the railroads, despite an actual attitude of highly sympathetic disinterest. In one speech, for example, he warned against hostility to the railroads that might damage "the welfare not merely of some few rich men, but of a multitude of small investors, a multitude of railroad employees, wage workers, and most severely against the interest of the public as a whole."[39] As we saw in Chapters 1 and 8, the welfare of the small investors has been similarly invoked by defenders of the Comsat arrangement.

Kolko's story ends with the Transportation Act of 1920, but others have followed the record of the ICC up to the present day. Judge Henry J. Friendly has shown how the Transportation Act of 1958, an amendment to the Interstate Commerce Act, emerged just like the original almost solely from railroad pressure, while the debate and revisions of it primarily considered the needs of other ICC clients.[40] Robert Fellmeth's 1970 study for Ralph Nader showed that the ICC still operates conservatively, to restrict entry and discourage competition, and that its fealty is still, as Kolko says it was in the nineteenth century, "to the existing economic order" and, within it, to the transportation sector.[41]

Since 1887, other sectors of "the existing economic order" have perceived the advantages of creative government intervention in the American economic system. The railroad experience of subsidy followed or accompanied by regulation has been repeated, and in accelerating cycles. "Alienation of the public domain and grants of privilege laid the foundations for powerful private monopolies and at the same time placed them pretty effectively beyond the reach of the police power," writes Walter Adams, another early and influential regulatory agency critic.[42] Regulation has become so widespread—and the rationale for it by legislators, courts, and economists so murky—that, according to another economist, "there is no longer any distinction between the public utilities and other industries."[43]

Judge Friendly says that the regulatory agencies that grew up in the ICC tradition "did not combine the celerity of Mercury, the wisdom of Minerva, and the purity of Diana to quite the extent we had been taught to expect."[44] The stories are familiar. Federal western land and water policies have, beyond benefiting the railroads, greatly encouraged cartelization of the utility industry and high concentration of agricultural holdings, while the Federal Power Commission and the Agricultural Department have established the requisite client relationships with the power groups thus nurtured. Through their licensing powers, the Federal Communications Commission (1933) and the Civil Aeronautics Board (1938) have supervised alienation of the radio spectrum and of air routes to private oligopolies; then they have protected the closed power groups that have resulted. The CAB takes its job so seriously that it has never approved a competitive new trunk line. The Atomic Energy Act of 1954 featured alienation of the $12 billion government investment in atomic energy and licensing provisions equally likely to discourage competition.

The ICC experience has been influential in both the techniques and the culture of the regulatory bureaucracy. Although the railroads did not invent lobbying, they were the first business interest group to practice it in Washington on a large scale, and their methods have been imitated by subsequent regulated industries, because they were so successful.

In the course of their first half century of relations with state and federal governments the railroads introduced most of the present day practice of lobbying and public relations. . . . While it is obviously impossible to assess the total effect of such activities, it is significant that the United States became the only major industrial nation without state-owned railroads.[45]

Cultural proof of the railroad industry's influence can best be seen in the growth of a standard regulatory language. With the establishment of the Interstate Commerce Railway Association in 1889, the railroads adopted the government's jargon as their own. Reference today to communications companies as "common carriers" derives from the ICC name for the railroads, and is one example of the continuing tradition of the business/government cultural exchange. Other examples are less innocuous. Phrases in the various ICC acts have been copied in subsequent regulatory legislation—for example, "the public convenience, interest or necessity." These words—ostensibly the standard by which regulatory decisions are to be made—appeared in the Transportation Act of 1920; they resurfaced in the Communications Act of 1934, the Motor Carrier Act of 1935, and the Civil Aeronautics Act of 1938. At this point, according to Friendly, they are legally "almost drained of meaning."[46] Adams points out that this "special vocabulary of rationalization"—terms such as "public interest," "public convenience and necessity," "fair value," "fair return," and "reasonable rates"— "has tended to obscure economic realities, to induce in the public mind a spirit of complacency, and to preclude the evolution of alternative arrangements."[47]

Enthusiasm for new regulatory agencies peaked during the 1930s. Since the end of World War II they have been frequently under attack, and public awareness of their failure has increased constantly. The case against the regulatory agencies has been made so persuasively and often that even those who reject the Adams/Kolko theories about their purpose have had to concede that if their intent was noble, their results have been less so. According to one social commentator—not an economist—it is now a commonly accepted belief "that Wall Street runs the Securities and Exchange Commission, the networks dominate the decisions of the Federal Communications Commission, and the private utilities control the Federal Power Commission."[48] With their failures exposed to the public, the regulatory agencies do their clients litle good as shields against public antagonism. Their roles as cartel managers and givers of dispensation from the antitrust laws become much harder, if not impossible, to sustain. The old regulatory agencies may stagger on, but it is increasingly likely that the regulatory agency solution will not be available to corporations hoping for a method of qualifying for government largesse in new fields.

This is where Comsat fits in. Here we have a new regulatory arrangement that remains largely uncriticized, one that can be used to legitimize new government giveaways and satisfy the public demand for government supervision without causing any trouble. Meanwhile the old regulatory agency is still around to bail out its regular clients in case the youngster gets out of hand. The Comsat model has all the advantages of the old solution, and, to those who are unaware of the Union Pacific's history, that of novelty as well.

To see why the Comsat solution is especially appropriate to our times and our nation, we need to understand that the regulatory arrangement is pretty much unique to the United States. Many of the industries that we regulate—airlines, railroads, communication—are operated in Europe as nationalized industries. Even in England under Tory rule, the Comsat problems would not likely have arisen; it would not have occurred to the British to create a monopoly for public policy reasons, then to turn it over to a private company. But the United States lacks the tradition of industrial socialism, even in its most restricted forms. This too is largely the result of the "frontier spirit" of individualism, which leads to an overwhelming belief in the superiority of private to public enterprise. A group of Harvard economists defined the "American Business Creed" in 1948: "Government is at best a necessary evil; at worst the evil far outweighs the necessity and, unchecked, can ruin society."[49] Ironically, the same national spirit of "manifest destiny," which requires government encouragement and financial backing of certain expansive enterprises like the Western railroads and space exploration, creates a strong prejudice in favor of private management. Americans ascribe to private enterprise the efficiency resulting from the legendary rigors of competition, even where no competition exists. The gouging that many state governments took from private railroad entrepreneurs in the 1850s somehow served to reinforce the impression that business should be left to businessmen.[50] Thus construction of the Union Pacific was turned over to private hands, despite the cries of contemporary critics that this represented "a crude attempt to raid the government treasury and nothing more," affirmed by recent scholarship proving that government construction not only would have produced a more "sound business institution," but "would have realized a tidy profit" for the Federal treasury.[51]

The superiority of competition to government as a means of control is the basic tenet of capitalist social ideology—Adam Smith's "invisible hand" writing large. It was most powerful in America during the nineteenth century, but remains influential today. However, with the decline of competition under the aegis of government programs at least as likely to please business as to displease it, capitalist ideology has become inappropriate to the debate, and even embarassing to its traditional advocates. The political scientist Theodore Lowi has suggested that its twentieth century equivalent is something slightly different. He argues that between the turn of the century and the height of the New Deal, a new "public philosophy" developed that combined capitalism's "invisible hand" with the theory of the group from pluralist democratic thought. This new "public philosophy" eliminated the need to condemn government interference. Lowi calls it "interest group liberalism."

> It may be called liberalism because it expects to use government in a positive and expansive role, it is motivated by the highest sentiments, and it possesses strong faith that what is good for government is good for the society. It is "interest group liberalism" because it sees as both necessary and good that the policy agenda and the public interest be defined in terms of the organized interests in society. . . . The role of government is one of ensuring access particularly to the most effectively organized [groups], and of ratifying the agreements and adjustments worked out among the competing leaders and their claims. This last assumption is supposed to be a statement of how our democracy works and how it ought to work.[52]

Through the regulatory agencies, the Commerce and Agriculture Departments, and so forth, the government *encouraged* formation of powerful private interest groups such as the Association of American Railroads, the Farm Bureau Federation, and the U.S. Chamber of Commerce. The result has been delegation of government authority to these groups at the very moment increased government authority was emerging, leading to "(1.) the atrophy of institutions of popular control; (2.) the maintenance of old and creation of new structures of privilege; and (3.) conservatism, in several senses of the word."[53] Acknowledging the existence of market power, interest group liberalism replaces competition with bargaining, but retains the myth of the invisible hand.

The trouble is, of course, that there is no guarantee that everyone will be represented. As Lowi explains, the public is excluded further because the process is exempt from accountability to the government and to absolute standards of justice. At the same time, the power of existing and created "structures of privilege" and their resistance to change are increased due to their affiliation with the government. Techniques of lobbying and legislative logrolling first developed by the railroads likewise become institutionalized, and "government by conflict-of-interest" is elevated "to a virtuous principle."[54] The results are available for all to see, not only in the failure of regulation (which Theodore Roosevelt said was intended as "exactly as much a square deal for the rich man as for the poor man"[55]) and in subsequent government policies from the New Deal to the New Frontier, but also in statements of policy makers and sympathetic intellectuals, such as Arthur Schlesinger, who wrote (with somewhat more sophistication than Teddy Roosevelt):

> What is the essence of a multi-essence administration? It is surely that the leading interests in society are all represented in the interior processes of policy formation—which can be done only if members or advocates of these interests are included in key positions of government.[56]

In 1862, the Western railroad was considered a unique problem, the semipublic solution to which was later regretted by most of its advocates. In 1887, the first federal regulatory agency likewise was considered a unique solution to a unique problem. But, says Lowi, "In the 1960s pluralist solutions have not been forced upon national leaders but are voluntarily pursued as the highest expression of their ideology."[57]

Comsat was the logical culmination of the history of government subsidy and regulation from the early nineteenth century through 1962, and it fits well into Lowi's theory. Kolko says of railroad regulation, "It was, in fact, an effort to use political means to solve economic problems while maintaining the essential theory of social priorities and values of a capitalist economy."[58] If a fifty-fifty distribution is the prototypical political settlement, then the Comsat arrangement represents "the effort to use political means to solve economic problems" par excellence. Ownership in the corporation was split fifty-fifty between the common carriers and the "general public," ownership of earth stations was split fifty-fifty between the carriers and Comsat; international communications business was split fifty-fifty between the carrier-owned cables and Comsat's satellite system.

Exactly 100 years after the first Union Pacific Act, Congress again alienated public domain to private hands for development. But Comsat is also the culmination of a century of experience, not only at alienation of public domain, but at regulatory techniques that delegate public control to private hands and at political thought that justifies both these actions. From the FCC's 1961 ad hoc carrier committee, to the division of stockholdings, to the series of domestic satellite decisions, the feeling was evinced that democracy and accountability were best served by absorbing into the decision-making process the appropriate interest groups, of which the "general public" is only one more. And it, too, according to the customary board of directors assignments, could be split into interest groups called "labor," "management," and "education." The critique of interest group liberalism—that it leads to irrational outcomes (because the "invisible hand" does not necessarily apply to bargaining) and fails to protect the public interest (because not everybody is represented in all areas by interest groups of equal strength)—applies both to regulation and to Comsat. The Comsat solution has an advantage of unfamiliarity.

The Comsat solution has a second advantage. Kolko comments on the ultimate failure of the railroads despite the protection of the ICC:

> The automobiles and trucking industries, and not the shippers or radical state legislatures, were to nullify the benefits to the railroads of the Transportation Act. Nothing could save the railroads from the impact of the revolution in American transportation that was beginning to roll off the assembly lines of Detroit.[59]

The Comsat solution has served to protect the terrestrial communications carriers from the revolution blasting off from the launch pads of Cape Kennedy. An arrangement like Comsat, unlike the regulatory one, guards its clients not only against other members of "the existing economic order," not only against the general public, but against technological change and the economic order of the future.

Comsat's success has not gone unnoticed. Just as the regulatory agency solution, in the years after it was first developed in the ICC Acts between 1887 and 1920, was adopted in several other industries with no easily identifiable mutual problem (such as natural monopoly), the Comsat solution has become popular with executives of private enterprises who wish to gain government subsidy without submission to government control, and with liberal politicians who have discovered that "bold" proposals for new agencies and commissions do not get the quick editorial praise they used to, but that new "semipublic corporations" do. John Chamberlain, the noted conservative columnist, wrote in 1966:

> The magic word in Washington today is "Comsat." Important people in both political parties are talking about a "Comsat-like" approach toward solving a whole host of public problems, from slum rehabilitation to the control of pollution in our streams, lakes and the surrounding atmosphere.[60]

Chamberlain pointed out that "this convergence of Left and Right in a new consensus is not without its ironies," considering the left-wing opposition to Comsat in 1962. He then praised the liberals' new insight.[61]

In 1971 the Committee for Economic Development, a prestigious group of "200 leading businessmen and educators . . . devoted . . . to develop findings and recommendations for private and public policy which will contribute to preserving and strengthening our free society," produced a report on the "Social Responsibilities of Business Corporations."[62] The report suggested:

> New hybrid types of public-private corporations may need to be developed to combine the best attributes of government . . . and of private enterprise (systems analysis, research and technology, managerial ability) in the optimum mix for dealing effectively with different kinds of major socio-economic problems such as modernizing transportation, rebuilding the cities, and developing backward regions of the nation. Public-private corporations not only could provide the essential framework for blending government and business capabilities but also could contribute to the synergistic effect that seems to be needed to solve problems that so far have defied conventional attacks. Prototypes of these future public-private institutions already exist. They include such organizations as Comsat (Communications Satellite Corporation), Amtrak (National Railroad Passenger Corporation), and the National Corporation for Housing Partnerships.[63]

The committee said that government's role would include "a major share of responsibility for financing through appropriations, public borrowing, loan guarantees," and "public accountability through a board of directors, partially elected and partially appointed, whose tenure (perhaps seven years) overlaps political terms to insulate the corporation from political pressure."[64] The CED report promises that "the government-business relationship is likely to be the central one in the last third of the twentieth century," whatever that means exactly.[65]

Amtrak and the National Corporation for Housing Partnerships are just two examples of Comsat-type corporations being set up and being given government money. Two of NCHP's founders, industrialist Edgar Kaiser and his Washington lawyer Lloyd Cutler, were founders of Comsat. Politicans have suggested "Comsats" for East-West trade and to replace Radio Free Europe, among others.[66] For a while, a "Comsat" was being suggested for development of supersonic transport. An editorial in the *New York Times* said:

> The American SST might be more safely and soundly developed if it commanded the combined resources of the entire American industry and the Government. There are obvious advantages in industrywide cooperation. It would promote a spread, rather than a narrowing of technology. It would mean less cost—and less risk—to taxpayers. And it would remove the threat that Government participation might eventually lead to Government control. . . . It would be preferable if the entire aerospace industry participated, along with the Government, in this big and speculative project. By setting up a new corporation along the lines of Comsat, the SST would have more chance of being a success while strengthening the industry without undue risk to the taxpayer.[67]

Here we have it: all the fallacies offered in defense of Comsat being put forward again—saving the taxpayers money and risk, the glories of cooperation among supposed competitors, the dangers of government bureaucracy. If the SST Comsat had gone through, it would have been a fine consolation prize for the aerospace industry after their loss of the original back in 1962.

The "Comsat solution" may be an idea whose time has come. The idea will appeal to private business as long as it appeals to legislators and the public—that is, as long as no one asks why direct government control of government-financed technology would be less efficient than private development with no competition and a whopping subsidy from the taxpayers. And in an age when, as Galbraith would have it, managerial control has replaced land and capital as the basis of power in society, delegation of power is itself a subsidy.

> Delegation of power has become alienation of public domain—the gift of sovereignty to private satrapies. The political barriers to withdrawal of delegation are high enough. But liberalism reinforces these through the rhetoric of justification and often even permanent legal reinforcement: Public corporations—justified, oddly, as efficient planning instruments—permanently alienate rights of central coordination to the directors and to those who own the corporate bonds.[68]

Conclusion:
The Last Frontier

In the second decade of the nineteenth century there was a working-class movement in England known as the Luddites. The Luddites gained notoriety by destroying labor-saving textile machinery, because they feared it would cause unemployment. Since that time the term "Luddite" has been applied to anyone who opposed technological progress because of conflict with some other, presumably more short-sighted, goal. In recent years this term of opprobrium has been reserved for people on the left—members of the ecology movements, or corporate critics like Ralph Nader. The forces of corporate capitalism have been pictured—even by their critics—as unreconstructed advocates of progress, still in blind and zealous pursuit of America's manifest destiny, leading us with undimmed enthusiasm toward the next frontier.

The proposition that modern American corporations are the strongest proponents and suppliers of technological progress needs to be reconsidered. I have tried to show in this book how the communications giants, primarily AT&T, have been able to prevent the application of satellite technology, which some day will revolutionize our daily lives. Other examples of what might be called corporate Luddism fill the daily newspapers. The energy crisis has reminded us of how the automobile makers and the highway lobby have slowed the development of rapid transit systems, and of what the oil companies have done to prevent the exploration of alternative energy sources. The broadcast interests have hamstrung the development of cable television. And all of this has been accomplished with the help of the various arms of the federal government.

We should consider whether this should be allowed to continue. The development of commercial satellite communication is a good focal point for such a discussion, because in at least three ways it represents the last of the American frontiers. It marks, of course, the beginning of the serious exploitation of outer space as a resource. Other than outer space, what physical options remain? The American West also seemed unlimited once, so we should be cautious in assuming that any mistakes we make in exploiting this resource are easily reversible.

Communications has now succeeded manufacture and transportation as the cutting edge of technological progress, and satellites represent the most advanced application of communications technology. When satellites permit us—as they almost can now—to transmit unlimited quantities of information at minimal cost between any two spots in the globe, using receivers small and cheap enough for any household, the communications revolution will be complete. It has been suggested that this imminent revolution will have a more profound effect on American life styles during the 1970s and 1980s than introduction of the motorcar had in the teens and twenties. Just for example, Dr. Peter Goldmark, the communications visionary who invented color television and the long-playing record, has suggested that such a breakthrough could solve the urban crisis and the population explosion by encouraging people to move from the cities back to moderately-sized towns. Cheap satellite communication could keep corporations that relocated in these towns as much in touch with one another as if they were all along the same street in Manhattan. Meanwhile their employees would not need to miss the cultural, entertainment, and informational offerings of the big cities (some of which even city dwellers today have difficulty taking advantage of because of crime and congestion). All these things could be broadcast direct from satellites to high-resolution screens in people's homes. Americans would have the best of both worlds—the city and the small town—whereas now many sit in suburbs enjoying the benefits of neither.[1] The potential benefits to underdeveloped countries are even greater. Yet the corporate Luddites have succeeded in denying people these benefits.

The final sense in which commercial satellite communication represents America's last frontier concerns its unique economic structure, the ultimate refinement—the evolution of which was traced in the previous chapter—in American capitalism's attempt to adjust to the anomalies that have grown up within it. As we have seen, this refinement has two aspects: the so-called semigovernment corporation, and the regulatory agencies.

In the years since the passage of the Communications Satellite Act the special provisions intended to make it a unique experiment in government/business cooperation have atrophied. The carriers have sold their interest in the company, the White House has abandoned its duty to appoint government representatives to the corporate board, and Congress has failed completely in any supervisory function it may have thought it was allocating to itself in 1962. Perhaps the quiet burial of the Comsat solution in its original application will prevent its application in other areas where it is equally inappropriate. This, unfortunately, will not solve the problems that have accumulated already in satellite communication. A review of some of the factors responsible for these problems suggests what might be done now to solve these problems and prevent others like them from occurring.

The Federal Communications Commission.   Federal Communications commissioners had at every point along their tortuous path the option of making better decisions than the ones they made, without any changes in the standards or methods by which such decisions are made. The decisions reviewed in this book appear to be the products of inferior minds or, at the very least, minds somewhat distracted from the public weal. The simplest solution to the problems of commercial satellite communication might simply be to improve the calibre of FCC commissioners.

Most FCC appointments suffer from some combination of a few common weaknesses, shared by appointments to the other Washington regulatory commissions. Sometimes they are political appointees—defeated politicians or loyal party workers with little knowledge of economics or communication, unable to challenge the expertise of the companies they regulate. Worse, they are broadcasting or communications executives (often influential in local and regional politics) with clear, vested interests in various aspects of the status quo.

Besides reform of the political system, which is beyond the scope of this book, there is little that can be done about such appointments (although a President some day might aspire to set a higher standard, and then be emulated by his successors). However, some simple regulations could prevent the insidious system whereby lawyers who are on the FCC or its staff leave after a few years to open lucrative Washington practices (as Dean Burch did, for example, on leaving the White House in 1974) in which they represent the same corporations which as commissioners they were supposed to regulate. Ralph Nader has aptly termed this the "deferred bribe."

The Adversary System   The hegemony of lawyers in all aspects of regulation suggests the next thing that deserves review. Nothing can prevent incompetent or corrupt commissioners from making bad regulatory decisions if they wish to. But the arduous process at the end of which FCC decisions are made, the adversary system, greatly facilitates the making of bad decisions by camouflaging the real issues, by giving a false impression of judicial fairness, and by causing unnecessary delay. The adversary proceeding cannot be described as the process *by which* decisions are made. As we have seen, the final decisions are likely to have no relation to the arguments and preliminary decisions that preceded them.

As explained in the last chapter, there is no guarantee that human commissioners can direct the cycle of contesting claims by interest groups of varying strengths as effectively as the invisible hand directs the cycle of bargains struck by producers and consumers in the unregulated competitive market. Indeed, Commission decisions are remarkably inferior even to what a reasonably intelligent and patient outside observer might decide, given the power. Surely, then, there is no need to pretend that these endless adversary proceedings represent some sort of dialectical progression toward an otherwise unapprehendable truth, because in all the cases studied here the same decision, if not a better one, could have been made at any point along the way. Often the information most relevant to an important decision—for example, the relative cost of a proposed cable and an equivalent satellite—does not even emerge from these avalanches of paper.

Obviously, corporations should be allowed to advance facts and arguments in their own self-interest, when decisions are to be made that affect them. But these should be a relatively minor and expeditious part of the decision-making process. And there should be no suggestion that these corporations are required to consider or advance the *public* interest in their filings, since this suggestion presently encourages the most embarassing sort of hypocrisy. Let the commissioners worry about the public interest, based on their own resources of expertise and good sense, and make their decisions on that basis.

Rate-Base Regulation.   As we have seen, not only are the regulatory agencies dominated by the companies they are supposed to regulate, but their method of regulation by rate base and rate of return actually encourages corporations to avoid technological innovations that will reduce the amount of investment they are able to make per unit of output. Proper regulation under the rate-base method would require the Commission to make an independent determination of whether each expenditure of a regulated company is the least expensive method of providing a certain service, *followed* by consideration of whether demand will be sufficient to justify it at a price set equal to long-run marginal cost. Any attempt to enforce rate-base regulation across the whole spectrum of markets that the FCC must supervise would require a staff many times the size of the FCC's current staff, and might become so involved that it would seriously hamper the operation of the companies under scrutiny.

As things stand, the pretense that Commission decisions are constrained by the rules of rate-base regulation is barely supportable. In 1975 the FCC had been regulating the rates of Comsat for a decade, but a study begun in 1965 of what Comsat's rate base and rate of return should be still had not been completed.

The Structure of the Communications Industry.   Rate-base regulation, along with the rest of the baggage of the regulatory system, clearly form a second-best solution to the insoluble problems created by the anachronistic structure of the American communications industry. The semigovernment corporation is not even second-best. The episodes chronicled in this book have convinced me, and I hope the reader, that these ambiguous relationships between business and government are thoroughly undesirable. Either we should admit that, at least in certain industries such as communication, the internal inconsistencies are inevitable, and move on to full government ownership and control; or we should give the capitalist verities a real test, such as they have not had for a long time.

The absence in the United States of any tradition of industrial socialism, even in its most restrictive forms, apparently is bound up with the notion—the historical cause of which was discussed in the previous chapter—that government operations inevitably are more wasteful and less productive than private ones. This is why the notion of a government-operated communications satellite program, in which the profits would be guaranteed to the taxpayers who made them possible, and development of the system would follow a pattern most beneficial to the public as a whole, received such short shrift in 1962. Even a Western European government would be unlikely to create a monopoly for public policy reasons, and then turn it over to a private company. But in this country we apparently ascribe to private enterprise the efficiency resulting from the legendary rigors of competition, even when no element of competition exists.

Could anyone who has followed the development of commercial satellite communication seriously contest the proposition that creating a semigovernment corporation in a heavily regulated environment has led to the worst excesses of both government and private enterprise? It is not clear that the socialist solution would have been the best one for development of satellite communication. But in terms of bureaucratic delay and costly inefficiency, it could not have been worse than what we have now. It is time to stop letting worn-out shibboleths prevent serious consideration of the socialist alternative, especially in areas so closely related to the government function.

There is, however, much to be said for competition, too. It certainly would not be fair to let something like Comsat represent this much-abused concept in any ideological confrontation. Indeed true competition is about as much untried in the communications industry as is true socialism. Since it is too late (or perhaps still too early) for the socialist alternative, much good could be done by attempting to promote competition in the communications satellite area. For a start, the Authorized Users and Earth Stations decisions could be repealed to free Comsat to sell circuits to whomever it wants. In addition, a wide variety of domestic satellite systems could be encouraged. The FCC claims to be following the latter policy, though it cannot seem to bring itself to abandon all the various control and delay mechanisms at its disposal. The Justice Department's 1974 antitrust suit against AT&T may also be a promising step in the right direction, though any results remain years and piles of expensive litigation into the future, and the Justice Department's record concerning AT&T and antitrust is not an enviable one.[2]

It is important to remember the limits of any "competition" that may be brought to the communications industry. For obvious financial and technological reasons the number of satellite communications systems, for example, will never be so large that each owner will be without any market power, in the classic Adam Smith concept of competition. But this is no reason to straightjacket the industry even more with needless regulation. Satellite communication is a good example in support of the well-known thesis of the economist Joseph Schumpeter, that large corporations are necessary for technical progress because only their size and their oligopoly profits can finance it. But Schumpeter relied on fierce competition between the large corporations in each industry to provide what he called the "perennial gale of creative destruction," by which the companies would take turns making one another's innovations obsolete.[3] Without competition the incentive for innovation disappears. And with it goes technological progress, of which commercial satellite communication has been held to be such a shining example.

Notes

CHAPTER ONE

1. Quoted in W. Wallace Kirkpatrick, "Antitrust in Orbit," *George Washington Law Review,* **33**:1 (October 1964).
2. Quoted in Hugo Young, Bryan Silcock, and Peter Dunn, "From the Bay of Pigs to the Sea of Tranquility: Why We Went to the Moon," *Washington Monthly,* April 1970, p. 29.
3. U.S. Congress, Senate, Committee on Foreign Relations, *Hearings on the Communications Satellite Act of 1962,* 87th Cong., 2d sess., August 3, 6, 7, 8 and 9, 1962, p. 34.
4. U.S. Congress, Senate, Subcommittee on Monopoly of the Select Committee on Small Business, Hearings on Space Satellite Communications, 87th Cong., 1st sess., August 2, 3, 4, 9, 10, and 11, 1961, p. 291.
5. Young, Silcock, and Dunn, *op. cit.* (note 2 above), p. 38.
6. *Ibid.,* p. 29.
7. *Ibid,* p. 29.
8. U.S. Congress, Senate, Committee on Foreign Relations, *op. cit.* (note 3 above), p. 188.
9. U.S. Congress, Senate, Senator Paul Douglas and Senator Albert Gore speaking on the Commercial Communications Satellite System, H.R. 11040, 87th Cong., 2d sess., July 30, 1962, *Congressional Record* (unbound), p. 14074. (Hereafter cited as *Senate Comsat Debate.* References are to pages in the unbound edition unless otherwise indicated.)
10. "Extra-Terrestrial Relays, Can Rocket Stations Give World-Wide Radio Coverage?" Arthur C. Clarke, *Wireless World,* October 1945, pp. 305–308.
11. Young, Silcock, and Dunn, *op. cit.* (note 2 above), pp. 40–46.

12. U.S. Congress, Senate, Subcommittee on Monopoly of the Select Committee on Small Business, *op. cit.* (note 4 above), p. 255.

13. U.S. Congress, House, Representative William Fitts Ryan speaking on the NASA budget, 88th Cong., 1st sess., August 1, 1963, *Congressional Record* (unbound).

14. *Senate Comsat Debate,* Senator John Pastore, June 18, 1962, p. 9869.

15. *Senate Comsat Debate,* Senator Albert Gore, July 30, 1962, p. 14085.

16. Kennedy statement reprinted in U.S. Congress, Senate, Committee on Aeronautical and Space Sciences, *Staff Report: Documents on International Aspects of the Exploration and Use of Outer Space,* 88th Cong., 1st sess., May 9, 1963, p. 229; Justice Department proposal reprinted in U.S. Congress, Senate, Committee on Foreign Relations, *op. cit.* (note 3 above), p. 35.

17. U.S. Congress, House, *Communications Satellite Act of 1962,* Pub. L. 87-624, 87th Cong., 2d sess., 1962, H.R. 11040.

18. *CQ Weekly,* April 27, 1962. The section on Comsat in Joseph C. Goulden's book on AT&T, *Monopoly* (New York: Pocket Books, 1970), pp. 96–131, was very useful in preparing this chapter. However, Goulden seems to have missed the point on this particular incident. He confuses the original Kennedy bill with the compromise one that actually passed. Kerr introduced Kennedy's January bill, but his own bill for complete carrier ownership was still alive at the time, according to *CQ Weekly* of February 9, 1962.

19. Kennedy statement cited in note 16 above; U.S. Congress, House, *Communications Satellite Act of 1962,* cited in note 17 above, Section 102(d); U.S. Congress, Senate, Committee on Foreign Relations, *op. cit.* (note 3 above), pp. 375–76.

20. U.S. Congress, Senate, Subcommittee on Monopoly of the Select Committee on Small Business, *op. cit.* (note 4 above), p. 52.

21. *Ibid.,* p. 34.

22. *Ibid.,* p. 48.

23. U.S. Congress, House, Committee on Interstate and Foreign Commerce, *Hearings on Communications Satellites,* 87th Cong., 2d sess., March 13–16, 20–22, 1962, p. 565.

24. U.S. Congress, Senate, Committee on Foreign Relations, *op. cit.* (note 3 above), p. 36.

25. *Ibid.,* p. 38.

26. *Ibid.,* p. 30 (reprint of Katzenbach letter).

27. U.S. Congress, Senate, committee on Foreign Relations, *op. cit.* (note 3 above), p. 69.

28. U.S. Congress, Senate, Subcommittee on Monopoly of the Select Committee on Small Business, *op. cit.* (note 4 above), p. 251.

29. *Ibid.,* p. 257.

30. U.S. Congress, House, Committee on Interstate and Foreign Commerce, *op. cit.* (note 20 above), p. 518.

31. U.S. Congress, Senate, Committee on Aeronautical and Space Sciences, *Hearings on Communications Satellite Legislation,* 87th Cong., 2d sess., February 27, 28, March 1, 5–7, 1962, p. 313.

32. U.S. Congress, Senate, Subcommittee on Monopoly of the Select Committee on Small Business, *op. cit.* (note 4 above), p. 254.

33. U.S. Congress, House, Committee on Interstate and Foreign Commerce, *op. cit.* (note 20 above), p. 549.

34. U.S. Congress, Senate, Committee on Aeronautical and Space Sciences, cited in note 31 above, p. 309.

35. U.S. Congress, House Committee on Interstate and Foreign Commerce, cited in note 20 above, p. 507.

36. *Senate Comsat Debate,* Senator Russell Long, June 18, 1962, p. 10225.

37. U.S. Congress, House, Committee on Interstate and Foreign Commerce, cited in note 20 above, p. 601.

38. Goulden, *op. cit.,* p. 96.

39. *Senate Comsat Debate,* Senator Ralph Yarborough, June 18, 1962, p. 9917.

40. *Senate Comsat Debate,* Senator Russell Long, June 18, 1962, p. 10226.

41. *Senate Comsat Debate,* Senator Ernest Gruening, July 26, 1962, p. 13878; Senator Wayne Morse, July 26, 1962, p. 13887.

42. *Senate Comsat Debate,* Senator Wayne Morse, July 27, 1962, p. 13903; Senator Everett Dirksen and Senator Wayne Morse, July 26, 1962, p. 13884.

43. *Senate Comsat Debate,* Senator Wayne Morse, July 27, 1962, p. 13903.

44. *Senate Comsat Debate,* Senator Maurine Neuberger, July 30, 1962, p. 14604.

45. *Senate Comsat Debate,* Senator Robert Kerr and Senator Stuart Symington, August 13, 1962, p. 15337; Senator Barry Goldwater, July 31, 1962, p. 14177; Senator John Pastore, June 15, 1962, p. 9869.

46. *Senate Comsat Debate,* Senator Albert Gore and Senator Robert Kerr, August 13, 1962, p. 15337.

47. *Senate Comsat Debate,* July 27, 1962, p. 13908.

48. William S. White, *Washington Star,* August 13, 1962; Marquis Childs column and editorial, "The Issue Before The Senate," *Washington Post,* August 13, 1962.

49. Dirksen quoted in the *New York Times,* August 15, 1962.

50. AT&T advertisement in the *New York Times,* August 14, 1962.

51. *Senate Comsat Debate,* Senator Maurine Neuberger, August 14, 1962, p. 16421 (bound edition).

52. *Senate Comsat Debate,* Senator Russell Long, August 14, 1962, p. 16418 (bound edition).

53. *Senate Comsat Debate,* Senator Paul Douglas, August 14, 1962, p. 16421.

54. *Senate Comsat Debate,* Senator Wayne Morse, August 14, 1962, p. 16427 (bound edition).

55. *Senate Comsat Debate,* Senator Hubert Humphrey, August 16, 1962, p. 16694.

56. *Senate Comsat Debate,* Senator John Pastore, August 17, 1962, p. 16926.

57. James A. Weschler, "Satellites, Inc.," *The Progressive,* October 1962, reprinted in U.S. Congress, Senate, 88th Cong., 1st sess., April 24, 1963, *Congressional Record* (unbound), p. 6623.

58. FCC recommendation quoted in Goulden, *op. cit.,* p. 106; Horace Moulton, "Communications Satellites," *Business Lawyer,* 18:173 (November 1962).

59. AT&T's 1971 annual report indicates 50 million preferred and 549 million common shares outstanding. The company prides itself on "over 3 million" stockholders.

60. Quoted in the *Wall Street Journal,* June 2, 1964.

61. Comments of Communications Satellite Corporation enclosed with letter of January

31, 1972, in response to questions submitted by Ralph Nader Study Group, July 29, 1971 (in future references, *Comsat Q&A*), p. 8–1.

62. Quoted in *Newsweek,* March 16, 1964.

63. U.S. Congress, Senate, Subcommittee on Monopoly of the Select Committee on Small Business, *op. cit.* (note 4 above), pp. 206, 207.

64. U.S. Congress, House, Representative William Fitts Ryan speaking on the NASA budget, 88th Cong., 1st sess., August 1, 1963, *Congressional Record* (unbound).

65. *Senate Comsat Debate,* Senator Estes Kefauver, August 11, 1962, p. 15237.

66. U.S. Congress, House, Committee on Interstate and Foreign Commerce, *op. cit.* (note 20 above), pp. 518, 521.

67. "In the matter of American Telephone and Telegraph Company, ITT World Communications, Inc., RCA Global Communications, Inc., Western Union International, Inc., Application for authority to participate in the construction and operation of the TAT-6 SG submarine cable system between the United States and France," FCC 72-613, July 7, 1972; Jack Gould, "Ford Fund Urges F.C.C. To Consider New TV Satellite," *New York Times,* August 2, 1966, p. 1.

68. *Comsat Q&A,* p. 11–6.

69. "Debate on Split-Second Slows Comsat," *Washington Post,* September 30, 1963.

70. Staff economist Benjamin Gordon was particularly insistent on this point during Senator Long's Monopoly Subcommittee hearings of August 1961 (cited note 4 above), the transcript of which provides documentation of it.

71. U.S. Congress, House, Committee on Interstate and Foreign Commerce, *op. cit.* (note 20 above), p. 520; U.S. Congress, Senate, Subcommittee on Monopoly of the Select Committee on Small Business, *op. cit.* (note 4 above), p. 261.

72. *Comsat Q&A*), p. 11–6.

73. FCC Docket 16495, "In the Matter of the Establishment of Domestic Communications Satellite Facilities by Nongovernmental Entities," *Comments of the Ford Foundation, Vol. III: Technical and Economic Data,* December 12, 1966, pp. 77–92.

74. U.S. Congress, Senate, Committee on Foreign Relations, *op. cit.* (note 3 above), pp. 32, 26–27.

75. Quoted in *Newsweek,* March 16, 1964.

76. FCC Docket 16495 (cited in note 73 above), *Reply Comments of Communications Satellite Corporation,* July 12, 1971, p. 20.

77. *Comsat Q&A,* p. 11–2.

78. *Senate Comsat Debate,* Senator Russell Long, August 11, 1962, p. 15166.

79. 15 *U.S.C.* s.s. 80a-2a(9).

80. *U.S.* v. *E. I. du Pont de Nemours & Co.,* 353 U.S. 586 (1957).

81. *Comsat Q&A,* annex 8B and figures derived therefrom.

82. FCC Docket 16495 (cited in note 23 above), Commission *Report and Order,* December 22, 1972; Executive Offices of the President, Office of Telecommunications Policy, *International Communications–Objectives and Policy,* mimeo, February 1973.

83. Letter from Richard W. McLaren, Assistant Attorney General, Antitrust Division, to Senator Mike Gravel, January 7, 1971; Executive Office of the President, Office of Telecommunications Policy, Press Release, January 7, 1971.

CHAPTER TWO

1. Gene Smith, "Boom Seen in Overseas Phoning," *New York Times,* July 16, 1973.

2. Communications Satellite Corporation, *Annual Report,* 1971, pp. 6, 7.

3. Press release from American Telephone & Telegraph Company. October 30, 1967, accompanying response to FCC letter of October 4, 1967, "Requesting Data Relating to Communication Facilities in the Atlantic Basin Area." The FCC clearly concurred in this logic. See concurring statement of Commissioner Kenneth Cox, with Commission *TAT-5* letter, February 16, 1968, FCC 68-210 12512, p. 1.

4. FCC *TAT-5* decision, File Nos. P-C-7022 and S-C-L-40, "In the Matter of American Telephone and Telegraph Company et al., Applications for Authorization to Participate in the Construction and Operation of an Integrated Submarine Cable and Radio System . . . [etc.]," May 31, 1968, p. 10.

5. U.S. Congress, House, *Communications Satellite Act of 1962,* Pub. L. 87–624, 87th Cong., 2d sess., 1962, H.R. 10040, s.s. 305(a)(4).

6. FCC *TAT-6* decision, "In the Matter of American Telephone and Telegraph Company, ITT World Communications Inc., RCA Global Communications, Inc., Western Union International, Inc., Application for authority to participate in the construction and operation of the TAT-6 SG submarine cable system between the United States and France," FCC 72-613, July 7, 1972.

7. FCC Docket 16495, "In the Matter of the Establishment of Domestic Communications Satellite Facilities by Nongovernmental Entities," *Reply Comments of Communications Satellite Corporation,* July 12, 1971.

8. *Ibid.,* p. 24.

9. Herman Schwartz, "Comsat, The Carriers and the Earth Stations: Some Problems With Melding Variegated Interests," *Yale Law Journal,* **76**:3 (January 1967), p. 454; Comments of Communications Satellite Corporation enclosed with letter of January 31, 1972, in response to questions submitted by Ralph Nader Study Group, July 29, 1971 (hereafter *Comsat Q&A*), p. 5–1; FCC *TAT-5* decision (cited in note 4 above), p. 11.

10. "Commission Rejects Comsat Settlement . . .," *Telecommunications Reports,* August 5, 1974.

11. FCC Docket 19129, "In the Matter of American Telephone and Telegraph Company and the Associated Bell System companies, Charges for Interstate Telephone Services," *Proposed Findings of Fact and Conclusions of Law of the Trial Staff of the Common Carrier Bureau,* July 12, 1971. The most lucid short discussion of the theoretical problems with rate-base regulation and the alternatives to it can be found among the staff papers of the 1967–1968 President's Task Force on Communication Policy ("Central Staff Working Paper on the Regulation of Communications Common Carriers," mimeo, dated June 11, 1968). For a quick review of the administrative hassles involved in regulating the telephone company, see Nicholas Johnson, "Why Ma Bell Still Believes in Santa," *Saturday Review,* March 11, 1972, p. 57.

12. Harvey Averch and Leland L. Johnson, "Behavior of the Firm under Regulatory Constraint," *American Economic Review,* **52** (December 1962), pp. 1052–1069. This discussion also relies heavily on Alfred E. Kahn, *The Economics of Regulation: Principles and Institutions* (New York: Wiley, 1971), especially Vol. 2, pp. 48–59.

13. For a thorough discussion and several detailed examples, see William M. Capron, ed.,

Technological Change in Regulated Industries (Washington, D.C.: Brookings Institution, 1971).

14. "Taking a Flyer in Outer Space," *Newsweek*, March 16, 1964; *Communications Satellite Act of 1962* (cited in note 5 above), s.s. 201 (c) (7); U.S. Congress, Senate, Committee on Aeronautical and Space Sciences, *Hearings on Communications Satellite Legislation,* 87th Cong., 2d sess., February 27, 28, March 1, 5–7, 1962, pp. 309–313.

15. "Ground Stations Plea by Comsat," *New York Herald Tribune,* October 24, 1964.

16. *Telecommunications Reports,* November 2, 1964.

17. ITT filing quoted in "Comsat Ground Station 'Go' Fears: Who'll Win The Monopoly Game?" *Electronic News,* November 9, 1964.

18. "Comsat Bid to Operate Ground Stations Itself Gets AT&T Support," *Wall Street Journal,* January 6, 1965.

19. Schwartz, *op. cit.* (see note 9 above), p. 454. Schwartz relied heavily on testimony before the Holifield Committee: U.S. Congress, House, Military Operations Subcommittee of the Committee on Government Operations, *Hearings on Government Use of Satellite Communications,* 89th Cong., 2d sess., August 15–19, 29–31, September 1, 6, 7, 12–14, 1966.

20. U.S. Congress, House, Military Operations Subcommittee of the Committee on Government Operations, *op. cit.* (cited in note 19 above), p. 515.

21. Interview, Washington, D.C., July 1971.

22. "Early Bird Rings the Bell," *Business Week,* May 1, 1965.

23. FCC Public Notice, May 12, 1965, accompanying FCC Docket 15735, "Interim Policy to Govern Issuance of Authorizations for Initial Communications Satellite Earth Stations," *Commission Report and Order,* May 12, 1965.

24. See "Comsat Wins Stations Case," *Washington Star,* May 12, 1965. Only the *Wall Street Journal,* of all reports at the time, emphasized the time limit.

25. FCC Docket 15735, Commission *Report and Order,* May 12, 1965.

26. *Ibid.*

27. *Washington Post,* June 12, 1965; *Telecommunications Reports,* February 28, 1966; *Telecommunications Reports,* February 28, 1966; *Telecommunications Reports,* July 19, 1965; *Electronics News,* January 24, 1965.

28. *Telecommunications Reports,* February 28, 1966.

29. Communications Satellite Corporation, internal memorandum, mimeo, unsigned, March 1968.

30. *Electronics Reports,* January 24, 1966.

31. ATT filing quoted in *Telecommunications Reports,* May 16, 1966.

32. *Wall Street Journal,* May 12, 1966; Comsat filing quoted in *Telecommunications Reports,* June 6, 1966; FCC Public Notice, "Report on Meeting on Second Eastern Earth Station," August 22, 1966.

33. *Broadcasting,* September 9, 1966; *Telecommunications Reports,* October 3, 1966.

34. Communications Satellite Corporation, press release, October 6, 1966, cited in Schwartz, *op. cit.,* p. 458 (footnote 81).

35. *Telecommunications Reports,* November 14, 1966.

36. FCC Docket 15735, Commission *Report and Order,* December 8, 1966.

37. *Ibid.*

39. This memorandum, cited in note 29 above, was not obtained from its author.

40. *Comsat Q&A*, pp. 5–1, 5–2.

41. *Telecommunications Reports*, December 27, 1966.

42. Speech before the American Institute of Aeronautics and Astronautics in San Francisco, quoted in *Telecommunications Reports*, April 8, 1968.

43. "Hughes Proposes Low Cost Ground Terminal for Comsat," *Electronics News*, November 23, 1964; "Comsat Ground Station 'Go' Fears: Who'll Win The Monopoly Game?" *Electronics News*, November 16, 1964; "Earth Station Approved for West Virginia," *Washington Evening Star*, June 5, 1967.

44. Phil Showell, "COMSAT Earth Station: Big Dish for a Little Town," *Western Electric Magazine*, September 1967.

45. Testimony of Martin J. Votaw, assistant vice-president, Communications Satellite Corporation, quoted in *Telecommunications Reports*, March 13, 1972.

46. *Telecommunications Reports*, May 6, 1968; *Telecommunications Reports*, August 26, 1968; *Telecommunications Reports*, November 18, 1968; *Telecommunications Reports*, April 21, 1969; *Telecommunications Reports*, June 9, 1969; *Telecommunications Reports*, July 7, 1969; *Telecommunications Reports*, August 25, 1969.

47. FCC press release, December 4, 1969.

48. *Telecommunications Reports*, April 27, 1970.

49. *Telecommunications Reports*, June 22, 1970.

50. Remarks of Dr. Joseph V. Charyk, president, at Communications Satellite Corporation annual shareholders meeting, May 9, 1972, quoted in *Comsat News Magazine*, June 1972.

CHAPTER THREE

1. Concurring statement of Commissioner Kenneth Cox, in which Commissioner Lee Loevinger joins, with letter from Commission to interested parties of intent to approve *TAT-5* cable, FCC 68-210, February 16, 1968.

2. FCC *Authorized Users* decision, "In the Matter of Authorized Entities and Authorized Users under the Communications Satellite Act of 1962," 4 FCC 2d 421; concurring statement of Commissioners Kenneth Cox with FCC *TAT-5* decision, "In the Matter of American Telephone and Telegraph Company et al., Applications for Authorization to participate in the construction . . . etc.," File Nos. P-C-7022 and S-C-L-40, May 31, 1968.

3. U.S. Congress, Senate, Senator Albert Gore and Senator John Pastore speaking on the Commercial Communications Satellite System, H.R. 11040, 87th Cong., 2d sess., June 14, 1962, *Congressional Record* (unbound), p. 9868.

4. *Telecommunications Reports*, January 25, 1965; *Washington Star*, January 12, 1965; Leo D. Welch, speech before the Broadcast Advertising Club of Chicago, quoted in "Success of Comsat Tied to Telephone," *Chicago Sun-Times*, October 14, 1964; *Telecommunications Reports*, April 26, 1965; *Washington Post*, May 13, 1965; *New York Times*, May 12, 1965; *Telecommunications Reports*, June 7, 1965; *195 Magazine* (house organ of AT&T headquarters at 195 Broadway, New York City), June 1965.

5. *Wall Street Journal*, June 24, 1965; *Washington Post*, July 16, 1965; "Early Bird: Priced Out of Reach?" *Broadcasting*, June 7, 1965; *Variety*, July 7, 1965.

6. Summary of Authorized Users submissions from *Washington Post*, November 4, 1965; *Washington Star*, November 2, 1965; "Inconceivable" quote from "Industry Fighting to Limit Comsat," *New York Times*, July 1, 1966.

7. "Middle position" quote is from "Who's Entitled to Wholesale Comsat Rates?" *Washington Post,* November 4, 1965.

8. *Wall Street Journal,* March 7, 1966; Claudia Dale Goldin, *The Economic Effects of the Introduction of Satellite Communications in the International Communications Industry,* unpublished undergraduate thesis, Cornell University, May 1967, pp. 21–22.

9. FCC *Authorized Users* decision (cited in note 2 above).

10. Goldin, *op. cit.,* p. 59.

11. FCC *Authorized Users* decision (cited in note 2 above).

12. Interview with Asher Ende, deputy director, FCC Common Carrier Bureau, FCC offices, Washington, D.C., July 13–14, 1971.

13. FCC *Authorized Users* decision (cited in note 2 above).

14. Dissenting opinion of Commissioner Nicholas Johnson, with FCC *TAT-5* decision (cited in note 2 above), p. 1.

15. Interview with Roger Noll, staff economist, Brookings Institution, Washington, D.C., July 7, 1971.

16. Richard A. Posner, "Taxation by Regulation," *Bell Journal of Economics and Management Science,* **2**:1(Spring 1971), p. 32.

17. Goldin, *op. cit.,* p. 55.

18. Alfred E. Kahn, *The Economics of Regulation: Principles and Institutions, Vol. 2: Institutional Issues* (New York: Wiley, 1971), p. 231. This discussion relies heavily on Kahn, Vol. I, pp. 166–175, and Vol. II, pp. 223–233; also Posner, *op. cit.,* pp. 22–50.

19. *Ibid.,* p. 224.

20. FCC Docket 16509 (Specialized Common Carriers), "In re Applications of Microwave Communications, Inc. for construction permits to establish new facilities in the Domestic Public Point-to-Point Microwave Radio Service at Chicago, Illinois, St. Louis, Missouri and Intermediate Points," Commission *Report and Order,* p. 17.

21. FCC Public Notice, June 23, 1966, accompanying *Authorized Users* decision (cited in note 2 above).

22. Comments of Communications Satellite Corporation enclosed with letter of January 31, 1972, in response to questions submitted by Ralph Nader Study Group, July 29, 1971, p. 5–1.

23. *Wall Street Journal,* July 7, 1966.

24. U.S. Congress, House, *Communications Satellite Act of 1962,* Pub. L. 87–624, 87th Cong., 2d sess., 1962, H.R. 11040, s.s. 404(a) and (b).

25. Interview with former Comsat executive who asked not to be identified, July 1971.

26. Interview with Nicholas Zapple, staff director, Subcommittee on Communications of the Senate Commerce Committee, July 12, 1971.

27. FCC Docket 16828 (ITT-ABC merger), statement by Harvey J. Levin, "Carrier and Noncarrier Interests in Satellite Organizational Structure."

28. Goldin, *op. cit.,* p. 71.

29. U.S. Congress, House, Committee on Government Operations, *Government Use of Satellite Communications,* House Report No. 2318, 87th Cong., 2d sess., October 19, 1966, p. 53.

30. Communications Satellite Corporation, internal memorandum, mimeo, unsigned, March 1968, p. 14; *Telecommunications Reports,* February 6, 1967.

31. Speech before the American Institute of Aeronautics and Astronautics, San Francisco, quoted in *Broadcasting*, April 15, 1968.

32. *Telecommunications Reports*, November 18, 1968; *Telecommunications Reports*, December 16, 1968; AT&T press release, January 30, 1969.

CHAPTER FOUR

1. Letter from G. Canestrari, Deputy Director of Rates and Tariffs, ITT World Communications, Inc., to Claudia Dale Goldin, March, 1967; Communications Satellite Corporation, *Revised Report on Rates and Revenue Requirements*, November 10, 1966, Section B, p. 3. Both are cited in Claudia Dale Goldin, *The Economic Effects of the Introduction of Satellite Communications in the International Communications Industry*, unpublished undergraduate thesis, Cornell University, May 1967, p. 30.

2. FCC Docket 18875, "Inquiry into policy to be followed in future licensing of facilities for overseas communications," *Comments of American Telephone and Telegraph Company*, August 19, 1970, Appendix 10, pp. 4, 7.

3. *Ibid.*, Annex A to Appendix 3, p. 1.

4. Merrill, Lynch, Pierce, Fenner & Smith, Incorporated, et al., *Prospectus: 10,000,000 Shares, Communications Satellite Corporation*, June 2, 1964, p. 27.

5. Communications Satellite Corporation, *1974 Report to The President and Congress*, p. 5.

6. *Telecommunications Reports*, April 5, 1971.

7. Gerald R. Engel, "Satellite Communication," *Telephone Engineer and Management*, November 15, 1971.

8. Jack Anderson, "The Washington Merry-Go-Round: U.S. Military Communications Archaic" *Washington Post*, February 5, 1973.

9. This example comes from Executive Offices of the President, Office of Telecommunications Policy, *International Facilities* Study, May 1971, pp. 116–117.

10. *Ibid.*

11. Interview with Dr. Reinhold Steiner, Representative to Intelsat from Switzerland/Austria/Liechtenstein, Swiss Embassy, Washington, D.C., August 26, 1971.

12. The point is also made in *International Communications Policy Initiatives*, study prepared by the staff of the Office of Telecommunications Policy, quoted in "Separation From AT&T of Overseas Long Lines Operations . . .," *Telecommunications Reports*, March 12, 1973.

13. "Communications in Conflict: Comsat Clashes with AT&T, ITT on Plan to Lay New, High-Capacity Marine Cable," *Wall Street Journal*, May 31, 1966; "Comsat Disputes ITT, AT&T on Phone Cable to Islands in Caribbean," *Wall Street Journal*, June 13, 1966.

14. Commission *Report and Order* on United States–Puerto Rico Cable, December 7, 1966, 5 FCC 2d 823.

15. FCC Docket 18875 (cited in note 2 above), *Comments of American Telephone and Telegraph Company*, August 19, 1970, Annex A to Appendix 3, p. 1, and Annex B to Appendix 1, p. 4. In the same docket, *Comments of Communications Satellite Corporation*, September 14, 1970, Appendix A, p. 11.

16. *Telecommunications Reports,* September 11, 1967.

17. Katherine Johnsen, "US Discloses Satellites vs. Cable Policy," *Aviation Week and Space Technology,* February 26, 1968.

18. Letter from Rosel H. Hyde, chairman, Federal Communications Commission, to Mr. H. M. Botkin, American Telephone and Telegraph Company, October 4, 1967. This letter states that a similar one was being sent to Comsat.

19. Letter from R. R. Hough, vice-president, American Telephone and Telegraph Company, to Honorable Rosel H. Hyde, chairman, Federal Communications Commission, October 30, 1967, plus enclosed appendices A through N.

20. *Ibid.*

21. *Ibid.*

22. *Ibid.*

23. *Ibid.*

24. "Comsat, AT&T in Bitter Dispute Over Satellites v. Cables," *CQ Fact Sheet,* March 13, 1968, p. 3.

25. See note 19 above.

26. AT&T Press Release, October 10, 1967.

27. See note 17 above.

28. Letter from James McCormack, chairman, Communications Satellite Corporation, to Honorable Rosel H. Hyde, chairman, Federal Communications Commission, October 30, 1967.

29. "AT&T and Comsat Exchange Sharp Criticisms . . . ," *Telecommunications Reports,* January 8, 1968.

30. *Telecommunications Reports,* May 23, 1966.

31. *Washington Star,* May 19, 1966.

32. Interview with Asher Ende, deputy director, FCC Common Carrier Bureau, FCC offices, Washington, D.C., July 13–14, 1971.

33. "AT&T and Comsat Exchange Sharp Criticisms . . . ," *Telecommunications Reports,* January 8, 1968.

34. *Ibid.*

35. Letter from Dr. Joseph Charyk, president, Communications Satellite Corporation, to Honorable Rosel H. Hyde, chairman, Federal Communications Commission, January 4, 1968.

36. *Ibid.*

37. "AT&T and Comsat Exchange Sharp Criticisms . . .," *Telecommunications Reports,* January 8, 1968.

38. Letter from Dr. Joseph Charyk to Honorable Rosel Hyde, January 4, 1968.

39. Letter from Rosel H. Hyde, chairman, Federal Communications Commission, to Mr. Richard R. Hough, vice-president, American Telephone and Telegraph Company, FCC 68–212, February 16, 1968.

40. Letter from Rosel H. Hyde, chairman, Federal Communications Commission, to Mr. James McCormack, chairman, Communications Satellite Corporation, FCC 68–211, February 16, 1968; Katherine Johnsen, "US Discloses Satellites vs. Cable Policy," *Aviation Week and Space Technology,* February 26, 1968.

41. Letter from Rosel H. Hyde, chairman, Federal Communications Commission, to

Honorable Eugene V. Rostow, undersecretary, Department of State, FCC 68–210, February 16, 1968.

42. Associated Press news wire, February 13, 1968, 66819P–13; "Service on Two Trans-Atlantic Cables Interrupted by Trawler Damage," *Telecommunications Reports*, February 19, 1968.

43. *Dissenting Opinion of Commissioner Nicholas Johnson*, February 16, 1968, accompanying letters cited in notes 39–41 above.

44. *Ibid.*

45. *Ibid.*

46. *Concurring Statement of Commissioner Kenneth A. Cox in which Commissioner Lee Loevinger Joins*, February 16, 1968, accompanying letters cited in notes 39–41 above.

47. See note 43 above.

48. See note 46 above.

49. "Carriers' TAT-5 Applications Need Clarification, Comsat Says . . .," *Telecommunications Reports*, April 29, 1968.

50. See note 46 above.

51. "TAT-1 Cable Service Interrupted . . .," *Telecommunications Reports*, April 29, 1968.

52. "U.S. Carriers, In Application to FCC for TAT-5 Cable Authority . . .," *Telecommunications Reports*, April 8, 1968.

53. FCC *TAT-5* Decision, File Nos. P–C–7022 and S–C–L–40, "In the Matter of American Telephone and Telegraph Company et al., Applications for Authorization to Participate in the Construction and Operation of an Integrated Submarine Cable and Radio System . . . [etc.]," May 31, 1968.

54. *Ibid.*

55. "Anticipated Traffic Requirements Indicate Urgent Need . . .," *Telecommunications Reports*, July 29, 1968; "ICSC Approves Contract with Hughes . . .," *Telecommunications Reports*, October 7, 1968.

56. See note 53 above.

57. *Dissenting Opinion of Commissioner Nicholas Johnson* and *Concurring Statement of Commissioner Kenneth A. Cox*, accompanying FCC *TAT-5* decision, cited in note 53 above.

58. *Ibid.*

59. See note 48 above.

60. See note 54 above.

61. See note 57 above.

62. Information derived from figures in FCC Docket 18875 (cited in note 2 above), *Comments of American Telephone and Telegraph Company*, August 21, 1970, Annex B to Appendix 1, pp. 1–4; and in the same docket, *Comments of Communications Satellite Corporation*, September 14, 1970, Appendix A, pp. 6–19.

63. "Comsat Still Disagrees With Carriers . . .," *Telecommunications Reports*, February 23, 1970.

64. Letter from Rosel H. Hyde to Mr. Richard R. Hough, cited in note 39 above.

65. "Comsat Still Disagrees With Carriers . . .," *Telecommunications Reports*, February 2, 1970; "ITT Worldcom Submits Views from 11 Countries . . . ," *Telecommunications Reports*, February 23, 1970.

66. "Three Record Carriers Defer Use . . . ," *Telecommunications Reports*, April 6, 1970;

"ITT Worldcom and Comsat, In Latest Moves . . . ," *Telecommunications Reports,* April 20, 1970.

67. "Record Carriers File Tariffs for TAT-5 . . . ," *Telecommunications Reports,* May 4, 1970; "FCC Says Additional Capacity of (F-7) . . . ," *Telecommunications Reports,* May 11, 1970.

68. "ITT Worldcom Asks Delay . . . ," *Telecommunications Reports,* December 21, 1970.

69. "ITT Worldcom Is Endeavoring to Upset . . . ," *Telecommunications Reports,* January 11, 1971.

70. "AT&T, Opposing Comsat's Move to Defer Action . . . ," *Telecommunications Reports,* January 11, 1971.

71. See Anthony Sampson, *The Sovereign State: The Secret History of ITT* (London: Coronet Books, 1974), pp. 134 ff. (Dita Beard's memorandum, p. 180.)

72. "ITT Worldcom Asks OTP Support . . . ," *Telecommunications Reports,* January 25, 1971; "First Intelsat IV Satellite Successfully Shot . . . ," *Telecommunications Reports,* February 1, 1971.

73. "ITT Worldcom Objects to Comsat Request . . . ," *Telecommunications Reports,* March 15, 1971; "Condition Attached to Temporary Authorization . . . ," *Telecommunications Reports,* April 19, 1971.

74. "AT&T Proposes Activating Five Additional Satellite Circuits . . . ," *Telecommunications Reports,* April 26, 1971; "Commission Order Sets Satellite/Cable 'Proportional Fill' . . . ," *Telecommunications Reports,* May 10, 1971.

75. "European Correspondents Unhappy with FCC's 'Proportional Fill' Order . . . ," *Telecommunications Reports,* June 7, 1971; "Significant Modification Soon of FCC's 5:1 'Proportional Fill' Order . . . ," *Telecommunications Reports,* October 4, 1971; FCC 71–1079 (decision redefining proportional fill).

76. FCC 71–1079.

77. "ITT Worldcom Opposes Any Plans by Comsat . . . ," *Telecommunications Reports,* November 20, 1970; "Comsat, as U.S. Entity, Being Urged to 'Go Slow' . . . ," *Telecommunications Reports,* December 18, 1972; "Intelsat 4.5 Decision Delayed to March," *Aviation Week and Space Technology,* January 1, 1973.

78. "ITT Worldcom Wants to Inspect 'Summary Record' . . . ," *Telecommunications Reports,* January 8, 1973.

79. "Comsat Reportedly Gets Nod from FCC . . . ," *Telecommunications Reports,* January 22, 1973.

80. "Plans for New Telephone Calls in Atlantic and Pacific . . . ," *Telecommunications Reports,* September 2, 1969.

81. *Ibid.*

82. FCC interoffice memorandum, June 8, 1971, "To: Files, From: Asher Ende, Subject: AT&T Plans for future transpacific cables." This memo was not obtained from Mr. Ende.

83. "U.S. Policy for Assigning Total Traffic Between Cables, Satellites . . . ," *Telecommunications Reports,* September 8, 1969.

84. Katherine Johnsen, "FCC Launches Cable-Satellite Investigation to Establish Policy," *Aviation Week and Space Technology,* December 8, 1969.

85. "FCC Initiates Inquiry into Overseas Services and Facilities . . . ," *Telecommunications Reports,* June 15, 1970.

86. FCC Docket 18875 (cited in note 2 above), *Comments of American Telephone and Telegraph Company,* August 21, 1970.

87. *Ibid.*

88. "Transatlantic Traffic Shifted to Intelsat IIIs After Break in TAT-5," *Telecommunications Reports,* March 29, 1971; Robert J. Samuelson, "Happiness for Comsat Is a Ruptured Cable," *Washington Post,* February 12, 1972.

89. See note 86 above.

90. See note 86 above.

91. "AT&T, Filing for Authority to Construct TAT-6 Cable . . . ," *Telecommunications Reports,* September 8, 1970.

92. FCC Docket 18875 (cited note 2 above), *Comments of Communications Satellite Corporation,* September 14, 1970.

93. *Ibid.*

94. Letter from Melvin Laird, Secretary of Defense, to Honorable Dean Burch, chairman, Federal Communications Commission, December 18, 1970.

95. Letter from Louis A. deRosa, assistant to the Secretary of Defense (Telecommunications), to Honorable Dean Burch, chairman, Federal Communications Commission, May 6, 1971.

95. Executive Offices of the President, Office of Telecommunications Policy, *Policy Recommendations and Conclusions for International Facilities,* accompanying letter from Clay T. Whitehead, director, to Honorable Dean Burch, chairman, Federal Communications Commission, May 21, 1971.

96. *Ibid.*

97. *Ibid.*

98. Executive Offices of the President, *Office of Telecommunications Policy,* International Facilities Study, May 1971.

99. Letter from Ted B. Westfall, ITT World Communications, Inc., to Honorable Dean Burch, chairman, Federal Communications Commission, June 14, 1971.

100. FCC Docket 18875 (cited in note 2 above), *Informal Conference on Transatlantic Communications,* Official Report of Proceedings, Washington, D. C., June 17, 1971.

101. FCC Docket 18875 (cited in note 2 above), Commission *Statement of Policy and Guidelines,* FCC 71-659, June 24, 1971.

102. FCC Docket 18875 (cited in note 2 above), American Telephone and Telegraph Company, *Petition for Partial Reconsideration,* July 23, 1971; "ITT Worldcom, RCA Globcom Urge Partial Reconsideration . . . ," *Telecommunications Reports,* August 2, 1971; "Comsat, Opposing Carriers' Request for FCC Reconsideration . . . ," *Telecommunications Reports,* August 16, 1971.

103. "Plans for Major Increase in Transatlantic Facilities . . . ," *Telecommunications Reports,* December 13, 1971.

104. AT&T letter to FCC, February 25, 1971, referred to in FCC interoffice memorandum, April 15, 1971, "To: The Commissioners, From: Chief, Common Carrier Bureau."

105. "ITT Worldcom, In Application for Participation in TAT-6 Cable . . . ," *Telecommunications Reports,* January 17, 1972.

106. FCC *TAT-6* decision, "In the Matter of American Telephone and Telegraph Company, ITT World Communications, Inc., RCA Global Communications, Inc., West-

ern Union International, Inc., Application for authority to participate in the construction and operation of the TAT-6 SG submarine cable system between the United States and France," FCC 720613, July 7, 1972.

107. FCC interoffice memorandum, June 8, 1971, "To: Files, From: Asher Ende, Subject: AT&T Plans for future transpacific cables." This memo was not obtained from Mr. Ende.

108. "As First Phase in Comprehensive Pacific Cable Facilities Plan . . . ," *Telecommunications Reports,* September 27, 1971.

109. "Comsat Not Opposed to New Mainland-Hawaii Submarine Cable . . . ," *Telecommunications Reports,* November 1, 1971.

110. "FCC Action on New Mainland-Hawaii Cable . . . ," *Telecommunications Reports,* March 6, 1972.

111. "Application Filed for Pacific Cable Link . . . ," *Telecommunications Reports,* October 9, 1972.

112. "ITT Worldcom and WUI File Proposed Hawaii/Okinawa Cable Applications . . . ," *Telecommunications Reports,* October 21, 1972.

113. "Comsat Sees Economic Burden on Ratepayers as 'Basic Question' . . . ," *Telecommunications Reports,* February 5, 1973.

114. "Commission Authorizes SF Pacific Cables to Hawaii and Okinawa . . . ," *Telecommunications Reports,* June 18, 1973.

115. *Ibid.*

CHAPTER FIVE

1. "The Tail and The Dog," *The Economist,* August 9, 1969.

2. U.S. Department of State, *International Telecommunications Satellite Consortium (Intelsat): Agreement Between the United States of America and Other Governments,* done at Washington, August 20, 1964, Treaties and International Acts Series #5616.

3. *Comments of Communications Satellite Corporation* enclosed with letter of January 31, 1972, in response to questions submitted by Ralph Nader Study Group, July 29, 1971 (in further references, *Comsat Q&A*), p. 6–4.

4. Quoted in the *New York Times,* April 22, 1965.

5. *Toronto Globe,* May 2, 1965.

6. Interview with José Alegrett, representative to Intelsat from Venezuela, Venezuelan Embassy, Washington, D.C., August 5, 1971.

7. Interview with former Comsat employee, IDD division, who asked not to be identified, August 1971.

8. Interview with Dr. Reinhold Steiner, representative to Intelsat from Switzerland/Austria/liechtenstien, Swiss Embassy, Washington, D.C., August 26, 1971.

9. *Ibid.*

10. Interview with former Comsat employee, who asked not to be identified, July 1971.

11. See note 6 above.

12. Booz, Allen & Hamilton, management consultants, *Intelsat Management Review,* conducted at the request of the Interim Communications Satellite Committee, Washing-

ton, D.C., under the terms of negotiated contract (No. CSC–55–231) with the Communications Satellite Corporation, May 1970.

13. See note 6 above.

14. These complaints were referred to in the Booz, Allen report (see note 12 above), and confirmed by Mr. Alegrett and Dr. Steiner in interviews.

15. See note 12 above.

16. Quoted in *Aviation Week and Space Technology,* August 28, 1972.

17. Interview with Asher Ende, deputy director, Common Carrier Bureau, Federal Communications Commission, FCC offices, Washington, D.C., July 13 and 14, 1971.

18. James L. Weeks, *Who Will Rule the Talk of the World? The International Politics of Communications Satellites,* unpublished paper, Case Western Reserve University, January 12, 1969.

19. Murray C. Schwartz and Joseph M. Goldsen, *Foreign Participation in Communications Satellite Systems: Implications of the Communications Satellite Act of 1962,* Rand Corporation Memorandum RM 3434–RC (February 1963), pp. 28–29, quoted in Weeks, *op. cit.* (see note 18 above).

20. Booz, Allen & Hamilton, cited in note 12 above, Exhibit XV; *Air & Cosmos,* July 17, 1971 (translation by Comsat).

21. International Telecommunications Satellite Consortium, *Procurement Regulations for Intelsat,* mimeo, February 2, 1968.

22. Interview with Clay T. Whitehead, White House director of Telecommunications Policy, Office of Telecommunications Policy, Washington, D.C., August 25, 1971.

23. Weeks, (see note 18 above), pp. 25–27.

24. *Comsat Q&A,* p. 6–5.

25. Booz, Allen & Hamilton, *op. cit.* (note 12 above), p. 34.

26. *Ibid.*

27. *Ibid.,* pp. 34 ff.

28. Interview with Dr. Reinhold Steiner, cited in note 8 above.

29. Interviews with José Alegrett and Dr. Reinhold Steiner, cited in notes 6 and 8 above.

30. Resumed Plenipotentiary Conference on Definitive Arrangements for the International Telecommunications Satellite Consortium, *Operating Agreement Relating to the International Telecommunications Satellite Organization "Intelsat,"* Document 233, May 19, 1971.

31. Interview with former Comsat employee, who asked not to be identified, July 1971.

32. Statement by the representative of Switzerland/Austria/Liechenstein, *Agenda Item No. 6 Consideration of Procurement of Additional Intelsat IV Satellites,* ANNEX to ICSC-44-3E W/12/69; FCC Docket 16495, "In the Matter of Establishment of Domestic Communications Satellite Facilities by Non-Government Entities."

33. *Comments of MCI Lockheed Satellite Corporation on Proposed Second Report and Order,* April 19, 1972, pp. 40–47.

34. See note 8 above.

35. Statement by Dr. Reinhold Steiner, quoted in *Comments of MCI Lockheed Satellite Corporation,* cited in note 30 above, p. 45.

36. Citation for permanent operating agreement is given in note 30 above. The other half of the permanent agreement, that between the signatory countries, is called *Agreement*

Relating to the International Telecommunications Satellite Organization "Intelsat" and is Document 232 dated May 19, 1971.

37. "1974 Will See US–USSR 'Hot Line' via Intelsat IV and Molniya II," *Air & Cosmos,* January 13, 1973 (translation by Comsat).

38. Interview with Mr. Abdel Razik, Intelsat public relations officer, Washington, D.C., June 3, 1975.

CHAPTER SIX

1.   "AT&T Attacks Ford Figures on TV Satellite," *New York Times,* August 19, 1966.

2.   FCC Docket 16495, letter from McGeorge Bundy to FCC Chairman Rosel H. Hyde, accompanying *Comments of the Ford Foundation in Response to the Commission's Notice of Inquiry,* August 1, 1966. The full title of FCC Docket 16495 is "In the Matter of Establishment of Domestic Communications-Satellite Facilities by Non-governmental Entities."

3.   Steven M. Aug, "Keeping the FCC In Step;" *The Sunday Star,* April 23, 1972.

4.   *The Economist,* August 6, 1966.

5.   U.S. Congress, Senate, Subcommittee on Monopoly of the Select Committee on Small Business, *Hearings on Space Satellite Communications,* 87th Cong., 1st sess., August 2, 3, 4, 9, 10, and 11, 1961, pp. 257–258.

6.   *Ibid.,* p. 47.

7.   U.S. Congress, Senator Russell Long speaking on the Commercial Communications Satellite System, H.R. 11040, 87th Cong., 2d sess., 1962, *Congressional Record* (bound), p. 16213.

8.   U.S. Congress, House, *Communications Satellite Act of 1962,* Pub. L. 87–624, 87th Cong., 2d sess., H.R. 11040, Sec. 102(d).

9.   *Senate Comsat debate* (cited in note 7 above), Senator Maurine Neuberger, July 30, 1962, *Congressional Record* (unbound), p. 14045.

10. *Ibid.,* Senator John Pastore, 1962, *Congressional Record* (bound), p. 15124.

11. *Ibid.,* Senator Jacob Javits, 1962, *Congressional Record* (bound), p. 16574.

12. Interview with former Comsat official, who asked not to be identified, July 1971.

13. AT&T Vice President Richard Hough, quoted in *Telecommunications Reports,* May 31, 1965.

14. Senate Comsat debate (cited in note 7 above), Senator John Pastore, June 15, 1962, *Congressional Record* (unbound), p. 9842.

15. *Ibid.,* Senator Robert Kerr and Senator Russell Long, June 19, 1962, *Congressional Record* (unbound), p. 10247.

16. FCC Docket 16495, AT&T *Petition for Reconsideration,* July 17, 1972, p. 19.

17. FCC Docket 16495, Concurring Opinion of Commissioner Nicholas Johnson, accompanying Commission *Second Report and Order,* June 16, 1972, p. 8.

18. *New York Herald Tribune,* November 18, 1964.

19. *Aviation Week and Space Technology,* February 1, 1965.

20. Speech to the 24th plenary session of the Diebold Research Program, quoted in "Marks Sees 'Risk' . . . ," *Telecommunications Reports,* November 16, 1970.

21. Letter from Bernard Gold, assistant general attorney, National Broadcasting Company, to Michael E. Kinsley, Center for Study of Responsive Law, July 30, 1971.

22. Interview with former Comsat executive, who asked not to be identified, August 1971.

23. *New York Times,* May 14, 1975; *Washington Post,* May 28, 1965; *Washington Star,* June 1, 1965; *Wall Stteet Journal,* September 22, 1965.

24. AT&T statement quoted in *Telecommunications Reports,* May 31, 1965.

25. Hough speech quoted in *Washington Post,* May 29, 1965.

26. Interview with Lee R. Marks, lawyer, Ginsberg, Feldman & Bress, Washington, D.C., July 7, 1971.

27. FCC Docket 16495, Comments of the Ford Foundation in Response to the Commission's Notice of Inquiry, August 1, 1966, p. 3.

28. Quoted in *Variety,* October 25, 1972.

29. Lawrence H. Rogers II, president, Taft Broadcasting Company, quoted in "Nixon Bill Would Check Local TV Stations on 'Bias' in Network News, Entertainment," *Wall Street Journal,* December 19, 1972.

30. Quoted in *Variety,* October 25, 1972.

32. John Carmody, "Public Broadcasting: New Chief, New Policy," *Washington Post,* September 21, 1972; John J. O'Connor, "Television: Moving In For the Kill?" *New York Times,* January 21, 1973.

33. Interview with Clay T. Whitehead, White House director of Telecommunications Policy, Washington, D.C., August 25, 1971.

34. *New York Times,* August 3, 1967.

35. Letter from Lowell F. Wingert, vice-president, American Telephone & Telegraph Company, to James McCormack, chairman, Communications Satellite Corporation, March 23, 1966.

36. *Ibid.*

37. Quoted in *Telecommunications Reports,* April 11, 1966.

38. "Comsat Opposes Rival Systems," *New York Times,* August 2, 1966.

39. Richard Harwood, "Networks Cool to Educational TV Proposal," *Philadelphia Inquirer,* August 24, 1966.

40. Interview with Lee R. Marks, lawyer, Ginsberg, Feldman & Bress, Washington, D.C., July 7, 1971.

41. "Comsat Opposes Rival Systems," *New York Times,* August 2, 1966.

42. FCC Docket 16495, *Ford Foundation Reply Legal Brief,* December 12, 1966, and Comsat brief quoted in it on pp. 18–23; FCC Docket 16495, *Ford Foundation Supplementary Legal Brief,* April 3, 1967, pp. 43–47, 9–15, and Comsat brief quoted in those pages.

43. Comsat comments of December 12, 1966 quoted in the *Washington Post,* December 13, 1966.

44. Senator Magnuson quoted in *Telecommunications Reports,* November 7, 1966.

45. *New York Times,* August 29, 1966.

46. *Variety,* August 31, 1966.

47. FCC Docket 16495, *Further Comments of the Ford Foundation,* September 18, 1967.

48. *New York Times,* December 18, 1966.

49. Comments of Communications Satellite Corporation enclosed with letter of January 31, 1972, in response to questions submitted by Ralph Nader Study Group, July 29, 1971, pp. 4–5; Harry Harris, "Ford Satellite Plan Would Prove Boon to Viewing Public," *Philadelphia Inquirer*, August 3, 1966; "The Amazing Story of Earth Satellites," interview with James McCormack, *U.S. News & World Report*, December 26, 1966; Communications Satellite Corporation, internal memorandum, mimeo, unsigned, March 1968.

50. FCC Docket 16495, *Public Interest Issues: Supplemental Comments of the Ford Foundation*, April 3, 1967, Appendix B: Hammet & Edison, Consulting Radio Engineers, *An Evaluation of the Technical and Economic Comments of the Ford Foundation, Comsat, and AT&T in FCC Docket No. 16495*.

51. "Comsat Will Win Domestic Satellite," *Business Week*, June 17, 1967.

52. "Communication: Searching Eye, Questing Ear," *Forbes*, July 15, 1967.

53. O'Connell quoted in *Broadcasting*, July 3, 1967.

54. FCC Docket 16495, Commission *Second Report and Order*, FCC 72–531, June 16, 1972.

55. U.S. Congress, House, *Global Communications System*, Message from the President of the United States, 90th Cong., 1st sess., August 14, 1967, Doc. No. 157.

56. "AT&T Proposes Rate Increase," *Broadcasting*, January 29, 1968.

57. AT&T quarterly report to shareholders, October 1, 1968, quoted in "Domestic Satellite Economics Currently 'Uncertain' . . . ," *Telecommunications Reports*, October 7, 1968.

58. President's Task Force on Communications Policy, *Final Report*, December 7, 1968, U.S. Government Printing Office, pp. 28 ff.

59. Interview with former staff member of the President's Task Force on Communication Policy, who asked not to be identified, July 1971.

60. "FCC Promises Pilot Domestic Satellite by '70," *Variety*, March 5, 1969; "60 Channel CATV By Comsat?" *Variety*, June 25, 1969; "Suggestion of Joint Comsat/NASA Team . . . ," *Telecommunications Reports*, June 30, 1969.

61. "A Short Course in Cable, 1973," *Broadcasting*, June 18, 1973.

62. FCC Docket 16495, Concurring Opinion of Commissioner Nicholas Johnson accompanying Commission *Second Report and Order*, FCC 72–531, June 16, 1972, p. 2.

63. " 'Small Working Group' To Be Named . . . ," *Telecommunications Reports*, July 28, 1969.

64. "Hyde Says FCC Will Welcome . . . ," *Telecommunications Reports*, August 4, 1969.

65. "White House Working Group to Consider . . . ," *Telecommunications Reports*, August 18, 1969.

66. Jack Gould, "Stanton to Urge a Private System of TV Satellites," *New York Times*, October 15, 1969.

67. "Answer to AT&T," *Broadcasting*, October 20, 1969.

68. "AT&T Drops Opposition to TV Networks Operating Own Communications Satellites," *Wall Street Journal*, October 16, 1969.

69. Jack Gould, "Comsat Advances Satellite TV Plan," *New York Times*, October 19, 1969.

70. "Domestic Satellite Developments, Including Release . . . ," *Telecommunications Reports*, October 27, 1969.

71. "Washington Newsletter," *Electronics*, October 27, 1969.

72. Jack Gould, "New Satellite System Proposed to Carry All Traffic but Phones," *New York Times,* October 30, 1969.

72. Katherine Johnsen, "AT&T Calls for Indefinite Delay in Domestic Satcom Inception," *Aviation Week and Space Technology,* January 5, 1970.

CHAPTER SEVEN

1. White House Memorandum for Honorable Dean Burch, chairman, Federal Communications Commission, signed by Peter Flanigan, assistant to the President, January 23, 1970, reprinted as Appendix B, pp. 33–40, of FCC Docket 16495, Commission *First Report and Order,* FCC 70–306, March 24, 1970. The full title of FCC Docket 16495 is "In the Matter of Establishment of Domestic Communications-Satellite Facilities by Non-governmental Entities."

2. *Ibid.*

3. *Ibid.*

4. *Ibid.*

5. "Comsat Industries," *Forbes,* March 15, 1970.

6. Statement by Communications Satellite Corporation, released January 23, 1970.

7. "AT&T To Ask Authority . . . ," *Telecommunications Reports,* February 2, 1970.

8. "Burch Welcomes White House Views . . . ," *Telecommunications Reports,* January 26, 1970.

9. Katherine Johnsen, "Satcom Policy Spurs Immediate Response," *Aviation Week and Space Technology,* February 9, 1970.

10. FCC Docket 16495, Commission *First Report and Order,* FCC 70–306, March 24, 1970.

11. FCC Docket 16495, Commission *Further Notice of Inquiry and Proposed Rule Making,* September 23, 1970.

12. "Western Union With First Application . . . ," *Telecommunications Reports,* August 3, 1970.

13. See note 11 above.

14. John D. McDonald, "Getting Our Communication Satellite Off the Ground," *Fortune,* June 1972. Much of the information on the following pages comes from this excellent article or from a box entitled "Prospects for U.S. Domestic Systems Described" in *Aviation Week and Space Technology,* August 23, 1971.

15. "Some Problems Relating to Establishment . . . ," *Telecommunications Reports,* November 2, 1970.

16. FCC Docket 16495, *Joint Statement of ABC, CBS and NBC,* March 29, 1971.

17. Advertisement in *Aviation Week and Space Technology,* August 23, 1971.

18. See note 14 above.

19. FCC Docket 16495, Commission *First Report and Order,* FCC 70–306, March 24, 1970, Appendix B, pp. 31–32.

20. See the collected press releases from the Office of Senator Mike Gravel, especially 1970–1971. Interview with Perry Poirier, legislative assistant to Senator Mike Gravel, July 5, 1971.

21. "AT&T, Comsat Give Satellite Plan Details," *Wall Street Journal,* October 20, 1970.

22. "Companion Applications For Domestic Satellite Service . . . ," *Telecommunications Reports,* October 19, 1970.

23. See note 21 above.

24. "How AT&T Views Its Role in Space Race," *Broadcasting,* October 26, 1970.

25. "Comsat Multi-Purpose Domestic Satellite System to Provide Nationwide Communications Services," Comsat press release 71–13, March 1, 1971.

26. "Comsat to File Plans This Week . . . ," *Telecommunications Reports,* March 1, 1971.

27. FCC Docket 16495, letter from David C. Acheson, Comsat vice-president and general counsel, to Mr. Ben F. Waple, secretary, Federal Communications Commission, accompanying *Comsat Multi-Purpose Domestic Satellite Communications System,* March 1, 1971, Vol. I, pp. 1–11.

28. "Economics and Regulation of Domestic Satellite Communication," address by William H. Melody, associate professor of Communication and Economics, Annenberg School of Communication, University of Pennsylvania, to the session on Domestic Satellite Communication for the U.S., IEEE International Convention, New York Hilton Hotel, March 25, 1971.

29. *Ibid.*

30. FCC Docket 16495, *Comments of Communications Satellite Corporation,* May 12, 1971. Primary reference is to pp. 22–58.

31. *Ibid.*

32. *Ibid.*

33. FCC Docket 16495, *Reply Comments of MCI Lockheed Satellite Corporation,* July 12, 1971, pp. 8–9.

34. FCC Docket 16495, *Comments of AT&T,* May 12, 1971, quoted in "FCC Deluged with Ideas . . . ," *Telecommunications Reports,* May 17, 1971.

35. FCC Docket 16495, *Comments of the United States Department of Justice,* May 12, 1971, p. 22.

36. FCC Docket 16495, *Reply Comments of the United States Department of Justice,* July 12, 1971, p. 5.

37. FCC Docket 16495, *Comments of MCI Lockheed Satellite Corporation,* quoted in "FCC Deluged with Ideas . . . ," *Telecommunications Reports,* May 17, 1971. Unless separately cited, all quotations from or summaries of May 12 *Comments* come from this article.

38. FCC Docket 16495, *Reply Comments of MCI Lockheed Satellite Corporation,* July 12, 1971. See also FCC Docket 16495, *Comments of MCI Lockheed Satellite Corporation on Proposed Second Report and Order,* April 19, 1972.

39. See note 14 above.

40. FCC Docket 16495, *Comments of the United States Department of Justice,* May 12, 1971, p. 8.

41. "FCC deluged with ideas . . . ," *Telecommunications Reports,* May 17, 1971.

42. FCC Docket 16495, *Reply Comments of Communications Satellite Corporation,* July 12, 1971.

43. See note 14 above.

44. "Burch Comments on Domestic System . . . ," *Telecommunications Reports,* February 7, 1972.

45. Federal Communications Commission, "Domestic Communications Satellite

Facilities: Proposed Establishment by Non-Government Entities," *Federal Register,* Vol. 36, No. 56, March 22, 1972, Part II.

46. Stephen M. Aug, "Keeping the FCC 'In Step,' " *The Sunday Star,* April 23, 1972.

47. FCC staff report (cited in note 45 above), *Federal Register,* Vol. 36, No. 56, March 22, 1972, Part II.

48. "Limitations on Use of Domestic Satellite . . . ," *Telecommunications Reports,* March 27, 1972.

49. "DOD Says Limitations on AT&T Use . . . ," *Telecommunications Reports,* April 3, 1972.

50. *Ibid.*

51. "Domestic Satellite Communications System Applicants Generally Oppose . . . ," *Telecommunications Reports,* April 24, 1972. All references to this round of comments come from this article, unless separately cited.

52. "Comsat Backs Open Entry for Domestic Satellite Services," Comsat press release, April 21, 1972; "Comsat Favors Open Entry for Domestic Services," *Comsat News,* June 1972; "Parties to Domestic Satellite Communications Proceedings Not Reaching Any Consensus . . . ," *Telecommunications Reports,* April 9, 1972.

53. Stephen M. Aug, "Keeping the FCC 'In Step,' " *The Sunday Star,* April 23, 1972.

54. FCC Docket 16495, Commission *Second Report and Order,* FCC 72–531, June 16, 1972.

55. *Ibid.,* p. 7.

56. *Ibid.*

57. Robert J. Samuelson, "FCC Lifts Ban on Using Satellites for Domestic TV, Phones, Wires," *Washington Post,* June 17, 1972.

58. See note 54 above.

59. "Coming Uses for Satellites—Battle To Control the Business," *U.S. News & World Report,* August 7, 1972.

60. Katherine Johnsen, "Telesat Pre-Launch Sales Near Capacity," *Aviation Week and Space Technology,* November 6, 1972.

61. "Western Union Corp.'s Unit Proposes Rates for Satellite System," *Wall Street Journal,* March 21, 1973.

62. "AT&T Opposes General's Revised Domestic Satellite Application . . . ," *Telecommunications Reports,* December 4, 1972.

63. Stephen M. Aug, "COMSAT's Puente Hired By Competitor," *Washington Star-News,* February 13, 1973.

64. "Comsat Loses Another Aide to Fairchild," *Washington Star-News,* February?

65. FCC Docket 16495, AT&T *Petition for Reconsideration,* July 17, 1972, pp. 11–13, 19.

66. FCC Docket 16495, *Petition of Communications Satellite Corporation for Reconsideration of Second Report and Order,* July 17, 1972.

67. "Consummation of Comsat–MCI Lockheed Agreement . . . ," *Telecommunications Reports,* September 11, 1972.

68. FCC Docket 16495, *Comments of MCI Lockheed Satellite Corporation on Proposed Second Report and Order,* April 19, 1972, p. 48.

69. "Comsat Characterizes WUI Proposal . . . ," *Telecommunications Reports,* February 20, 1973.

70. "Comsat Responds to Opposition Comments . . . ," *Telecommunications Reports,* November 20, 1972.

71. "Consortium Plan Hit as Dodge of FCC Policy," *Broadcasting,* October 2, 1972.

72. "Comsat Sees Revenues Rising in Rest of '72, Doesn't Predict Net." *Wall Street Journal,* September 7, 1972.

73. FCC Docket 16495, *Commission Memorandum Opinion and Order,* FCC 72–1198, December 21, 1972, quoted in "FCC, In Final Domestic Satellite Order, Reverses June Decision . . . ," *Telecommunications Reports,* December 26, 1972.

74. Sanford L. Jacobs, "IBM and Comsat Will Jointly Run Satellite Concern," *Wall Street Journal,* July 8, 1974.

75. "FCC Tentatively Lets AT&T Cut Line Charge To Television Networks," *Wall Street Journal,* May 10, 1973.

CHAPTER EIGHT

1. Salomon Brothers, The First Boston Corporation, Merrill, Lynch, Pierce, Fenner & Smith, Inc., *Prospectus: 2,895,750 Shares, Communications Satellite Corporation,* June 12, 1973. (In future references, 1973 Prospectus.)

2. Quoted in "Comsat Opposes Rival Systems," *New York Times,* August 2, 1966.

3. Comptroller General of the United States, *Large Costs to the Government Not Recovered for Launch Services Provided to the Communications Satellite Corporation,* B–168707, Report to the Congress, October 8, 1971.

4. *Wall Street Journal,* October 1, 1963.

5. UPI wire report, October 13, 1964.

6. *Time* quoted in Joseph C. Goulden, *Monopoly* (New York: Pocket Books, 1970), p. 129.

7. Comments of Communications Satellite Corporation enclosed with letter of January 31, 1972, in response to questions submitted by Ralph Nader Study Group, July 29, 1971 (in future references, *Comsat Q&A*), p. 10–2.

8. Annual Report of Communications Satellite Corporation to the Federal Communications Commission for the Year Ended December 21, 1971 (in future references, *Comsat Form M*), schedules 70B, 42.

9. *Wall Street Journal,* July 7, 1965.

10. "Man in the News," *New York Times,* May 3, 1965.

11. Comsat Press Release No. 70–39, July 7, 1970.

12. *Comsat Form M* (see note 8 above), schedule 43, number 8 (i.e., this was the eighth largest contract of any type let by Comsat during 1971).

13. McCormack contract from SEC Closed File on Communications Satellite Corporation, #1–4929–2–12, and dated June 19, 1970.

14. *Comsat Form M* (see note 8 above), schedule 3.

15. *Comsat Form M* (see note 8 above), schedule 20C.

16. Barry Miller, "TWR to Develop Satcom for USAF, Navy," *Aviation Week and Space Technology,* November 20, 1972.

17. "Navy Awards Contract . . . ," *Telecommunications Reports,* March 5, 1972.

18. "International Record Carriers, In Show of Unity . . . ," *Telecommunications Reports,* March 26, 1973.

19. "Comsat Given Waiver . . . ," *Telecommunications Reports,* April 16, 1973; "FCC Approves Participation . . . ," *Telecommunications Reports,* September 3, 1973.

20. "Airlines Planning Two-Way Suncom Tests," *Aviation Week and Space Technology*, November 1, 1965; "Airlines Sell FAA on Prompt Use of Comsat," *Business Week*, January 15, 1966.

21. Interview with former Comsat official, who asked not to be identified, August 1971.

22. Robert J. Samuelson, "Satellites to Help Airlines Proposed,"*Washington Post*, May 12, 1970; Phillip J. Klass, "The Aerosat Controversy,"*Aviation Week and Space Technology*, November 8, 1971; Robert J. Samuelson, "White House Rejects Plans for U.S.-Europe Satellite," *Washington Post*, February 15, 1972; Katherine Johnsen, "U.S. to Press for Private Entity Aerosat, *"Aviation Week and Space Technology*, February 21, 1972.

23. "ESRO to Pick U.S. Aerosat Partner," *Electronics*, January 18, 1973; *1973 Prospectus* (see note 1 above), p. 31.

24. "Comsat General Buys Interest in Intercomsa, *"Washington Star-News*, November 25, 1974.

25. *1973 Prospectus* (see note 1 above), p. 11.

25. Quoted in Thomas Dimond, "ITT Sale of Stock in Comsat Blamed on Basic Conflict," *Washington Star*, December 8, 1968.

26. *Comsat Q&A*, p. 3–6.

27. In the United States Court of Appeals for the District of Columbia Circuit, ITT World Communications, Inc., Petitioner, v. Communications Satellite Corporation, Respondent, "Emergency Petition for Preliminary Injunction, Temporary Restraining Order and Other Relief in Aid of the Jurisdiction of the Court," No. 20263, June 22, 1966.

28. Interview with David Acheson, general counsel, Communications Satellite Corporation, Washington, D.C., July 1971.

29. FCC Docket 16495, "In the Matter of Establishment of Domestic Communications-Satellite Facilities by Non-governmental Entities," *Reply Comments of Communications Satellite Corporation*, July 12, 1971, p. 8.

30. Herman Schwartz, "Governmentally Appointed Directors in a Private Corporation—The Communications Satellite Act of 1962," *Harvard Law Review*, **79**:350 (1965). Citation for Robert Kennedy quotation is note 15, p. 353.

31. *Articles of Incorporation of Communications Satellite Corporation*, As Amended Through June 5, 1969, Section 8.03.

32. *Comsat Q&A*, pp. 3–1, 3–4.

33. *New York Times*, September 21, 1964.

34. Drew Pearson, "The Washington Merry-Go-Round," *Washington Post*, October 4, 1964.

35. Letter from Clark Kerr to Michael E. Kinsley, August 1971.

36. *Comsat Form Ms*, 1965–1971, schedule 3. (See note 8 above for 1971.)

37. "Peterson Is Nominated by Nixon . . . ," *Telecommunications Reports*, July 27, 1970.

38. *Comsat Form Ms*, 1965-1971, Schedule 70B. (See note 8 above for 1971.)

39. Mark Green, *The Closed Enterprise System*, mimeo (Washington: Center for Study of Responsive Law, 1971), p. 1131.

40. Letter from Richard W. McLaren, assistant attorney general, Antitrust Division, Justice Department, to Senator Mike Gravel, January 5, 1971; *Comsat Form M* (see note 8 above), schedule 70B; SEC Closed File on Communications Satellite Corporation/1–4929–2–12.

41. "Twelve Comsat Directors Elected by Shareholders," Comsat press release No. 73–27, May 15, 1973.

42. Letter from George Meany, president, AFL-CIO, to the President of the United States, February 11, 1972.

43. "Nixon Eyes Fitzsimmons for Meany Comsat Seat," *Wall Street Journal*, May 19, 1972.

44. Interview with Clay T. Whitehead, White House director of Telecommunications Policy, Washington, D.C., August 25, 1971.

45. "Comments on Proposed Changes . . . ," *Telecommunications Reports*, March 19, 1973.

46. Comsat 1974 Report to the President and Congress, p. 59.

47. "A Quiet Young Man with Power and the Will to Use It," *Broadcasting*, October 19, 1970.

48. *Ibid.*

49. *Telecommunications Reorganization*, Message from the President to the Congress of the United States, February 9, 1970. For a lengthy critique of Reorganization Plan No. 1, see Edwin B. Spievack, "Presidential Assault on Telecommunicwions," *Federal Communications Bar Journal*, **23,** 3 (Part I), [1970 (misidentified as 1969)]: 155–181.

50. Whitehead quoted in *Broadcasting*, February 16, 1970, p. 38.

51. Editorial, "Telecommunications Policy," *New York Times*, March 14, 1970.

52. "The Communications-Regulation Gap?" *Broadcasting*, July 19, 1971.

53. Letter from Senator Mike Gravel to the President of the United States, September 26, 1969; Letter from Peter M. Flanigan, assistant to the President, to Senator Mike Gravel, October 13, 1969.

54. Letter from Senator Mike Gravel to Richard W. McLaren, assistant attorney general, Antitrust Division, Department of Justice, February 12, 1970.

55. Letter from Richard W. McLaren to Senator Mike Gravel, January 5, 1971.

56. See Anthony Sampson, *The Sovereign State: The Secret History of ITT* (London: Coronet, 1974), especially pp. 151–158, 197–200.

57. Press release No. 266 from U.S. Senator Mike Gravel, January 7, 1971.

58. Stephen M. Aug, "U.S. Acts to Divorce AT&T, Comsat," *Washington Star*, January 7, 1971.

59. Executive Office of the President, Office of Telecommunications Policy, Press Release, January 7, 1971.

60. Interview with Joseph Bell, antitrust division, Department of Justice, Washington, D.C., July 13, 1971.

61. Interview with Clay T. Whitehead, White House director of Telecommunications Policy, Washington, D.C., August 25, 1971; Executive Office of the President, Office of Telecommunications Policy, *International Communications: Objectives and Policy*, February 1973.

CHAPTER NINE

1. Vice-President Hubert Humphrey, quoted in *Business Week*, April 10, 1965.

2. U.S. Congress, Senate, Senator Estes Kefauver speaking on the Commercial Communications Satellite System, H.R. 11040, 87th Cong., 2d sess., August 11, 1962, *Congressional Record* (unbound), 15151ff.

3. Carter Goodrich, *Government Promotion of American Canals and Railroads*, 1800–1890 (New York: Columbia University Press, 1965), p. 186.

4. *Ibid.*, p. 3.

5. Robert W. Fogel, *The Union Pacific Railroad: A Case Study in Premature Enterprise* (Baltimore: Johns Hopkins University Press, 1960), p. 17.

6. Goodrich, *Government Promotion*, p. 278.

7. Robert E. Riegel, *The Story of the Western Railroads* (New York: Macmillan, 1926), p. 276.

8. Fogel, *Union Pacific*, p. 20.

9. *Cong. Globe*, 33rd Cong., 2d sess., p. 55 (Union Pacific Debate), quoted in Fogel, *Union Pacific*, p. 41.

10. U.S. Congress, Senate, Senator Ralph Yarborough speaking on the Commercial Communications Satellite System, H.R. 11040, *Congressional Record* (unbound), 87th Cong., 2d sess., June 18, 1962, p. 9917.

11. Riegel, *Western Railroads*, pp. 19, 49.

12. Oscar Handlin and Mary Flug Handlin, *Commonwealth, A Study of the Role of Government in the American Economy: Massachusetts, 1774–1861* (New York: New York University Press, 1947), pp. 185–194; Goodrich, *Government Promotion*, p. 162.

13. Goodrich, *Government Promotion*, p. 186.

14. Riegel, *Western Railroads*, p. 63.

15. *Ibid.*, pp. 36–37, 42.

16. *Ibid.*, p. 44.

17. *Sen. Repts.*, No. 194, 31st Cong., 1st sess., (565), p. 2, quoted in Fogel, *Union Pacific*, p. 28.

18. FCC quoted in Goulden, *Monopoly*, p. 106.

19. See note 17 above.

20. Riegel, *Western Railroads*, p. 72.

21. Fogel, *Union Pacific*, p. 47.

22. Riegel, *Western Railroads*, p. 91.

23. Evert Clark, "Early Bird Orbited as First Link in a Global Communications Net," *New York Times*, April 7, 1965, p. 1.

24. Riegel, *Western Railroads*, p. 78; Fogel, *Union Pacific*, pp. 67–70.

25. Riegel, *Western Railroads*, p. 78.

26. Charles Francis Adams, Jr., quoted in Fogel, *Union Pacific*, p. 51.

27. Riegel, *Western Railroads*, p. 76.

28. *Ibid*, p. 94.

29. Goodrich, *Government Promotion*, p. 192.

30. Quoted in Goodrich, *Government Promotion*, p. 193.

31. Fogel, *Union Pacific*, p. 53.

32. Riegel, *Western Railroads*, pp. 46–47.

33. Riegel, *Western Railroads*, pp. 63, 285; Thomas C. Cochran, "The Social Impact of the Railroad," in Bruce Mazlish, ed., *The Railroads and the Space Program: An Exploration in Historical Analogy*, Technology, Space and Society Series prepared by the American Academy of Arts and Sciences (Cambridge: The MIT Press, 1965), p. 175; Robert L.

Brandford, "Political Impact: A Case Study of a Railroad Monopoly in Mississippi," in Mazlish, ed., *Railroads and the Space Program,* p. 191.

34. Goodrich, *Government Promotion,* pp. 273–276; Handlin and Handlin, *Commonwealth,* pp. 239–242; Riegel, *Western Railroads,* p. 144.

35. Riegel, *Western Railroads,* p. 142.

36. *Ibid.,* pp. 156, 199–219.

37. Gabriel Kolko, *Railroads and Regulation, 1877–1916* (Princeton, N.J.: Princeton University Press, 1962), pp. 231, 232.

38. Quoted in Thomas C. Cochran, "The Social Impact of the Railroad," in Mazlish, ed., *Railroads and the Space Program,* p. 176.

39. Kolko, *Railroads and Regulation,* p. 115.

40. Henry J. Friendly, *The Federal Administrative Agencies: The Need for Better Definition of Standards* (Cambridge: Harvard University Press, 1962), pp. 131–136.

41. Robert Fellmeth, *The Interstate Commerce Omission* (New York: Grossman, 1970), Chapters 4 and 5; Kolko, *Railroads and Regulation,* p. 235.

42. Walter Adams and Horace M. Gray, *Monopoly in America: The Government as Promoter* (New York: Macmillan, 1955), p. 54.

43. Alfred Kahn, *The Economics of Regulation: Principles and Institutions, II* (New York: Wiley, 1971), p. 8.

44. Friendly, *Federal Administrative Agencies,* p. vii.

45. Thomas C. Cochran, "The Social Impact of the Railroad," in Mazlish, ed., *Railroads and the Space Program,* p. 177.

46. Friendly, *Federal Administrative Agencies,* p. 55.

47. Adams and Gray, *Monopoly in America,* p. 56.

48. Peter Schrag, *The Decline of the WASP* (New York: Simon & Schuster, 1971), p. 134.

49. Francis X. Sutton, Seymour E. Harris, Carl Kaysen and James Tobin, *The American Business Creed* (Cambridge: Harvard University Press, 1948), p. 185.

50. Louis Hartz, *Economic Policy and Democratic Thought: Pennsylvania, 1776–1860* (Cambridge: Harvard University Press, 1948.

51. Fogel, *Union Pacific,* pp. 49, 110.

52. Theodore J. Lowi, *The End of Liberalism: Ideology, Policy and the Crisis of Public Authority* (New York: Norton, 1969), p. 71. This and subsequent quotations reprinted from *The End of Liberalism* by Theodore J. Lowi with the permission of the publisher. Copyright © 1969 by W. W. Norton & Company, Inc.

53. *Ibid.,* p. 86.

54. *Ibid.,* p. 65.

55. Theodore Roosevelt quoted in Kolko, *Railroads and Regulation,* pp. 112–113.

56. Arthur Schlesinger, Jr., quoted in Lowi, *The End of Liberalism, p. 78.*

57. *Ibid.,* p. 124.

58. Kolko, *Railroads and Regulation,* p. 238.

59. *Ibid.,* p. 230.

60. John Chamberlain, "These Days . . . The New Word Is 'Comsat,' " *Washington Post,* December 12, 1966.

61. *Ibid.*

62. Committee for Economic Development, "Social Responsibilities of Business Corporations" (New York, June 1971), back cover.

63. *Ibid.*, pp. 59–60.

64. *Ibid.*

65. *Ibid.*

66. Associated Press report, July 24, 1968; "Turning Off the Radios," *Time,* March 6, 1972.

67. Editorial, "Paying for the SST," *New York Times,* December 27, 1966; see also Periscope, "An SST Comsat?" *Newsweek,* September 30, 1968.

68. Lowi, *The End of Liberalism,* p. 289.

CONCLUSION

1. Douglass Cater, "A Communications Revolution?" *Wall Street Journal,* August 6, 1973.

2. See Joseph C. Goulden, *Monopoly* (New York: Pocket Books, 1970), Chapter 5.

3. Joseph A. Schumpeter, *Capitalism, Socialism and Democracy* (London: George Allen & Unwin, 1952), pp. 88ff.

Index